The Carolina Mountains

This portrait of Margaret Warner Morley was taken in Chicago in 1888. The embellishment surrounding the portrait is one of Morley's line drawings from A Song of Life, *published in 1899.*

The Carolina Mountains

Margaret Warner Morley

Historical Images
Fairview, North Carolina

Historical Images is an imprint of Bright Mountain Books, Inc.

Printed in the United States of America

ISBN-10: 0-914875-11-6 (Originally published by Houghton Mifflin Company, Boston and New York, 1913)
ISBN-13: 978-0-914875-11-6

We thank the following for their kind permission to reproduce photographs:
The Polk County Historical Association, Tryon, North Carolina (page ii)
The Harriet Beecher Stowe Center, Hartford, Connecticut (page xi)
The North Carolina Museum of History, Raleigh, North Carolina (pages xii-xiv, xvii, 29, 55, 61, 67, 129, 141, 161, 187, 201, 287, 304-358)

Library of Congress Cataloging-in-Publication Data

Morley, Margaret Warner, 1858–1923.
The Carolina mountains / Margaret W. Morley.
p. cm.
Includes index.
ISBN 0-914875-11-6 (pbk : alk paper)
1. North Carolina—Description and travel. 2. Appalachian Region, Southern—Description and travel. 3. Mountains—North Carolina—History—20th century. 4. Mountain life—North Carolina. 5. Mountain life—Appalachian Region, Southern. 6. North Carolina—Social life and customs—20th century. 7. Appalachian Region, Southern—Social life and customs—20th century. 8. Natural history—North Carolina. 9. Natural history—Appalachian Region, Southern. I. Title.
F259.M86 2006
975.6—dc21

2001005461

The
Carolina Mountains

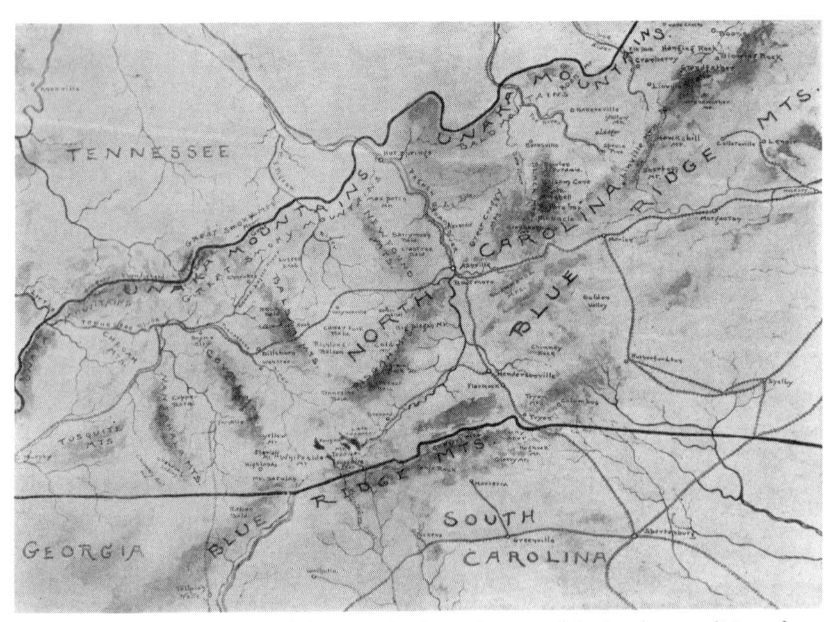

Amelia M. Watson painted this map for the endpapers of the hardcover edition of The Carolina Mountains *published by Houghton Mifflin Company in 1913.*

Contents

For Eric,
who also loved
the Carolina mountains.
1936–2002

Introduction to the Historical Images Edition

"No one will read this appreciation of the Carolina mountain region . . . without a longing for personal experience of their allurements."

Thus begins a review of *The Carolina Mountains* in *Literary Digest,* November 15, 1913. The book, written by Margaret Warner Morley, was published in 1913 by Houghton Mifflin Company of Boston. Her lyric descriptions of the region—from mountains and rivers to wildlife, trees, and flowers as well as the people who live there—paint a vivid, if not somewhat romantic, picture of the mountains at the beginning of the twentieth century.

Much of what we see reflected in her words is a product of her time and echoes the tone of the local color authors of the 1870–90s, some of whose writings she may well have read. Local color literature focuses on the unique characteristics of a geographic region, as told through the eyes of a narrator who is typically an outsider to the area. A dichotomy is established between the educated and urban narrator and the rural natives being observed. Far from looking down on the subjects portrayed, local color writers often romanticized the natives' primitive lives, industrialization is decried, and man's link to nature extolled.

Like many of the authors who preceded her, Miss Morley writes in enthusiastic and realistic terms about the mountain landscapes and regional geography, but tends to portray the people in generalities, whether complimentary or critical. These generalities and stereotypes appear to be intended to categorize and describe, not to demean or judge. Whether speaking of the white or black inhabitants of the region, her words, though somewhat patronizing, are never malicious. She often speaks of the mountaineers as childlike innocents, describing their kindness, honesty, cleverness, and hospitality. We see much the same treatment in Horace Kephart's *Our Southern Highlanders,* published in the same year as *The Carolina Mountains.*

Over the years, *The Carolina Mountains* has been both vilified and praised for its treatment of the mountaineer. Some critics say Morley followed in the "woeful" steps of many early writers who stereotyped the mountaineer as, at best, picturesque and primitive, and at worst, lazy and ignorant. In part, it was easy for native reviewers to discredit such writing purely based on the fact that the viewpoint was that of an outsider. Other critics have found lasting value in Morley's words and photographs. In spite of her frequently stereotypical treatment of the blacks and the mountaineers, one can see genuine admiration for those specific individuals about whom she writes. That warmth is lacking in her treatment of the Cherokee people. It appears that she spent little time in the Cherokee area, thus falling back on stereotypes for her descriptions.

While living in Tryon, Morley gathered material for *The Carolina Mountains*, touring widely through areas of upstate South Carolina and western North Carolina, photographing much of what she saw. Dressed in the cumbersome clothing of her day, she traveled by train, horse and buggy, donkey, or on foot over difficult terrain. Today's reader of *The Carolina Mountains* can trace Morley's travels throughout the mountains from Caesar's Head and Tryon to Asheville and Cashiers. Her detailed descriptions of Mount Mitchell and Roan Mountain remain largely true today. Her trained eye noted the tremendous variety of flora in the Southern Appalachian Mountains, and her delightfully descriptive writing allows us to see it as well. With very few exceptions, the details and accuracy of her journeys render her book a reliable guidebook nearly a century later.

Today, *The Carolina Mountains* offers an insightful glance at a time gone by. Miss Morley wistfully bemoans the "passing of the primitive life of the mountains" but acknowledges that it is inevitable. She refers to this change as the "exchange of Arcadia for Gotham." In the last chapter of her book she says, "The world may be coming, but the colors and the fragrances, the wonderful air and the ardent sun remain the same, and ever will." Would that she were correct. One wonders how Morley would address the devastation and the accompanying pollution brought to these mountains by the advances of man over almost a century since the publication of *The Carolina Mountains*. Perhaps she would be reassured to identify with the place-names and visit natural features that exist today much as they were nearly a century ago. Perhaps the answer lies in the last chapter where she confidently states:

> For Nature is long-suffering and very kind, so kind, indeed, that in moments of discouragement one has only to remember that even if the worst were to happen, and these beautiful mountains become devastated by ignorant invaders, when the time came, as come it would, that the profaner depart, Nature would begin anew her beneficent task of creating beauty.

About Margaret W. Morley

Little is known about Margaret Warner Morley beyond the books and articles which have survived her. She was born to Isaac and Sarah Robinson Warner Morley on February 17, 1858, in Montrose, Iowa. The family soon moved to Brooklyn, New York, where Margaret's public schooling was augmented by private instruction.

She was the product of Victorian America—an era rife with tension created by an insistence for prudence and a yearning for social evolution. It was also an age in which there were rapid advances in transportation, communication, and production of material goods. In addition, there was an increasing number of schools and colleges in America, as well as a greatly diversified curriculum within them—and an exciting increase in educational opportunity for women, from which Miss Morley benefitted.

Morley began her college education by attending Oswego Normal School, which is now part of the State University of New York system. She continued her studies at New York City Normal College, now Hunter College, graduating in 1878 at the age of twenty. After completing her undergraduate work, Morley pursued postgraduate studies at both Armour Institute in Chicago, now the Illinois Institute of Technology, and at Woods Hole Marine Laboratories in Massachusetts.

This picture, taken in the winter of 1893-94, shows Margaret Morley between Harriet Foote Taylor and George Henry Warner at the Warner home in Hartford, Connecticut.

Roughing it would have been normal for Morley's expeditions into the wilderness.

Upon completion of her formal education, Margaret Morley began a career as a teacher at Oswego Normal School. Following that, she taught in Milwaukee at the Wisconsin State Normal School, now part of the University of Wisconsin; and later in Leavenworth, Kansas, where she taught high school. She went on to Chicago, where she taught biology at the Armour Institute and served as an instructor for the Free Kindergarten Association Training Class. From Chicago, Morley moved to Boston to lecture on nature studies.

Margaret Morley made a career for herself as a classroom teacher, but she made a lasting name for herself as a writer. She wrote eighteen books on nature topics for children. Her books promoted the understanding and conservation of nature and compassion for wildlife. A sense of connectedness for all life permeates her writing. A pioneer of nature texts for the classroom, she wrote on the life of birds, insects, small mammals, and flowers. Sex education for children was taboo in Victorian America; however, in 1891, Morley published *A Song of Life,* a book that shocked many in its day. It describes in technical detail the reproductive cycle of plants, fish, frogs, birds, and mammals—including humans. In 1895, another volume followed, *Life and Love.* Of this book, the *Boston Journal* said:

> . . . a book which should be placed in the hands of every young man and woman. . . . It should result in the innocence of knowledge, which is better than the innocence of ignorance. Even a prude can find nothing to carp at in the valuable little volume.

Amelia Watson photographed Morley waiting while Dan and Tom drink at the ford. Note the footbridge in the background—a favorite subject of Morley's photography.

Many of Morley's books are illustrated with her own pen-and-ink drawings. Her detailed drawings are both scientifically accurate and whimsically engaging. In some instances, the words wrap around the illustrations in handset type, providing a most delightful visual experience. Morley's presentation of biological subject matter is often in story form for her young audience. A number of these books were used as texts when schools first began to teach nature studies.

Margaret was part of a community of New England authors, artists, and actors who often gathered at one another's homes for intellectual discussions. The literary colony known as Nook Farm in Hartford, Connecticut, was home to such notables as Mark Twain, Harriet Beecher Stowe, Charles Dudley Warner, and William Hooker Gillette. Artists exhibited and sold their works at nearby Wild Acres, home of Amelia Montague Watson and her sister, Edith Sarah Watson, both of whom were painters and photographers.

Though Margaret Morley wrote primarily for children, in 1900 she completed her first book for an adult audience, *Down North and Up Along,* a travel memoir of a trip to the maritime provinces of Canada. It is illustrated with photographs taken by the Watsons and Frank Gillette Warner, the son of Charles Dudley Warner.

In 1890, Margaret and Amelia Watson traveled to Tryon, North Carolina, to visit William Gillette. Gillette, the actor who first brought Sherlock Holmes to the stage in 1899, created the now-familiar image of the detective. Some years earlier, Gillette, stopping in Tryon to change trains, was so taken with the place that he built a home there which he

This road was the approach to William Gillette's Thousand Pines in Tryon, North Carolina. This unique house is currently a private home.

called Thousand Pines. Thousand Pines eventually became the property of Gillette's sister Elizabeth, the wife of George Henry Warner to whom *The Carolina Mountains* is dedicated. It is unknown whether Margaret was related to the Warner family, but it would seem likely, given her middle name.

It is Tryon that Morley refers to as Traumfest, "holiday of dreams," in her second book for an adult audience, *The Carolina Mountains.* Tryon at the turn of the century was a thriving artists' colony for creative men and, perhaps especially, creative women. With its mild climate, scenic surroundings, and freedom from the bustle of urban life, Tryon offered an idyllic setting for writing and painting and other artistic pursuits. Amelia Watson also lived part of the year in Tryon. The Houghton Mifflin edition of *The Carolina Mountains* was illustrated with Amelia's watercolor cover art, endpapers, and frontispiece.

Morley spent considerable time in Tryon, as a part-time visitor during the 1890s, and in 1915 bought a home there with her friend Annie Constance Snow. Their home on Melrose Avenue is no longer standing, but Margaret's studio still exists. Margaret and Constance sold their property in Tryon in 1920 during a period of failing health. Constance subsequently died in 1921. Margaret died from complications following emergency abdominal surgery in Garfield Memorial Hospital in Washington, D.C., December 12, 1923. She was sixty-five years old.

During her time in Tryon, Margaret Morley also gathered material for her book Little Mitchell: The Story of a Mountain Squirrel, *published in 1904 by A. C. McClurg & Company. According to the* Dictionary of American Biography, *Morley had a pet squirrel that she carried in her pocket. Since this photo appeared as the frontispiece of* Little Mitchell, *it is presumed to be Miss Morley and her Little Mitchell.*

Books by Margaret W. Morley

1891 *A Song of Life*, sex education for children
1895 *Life and Love*, sex education for children
1896 *Seed-Babies*, botany for children
1897 *A Few Familiar Flowers: How to Love Them at Home or in School*, botany for children
1897 *Flowers and Their Friends*, botany for children
1899 *The Honey-Makers*, bee studies for children
1899 *The Bee People*, bee studies for children
1899 *Little Wanderers*, botany for children
1900 *Down North and Up Along*, travelogue for adults
1900 *Wasps and Their Ways*, insect studies for children
1903 *The Insect Folk*, insect studies for children
1904 *Little Mitchell: The Story of a Mountain Squirrel*, fiction for children
1905 *Butterflies and Bees: The Insect Folk, Vol. II*, insect studies for children
1906 *The Renewal of Life: How and When to Tell the Story to the Young*, parents' guide
1907 *Grasshopper Land*, insect studies for children
1908 *Donkey John of the Toy Valley*, fiction for children
1913 *The Spark of Life: The Story of How Living Things Come into the World as Told for Girls and Boys*, sex education for children
1913 *The Carolina Mountains*, travelogue for adults
1913 *Will o' the Wasps*, insect studies for children
1915 *The Apple-Tree Sprite*, botany for children

Love of nature was a consuming passion for Morley throughout her life. Her friend Amelia Watson captured that feeling in this Tryon photo of her admiring the roses.

Historical Images Format and Editorial Changes

In the reprinting of Margaret W. Morley's *The Carolina Mountains* which follows, all elements of the original 1913 Houghton Mifflin edition have been retained. The words have been reset in a more contemporary font, and some editorial changes are noted below. Throughout the narrative, Morley's photographs have been placed approximately where they appeared in the original edition. Some of the relatively few extant pictures of Margaret Morley herself have been placed in the preceding pages, and a gallery of additional photographs from Miss Morley's camera follows the full text of *The Carolina Mountains.*

A special printing of *The Carolina Mountains* was produced for the Grove Park Inn in Asheville in 1926 by Houghton Mifflin Company. Two hundred and fifty printed but unbound books arrived in Asheville from Boston. On the grounds of the Grove Park Inn, the books were bound in blue homespun woven at Biltmore Industries and were placed in the guest rooms of the inn. Those keepsake volumes contained the following promotional insert praising both inn and book:

> At Asheville, N. C., the heart of the "Land of the Sky," is the finest and most wonderful resort hotel in the world—Grove Park Inn.
>
> It is built of great mountain boulders brought in from the coves where Nature left them countless centuries ago. It sits at the foot of Sunset Mountain and seems to be part of it. The walls of the Inn are as much as five feet thick in some places, and all solid mountain boulders, some weighing four and five tons each.
>
> There is an unusual atmosphere about the place such as one seldom finds.
>
> In each room there are two books—one the Bible, in large open-face type, bound in Roycroft binding, full of the beauty of the handwork of these incomparable craftsmen, and the other a copy of the *Carolina Mountains*, bound in hand-woven homespun.
>
> In addition to the many other interesting things to be found at the Inn is the largest hand-weaving industry in the world. This homespun industry was started by Mrs. George W. Vanderbilt as an industrial school nearly twenty years ago and later was bought by Mr. F. L. Seely, who built and operated Grove Park Inn. These industries have won two gold and one silver medal for hand-weaving and hand-carving, having won the gold medal at the Panama Exposition.
>
> No more delightful story of the Land of the Sky would be written than the *Carolina Mountains.* And no more fitting souvenir could possibly be conceived than a copy of it bound in hand-dyed, hand-woven homespun, the handiwork from start to finish of the mountain people, the story of whose lives make up this charming book.

For the Historical Images cover, the fabric look of the Grove Park Inn edition is combined with the Houghton Mifflin cover which utilized a watercolor painting by Margaret Morley's friend Amelia Watson. Watson's frontispiece is reproduced here on the back cover. The actual painting is now in the possession of a member of the Watson family and was brought to Tryon, North Carolina, in the summer of 2001 as part of the exhibit, Tryon Artists 1892-1942: The First Fifty Years.

A few typesetting conventions have been updated for the contemporary reader, and obvious typographical errors have been corrected. Some spellings and word usages we may now see as outmoded have been retained for accuracy and flavor; others have been modernized for today's reader. Such words as *Cæsar* employs the ligature *æ* as in the original text. Also left untouched are capitalization variations from the modern norm.

Contractions have been typeset here as one word instead of two words as in the original. Thus, *would n't* has been rendered as *wouldn't* in this edition. Hyphens have been removed from such words as *to-day* and *to-morrow*. A new index has been constructed to reflect changed page numbers, but the overall structure of the original index has been kept, with only slight modifications in spelling or capitalization for the sake of consistency.

Today's reader will quickly recognize Margaret Morley's writing to be from an earlier time. Savor her charming phrasing, appreciate her careful descriptions of the natural beauty of the mountains, and recognize the generosity of spirit she demonstrates toward the various people she encounters as she explores the countryside. Morley's writing predates present-day linguistic sensitivity, and no offense was intended by her use of the terms *Negro* or *red man*.

Finally, no effort has been made to correct Miss Morley's occasional errors of fact. They are few and will be readily apparent to the careful, knowledgeable reader of today. As an example, in her chapter on Asheville, she describes the journey by train from Flat Rock to Asheville, and she places the village of Tuxedo somewhere other than where it is. What is perhaps more noteworthy is the accuracy with which Margaret Morley observed and recorded the details of her journeys through the mountains and her appreciation of the land and its people. Nearly a century later, it is still a reliable guidebook.

Acknowledgments

Bright Mountain Books wishes to acknowledge the invaluable help of many people in researching the fascinating Margaret W. Morley and her photographs of the Southern Appalachians.

Eric V. Bright searched a variety of sources to acquire a complete set of Margaret Morley's known publications. The search was prompted by his interest in early textbooks published by Ginn and Company in Boston, the publisher for which he designed elementary texts in the 1960s. He found Morley's illustrations particularly appealing.

Our thanks to Frances Rooney, author of *Working Light: The Wandering life of Photographer Edith S. Watson.* She spoke at length with Cynthia Bright about her research which culminated in the publication of *Working Light* by Carleton University Press in 1996.

At the Grove Park Inn in Asheville, Alli Marshall consulted with Jerry Ball of Grovewood Galleries and the Homespun Shop. Together they delved into archived financial records to provide us with information on the blue homespun-bound *The Carolina Mountains.*

Michael J. McCue, a historical researcher and co-curator of the Tryon Artists exhibit at the Upstairs Gallery in Tryon, generously shared facts about the Watson sisters and others in the artists' colony. His research often paralleled ours as he searched for works of artists active in the Tryon area during the period Margaret Morley lived there.

In Raleigh, Eric N. Blevins, D. Kent Thompson, and the staff at the North Carolina Museum of History; and Stephen E. Massengill and his staff at the North Carolina Office of Archives and History provided access to their Morley photograph collections and shared their professional expertise.

Our sincere thanks to all.

THE CAROLINA MOUNTAINS

BY

MARGARET W. MORLEY

Author of "The Song of Life," "The Bee People," etc., etc.

WITH ILLUSTRATIONS

Published October 1913

TO

G. H. W.

INSPIRER, CRITIC, FRIEND

Contents

Illustrations

The Peach Trees Are in Bloom

March winds may howl, dull skies may lower, and chill airs pinch, up there in the frozen North, but down here—the peach trees are in bloom! They have opened like a burst of sunshine. On all sides, as far as the eye can reach, the landscape has over it the glow of peach blossoms.

If you happen to be crossing the State of North Carolina towards the mountains at this time, you will get a thrilling sense of the real mission of the peach tree. As the train sweeps over the country, one flower-wreathed picture follows another: here a tumble-down cabin with peach trees in ecstatic bloom at one corner, there a hollow filled with airy pink blossoms from the midst of which rises a farmhouse roof; the sordid little village, the unpainted house, the slope, the hilltop, each and everything your eye beholds is an adorable picture by grace of the blossoming peach trees. They seem to have alighted by chance, here, there, and everywhere, like wild flowers. You see them scattered over the cotton fields singly or in groups, covering the waste places, making long hedges, embowering the earth.

Occasionally these trees are in orchards that do not begin anywhere in particular, and trail off to nowhere, a ravishing maze of pink blossoms. Sometimes crowding close to the track, they fly past the car window a mere blur of color. Again a shining band of them stands still on the brow of a distant hill. The sky above is blue. The warm red earth is overlaid with tawny stubble, excepting where the plough has turned up a bright field. The air is soft and full of the smell of the earth. All Nature is in tune with the joyous peach trees.

In the yards are yellow bushes and daffodils. Snowy clusters of wild plums or of service blossoms shine out from the woods here and there, but the event of the day is the endless procession of blossoming peach trees. They go dancing by, hour after hour; trees, old and young, large and small, standing in all attitudes, graceful, laughing, exquisite—there is no end to them. From the sea to the mountains, the whole South is smiling through a veil of peach blossoms.

As finally you approach the mountains that form the western end of North Carolina, you catch glimpses of heights so divinely blue that you seem about to enter some dream world through their magical portals.

Through an opening between the mountains the train makes its way, and at an elevation of about a thousand feet leaves you at Traumfest, and continues its course up and over the difficult barrier of the Blue Ridge. For Traumfest lies in a nook of the Blue Ridge Mountains, and although it may not appear by that name on the maps, the place itself is a reality. The enfolding mountains, so dreamy, so enchanting in coloring when seen at their best moments, will explain the name and justify it, for translated into English "Traumfest" means "Holiday of Dreams," or, if one is willing to tamper a little with grammatical endings, it means, best of all, perhaps, "Fortress of Dreams." Here lingers a touch of summer even in midwinter, because of the evergreen trees and shrubs that so abound. And here spring comes early, for Traumfest, be it known, lies in the thermal belt, that magic zone where, although it may freeze, there is never any frost.

In this gentle land where even the cocks crow with a Southern accent, the newcomer, half-awake in the early morning, hears the great city he has recently left singing like a city of the blest. As consciousness emerges from the mists of sleep, however, one discovers that although the singing is real, it does not come from the town, now happily far away. It comes from the negroes down in the hollow, from the birds in the trees, and from the little children of the white people who live on the hilltops. All Traumfest seems to be singing. It makes one want to sing too. And that is the magic and the charm of the South; cares fly away and one wants to sing.

Mingling as it were with the singing of the people is the subtle smell of spring. One wonders what that odor of the Southern spring comes from, and suspects that the smoke of pine wood ascending like incense from the hearthstones in all the houses has something to do with it. It is a fragrance peculiar to the South, places, as well as animals, flowers, and races, having their distinguishing odors.

One soon discovers that the half-wild peach trees that make the foothills so lovely are also present in the mountains, where they bloom a little later and quite as enchantingly. To walk among them is quite as delightful as to fly past them on the train, and there is this advantage, one can hear as well as see them. If the blossoming trees do not sing aloud and clap their hands for joy, they at least draw to themselves a blissful chorus of happy creatures. Little things on wings have suddenly appeared. They seem to have blossomed with the peach trees, for yesterday they were not. Now the air hums with them, bees, wasps, flies, beetles, bugs, butterflies, all as busy as though they were of tremendous importance in the scheme of the universe. And walking thus among the blossoming trees, we can smell as well as hear and see them.

It is hard to tell which is best, the beauties of the day or the beauties of the night in this smiling land. The nights are so cool, so fragrant, and so enticing that one has an impulse to roam the woods in the magical moonlight and under the softly glowing stars. The stars hang big and dewy, dreamy lights in the vault of heaven. And there are so many of them, so bewilderingly many! That great star one sees in midwinter, glowing low towards the horizon and competing with Sirius in brilliancy, is Canopus of the Southern heavens, and, of a dark night, faint and twinkling lights may be seen near the horizon, small stars unknown in the Northern heavens, while that rare sight, the great cone of the zodiacal light, is sometimes to be seen just after the sun has set.

And the night here has its well-remembered sounds, the gentle breeze lightly sighing through the pines, the gust of wind striking the trees into deeper music, the trill of a bird, the muffled call of an owl, and in summer the insistent call of the whip-poor-will and the orchestral boom of a thousand insect performers. Besides these, there is one sound that never fails summer or winter. At stated intervals the cocks wake up and crow. They divide the night into watches of about three hours. You hear one clear call, a voice responds, then here and there and everywhere, like watchmen exchanging the signal, the cry goes forth; you hear the circle widening from that first challenge to distant margins where the voices are faint almost as memories—you imagine them circling on and on over the earth, and then all is still for another three hours. At the last crowing of the cocks, as though the sun were answering to their call, a gentle radiance flows up into the dome of the sky and

> "tenderly the haughty day
> Fills his blue urn with fire."

Traumfest on the Blue Ridge

The Blue Ridge! What mountains ever offered themselves to the sun so enchantingly as the long curve of the Appalachian chain where it passes through Virginia and North Carolina down to Alabama, running all the way full southwest! This battlement of heaven was not named by accident. It was named Blue because there was no other name for it. It is blue; tremendously, thrillingly blue; tenderly, evasively blue. And the sky that contains it is also entrancingly blue; even the storms do not make it sullen, and when they pass, the sun breaks out more radiantly than ever. Beyond the Blue Ridge in North Carolina, other and higher mountains rise like spirit forms into the deep sky, rank upon rank, height upon height, guarded as it were and protected by the encircling wall of the Blue Ridge.

Traumfest, Fortress of Dreams, rests in a vast amphitheatre on the eastern front of the Blue Ridge, an amphitheatre formed by a cordon of forest-covered mountains that nearly inclose the place, and among which are Hogback on the south and Tryon Mountain on the north, both descending towards the east in a series of ridges surmounted by low peaks, and leaving open between them a wide arc for the sun to enter. And how the sun does enter, flooding the place and also the mountains that inclose Traumfest as with loving arms.

The peculiar charm of Traumfest comes from the fact that it lies thus open to the east; it does not have to wait for the sun to climb and look in after his first morning freshness is dimmed. Its horizon is in reality the horizon of the plains. In the dewy morning one sees the sky lighten, and then the torch of day flash from hill-crest to hill-crest, the tree-tops kindling in masses, with night shadows yet intervening. If the day is clear, you may look far down the sea of color to where there rises as it were an island, long, rounded, and pale blue, or maybe the color of mist, and scarcely visible against the sky of which it seems a part. That faint, sweet island swimming in the mists is King's Mountain, where one of the bravest deeds in the history of the New World was once done by a little band of heroes from these mountains.

Because of its warm and beautiful location, and because the railroad came through that open door of the mountains, passing up the valley of the Pacolet and over the crest of the Blue Ridge to Asheville, Traumfest is not only the largest of the villages on the eastern slope of the Blue Ridge, but was among the first to become a resort for visitors from all parts of the country, here having grown up a friendly community representing more than two dozen states. Strangers say that Traumfest reminds them of an Old World village, with its bright painted houses and the little church with its square stone tower, the gift of one who lived here and loved the place. Like the peach trees, Traumfest seems to have happened, straggling about over a number of ridges separated from each other by deep hollows through which pass the connecting roads or paths, or down which run dancing brooks. Like the rest of the mountain villages, it is all up and down hill, most of the houses having their front door on the hilltop and the back door down below somewhere. It adds to the unstudied effect of the place that its houses are set at every angle, each person placing his as fancy dictates, but avoiding as by instinct planting any building square with the points of the compass.

Although Traumfest now contains enough new settlers considerably to temper the manner of life, its ancient quality is not all gone, as he who tries to get anything done on time, or done at all, will soon discover. That ox team slowly pulling a load of wood along Traumfest's main residence street also tends to dispel any illusion concerning the extent of change that may have taken place, while four oxen attached to one small cart sometimes hint at primitive roads not far away.

Traumfest's main street is bright red in color, for the Blue Ridge, although so enchantingly blue in the distance, has a soil composed largely of red clay, the characteristic soil of the whole mountain region, as also of the foothills. Consequently long threads of red and ochre and pink are woven through the sunny greens that here prevail as the roads mind uphill and down, over the heights and through the hollows. Red roads wind past houses with red-tinted foundations and chimneys chinked with red mud, and along through fields where the vegetation is sparse, as though loath to hide the fervid color of the soil, while here and there you will see a stream flowing with blood-red water. Even the wasps' nests that so plentifully adorn the walls and rafters are built of red mud. Men and boys have red ends to their trousers, and reddish-looking shirt-sleeves, horses have red hoofs and white mules have bright red legs. It must not be supposed, however, that all the earth is red; there is some gray soil, some that is brown, and much that is yellow; but red predominates to such a degree that you think of this as a red land.

Reinforcing the warm color of the soil is the sunny nature of the greens. One never sees here the cold dark greens of the North; even the pine trees have a warm tint as though soaked in sunshine, and on the eastern slopes of the Blue Ridge there is no greensward, the ground in summer being covered with sparse wild grasses, and little bushes and herbs that paint the landscape in many tones.

Lying as it does on the South Carolina state line, Traumfest, in addition to its other attractions, has a spice of border romance, for constantly crossing from one state to the other is that picturesque figure the "moonshiner," who persists in distilling corn whiskey in secret places and in passing the cup that cheers and most certainly inebriates to his willing neighbors, in defiance of the laws that declare such actions to be unlawful. Hogback and its companion, Rocky Spur, are in South Carolina, and between them and Traumfest, and also in South Carolina, lies one of those mysterious regions known as the "Dark Corners," into whose dread precincts one is warned with ominous head-shakings not to venture, for here generations of moonshiners have carried on the distillation of corn whiskey in a fashion nominally secret, undoubtedly reprehensible, and very picturesque.

The Southern sun that floods the mountains and beautifies the landscape has an irresistible influence over the people as well. No native thinks of disobeying its implicit command—"Thou shalt not hurry"; therefore the native-born of the Blue Ridge, no matter what else he may lack, is rich in time, a possession denied to the foreign invader who keeps his hoe in the tool-house where he can find it when he wants it. The mountain man leaves his in the field, and when he wants it, if he cannot find it, he drops the subject. That the ancient and honorable art of "settin' around" has been cultivated until it has grown into an integral part of life, you discover upon asking a mountain woman, who has waited in town half a day for some one to come, what she did with her time, and receive the illuminating reply, "Oh, I jest sot."

That the sun in time conquers even the most vigorous newcomer is a fact plainly discernible in Traumfest, where the people may be divided into three classes: Northerners who are always in a hurry, Southerners who are never in a hurry, and Northerners in process of southernization, who are sometimes but not always in a hurry. In course of time the Northern type becomes obliterated unless renewed from the original source.

The perfect type, of which the rest of us are but modifications, is illustrated by the man from Turkey Pen Gap, to see whom move is a revelation. It is as though eternity were ever present in his consciousness. It was he who said in his inimitable drawl, "I would rather go up a mountain than daown one. For when you go up, you *cain't* hurry, and when you come daown, you *have* to."

When a mountaineer unexpectedly completes a piece of work or makes some unwonted exertion, you may be tempted to think it the result of forethought, but if you ask him about it he will probably tell you it was because he "tuk-a-notion." Life has many consolations run on the "tuk-a-notion" principle.

"We're powerful poor around here, but we don't mean no

harm by it," is the cheery greeting you get when you visit an ancient native of the forest who you know does not think himself poor at all. He has plenty of time, the thing he values most. It was he who used to tell his reminiscences of the war, into which he had been drafted much against his will, and concerning the meaning of which he in common with his neighbors was not very clear. When you asked him about it he knit his brows, "studied" a minute, then slowly said, "Law, which side *was* I on?" But though the mountaineer may have been puzzled concerning the meaning and advantages of the War of the Rebellion, which he sometimes classified as "a rich man's war and a poor man's fight," and escaped if he could, it must not be supposed that he was either cowardly or uncertain where he understood the issue, a witness to the contrary being what occurred at King's Mountain that stormy day so long ago.

The village people, many of whom are native North Carolinians, are not to be classed with the mountaineers of the rural districts, for the villagers for the most part have come from the old plantations, or from less primitive regions below the mountains. But although the village shops have recently attained a high standard in both products and prices, it is a fact of far-reaching psychological significance that even now you cannot buy a darning-needle in the city of Traumfest. Yet your neighbors seem happy and respected by their fellows and totally unconscious of any gap in their lives.

Besides the white people, Traumfest is blessed with the negro, that true child of the sun who is found everywhere at the foot of the Blue Ridge, but is not so often seen in the higher mountains excepting in the larger villages. He prefers to linger near the cotton-line, the mountains being too sparsely settled to satisfy his gregarious instincts. Most of the negroes here are descended from slaves brought up on the plantations in the immediate neighborhood. They are good, and for the most part as industrious at least as the white people, and when you know them personally and intimately, you cannot help loving them. They believe in ghosts and signs and a hereafter, they are afraid of the comet, and they have good appetites. Many of them bear picturesque names bestowed upon them by the white people and yet more remarkable ones of their own selection, their feeling for rhythm alone often guiding them in their choice; hence the delightful name, Greenville Female Seminary Simms, proudly worn by a young girl of Traumfest.

By far the most interesting characters among them are the few survivors of the old *régime*, who are really proud of their slavery and the fact that they learned how to work and how to behave. Among them is Aunt Hootie, whose full name she will proudly tell you in a sort of rhythmical chant. This is it—"Anna Mar*i*a, Lucy Lees, Licif*i*er, Mary Ann, Markal*i*na, Gallahootie, Waters, Mooney. Aunt Hootie for short." Waters and Mooney were acquired by two excursions into matrimony, but the other names were bestowed at the baptismal font. Aunt Hootie is pious. When she comes to visit, which is generally about dinner-time, she graciously accepts an invitation to stay, never omitting reverently to "make a beginning," as grace before meat is expressed in the mountains. Aunt Hootie's "beginning" is simple, but to the point; folding her hands and composing her features she reverently remarks, "O Lord, thou knowest I need this," and proceeds to verify the assertion.

Near her picturesque cabin on the outskirts of Traumfest is that of Aunt Eliza, who, though a churchwoman, is not, properly speaking, pious. She has outlived slavery and her husband, for both which blessings she is duly grateful. "Now I can put my bread and cheese upon the shelf and nothing can blow cold upon me unless I let it, ha! ha!" she exclaims triumphantly when congratulating herself upon having weathered the perilous seas of matrimony. Aunt Eliza is a strong woman and works hard when she has to. When the bread and cheese get low, she goes to chopping down the pine trees on her piece of land. She converts them into firewood and hauls them to town on a home-made sled drawn by a very reluctant bull calf, whose neck she has subjected to the yoke despite his manifest disapproval. It used to be one of the diversions of Traumfest to see Aunt Eliza "wrastling" with her calf on the way to town, she at one end of the rope braced and inclined like a leaning tower, the calf at the other end, braced and rigid, leaning in the opposite direction. In her garden she raises, so she tells you, "oodles of gubers and taters," which translated means a great many peanuts and potatoes. Let not this appearance of energy, however, deceive or alarm any one, for Aunt Eliza manages to make her way without seriously disturbing the waters of idleness.

Some time since, Aunt Eliza got religion. She began going to church and profiting according to her light on the "preachment" and "taughtment" of the scriptures as there expounded, though her piety is intermittent, according to the long-suffering "preacher," who shakes his venerable head over her state as he remarks with a sigh, "Eliza is a mighty peace-breakin' woman."

The Forest

The first thing one notices upon approaching the mountains is that the Blue Ridge is wooded to the top, the beautiful Blue Ridge with all its outreaching spurs. And one later discovers that this is also true of the high mountains back of it, for the Southern Appalachian forests are not only the highest-lying of all the hardwood forests in North America, but the largest left in this once forest-covered country. Some six thousand square miles of them lie spread, a shining web of lights and colors, over the North Carolina mountains alone.

But although trees clothe the mountains here as with a garment, their boundless expanse is not oppressive, for the forest floor, unobstructed by glacial boulders and wet hollows, is easily traversed. As a rule its trees stand apart, tall, clean columns beneath which little green things and wild flowers grow, while the sun shines through the leafy roof. One reason the floors are so clean is that they are frequently swept by the fires that break out every winter either through carelessness, or else on purpose to clear the ground that fresh green may start for the cattle. In the dry season smoke clouds ascend on all sides. At night cities with their twinkling lights seem to have sprung up as by magic on the slopes, or else lines and curves of fire gird the mountain-tops. The atmospheric effect of these fires is lovely; a tender haze envelopes the landscape, while the air is filled with that faint and exquisite fragrance of burning wood that one always associates with the South. The air is smoky, but how different these clouds of incense from the smoke of a city! Strong, sweet winds blow over the mountains, mingling the odor of growing things with that of the burning forest.

Such trees as fall from fire or other causes, in this ardent climate quickly resolve into their elements. If they do not burn up, they decompose, excepting the heartwood of mature pine trees that for years may lie embedded in the crumbling envelope of the outer wood, forming the fragrant "fat pine" of the South, a splinter of which kindles at the touch of a match. Heavy, translucent, and damp with resinous juices, it burns with fierce heat and fiercer flames, the smoke that ascends from it being heavy like lampblack, although it does not smell like that: it smells like the South. It is the same odor intensified that steals over the earth when the sun is on the pine trees. For here the pine is everywhere present to the eye and to the sense of smell. Of all the trees it is the one the stranger first notices, and the first thing the newcomer says is, "How bright the pine trees look," for, instead of sharing the sombre aspect of pines that grow in the North, these seem full of sunshine.

Perhaps the pine also owes its supremacy here as elsewhere to a certain atmosphere of antiquity clinging about it and unconsciously affecting the feelings of one looking at it. For we know its family to be the sole arboreal survivor in this country of the myriads of strange forms that covered the earth in past geological ages—long before there were any broad-leaved trees in existence. However that may be, the ancient form of the pine gives a characteristic aspect to the scenery of the Carolina mountains, as well as characteristic fragrance to the woods, and a characteristic note in the music of the forest as the wind sweeps over it.

The noblest tree among them, the tall *Pinus echinata,* in Traumfest known as the "armored pine," from the large plate-like scales of its bark, stands head and shoulders above the rest of the forest, its picturesque crown of twisted limbs overtopping the other trees along the crest of the ridges.

Quite different in appearance is the *Pinus Virginiana,* whose spreading crown is close-dotted with little dark cones that cling fast for several years, until the tree finally looks like a Japanese decoration. This charming tree appears more mundane than the towering armored pine, whose spirit seems to be engrossed with matters of the sky. One could imagine the *Pinus Virginiana* laughing, but never the armored pine. It is the *Pinus Virginiana* that gives that delicious fragrance to roads banked with its young trees, a fragrance like that of a freshly opened tangerine orange. Besides these two, there are three or four other species of pine that blend their plumes with each other and with the foliage of the hardwood trees, and which fill the air with incense.

On the high mountains west of the Blue Ridge are yet to be found grand primeval forests of mingled pines and hardwood trees; but the trees of the Blue Ridge, though there are noble exceptions, are generally small, the forests here being sweet rather than majestic. And how sweet they are!

Of the numberless hardwood trees that flourish here, the oaks perhaps stand first because of their numbers and the many forms in which they appear, from the lordly white oak to the little ridiculous jack oak. Conspicuous among them is that large tree that looks so like a chestnut, but which the native assures the newcomer is an oak, unanswerably clinching the argument with the information that "hit grows acorns," and with patience one learns in time to tell a chestnut leaf from the leaf of a chestnut oak. A generation ago the foothills and the lower mountains were covered with chestnut trees, some of them of enormous size. But these are gone, only a few stumps broad enough for a cabin floor remaining to tell the tale of the past. Where are they? The reckless wood cutter is not to blame this time, for there descended upon the chestnuts a blight that in a few years wiped them out until not a bearing tree was left on the lower slopes, though at higher levels they are yet so abundant that one looking at the mountains in early summer can clearly trace the ravines down their slopes by the rivers of chestnut bloom that brim them. The mountaineer's method of gathering chestnuts is characteristic. Going into the woods with an axe, he selects a tree loaded with ripe nuts and chops it down.

The most beautiful as well as the most valuable of the hardwood trees here is the noble tulip-tree, poplar the people call it, whose grand, clean gray column rises out of the forest, the

G. H. W. and His Armored Pine

crown of bright green leaves overtopping all but the tallest of the pines. *Liriodendron,* the pretty botanical name of the tulip-tree, means a tree bearing lilies. And looking far up to the crown of this forest giant as its leaves unfold in early spring, one discovers that it indeed bears lilies—upright, green and orange lilies, one on the end of each twig. In the autumn when the great trees stand leafless, each twig holds aloft a golden urn, the seed-pod, that remains in place, a unique and charming decoration, until the following spring. There is something of romance attaching to these trees that stand so lordly and alone in our forests. They belong to a genus of which there are only two species in all the world, one in the eastern United States, the other in Asia. We have one tulip-tree, China has the other.

Of course hickories, maples, elms, beeches, birches, and many other trees abound, although we lack the beautiful "American elm" that so adorns the old New England villages and lends romance to Northern valleys. And the spectral white birch is not with us. But the sugar-maple—"sugar-tree" the native here calls it—abundant in some regions, sweetens the corn-pone of the mountaineer as agreeably as in the cold North it embellishes the buckwheat cakes of a winter's morning. The sugar-trees might yield a good profit to thrifty harvesters, but the time-honored method of chopping a hole in the trunk and sticking in a bit of bark to conduct the sap into a wooden trough on the ground, although time-saving, does not produce results that command fancy prices, particularly as the rest of the process is equally free and easy. The troughs stand on the ground through the remainder of the year collecting water, twigs, leaves, and anything else that may chance to fall into them. In the winter all this freezes into a solid cake which the practical mountaineer has discovered can be turned out whole, thus giving less trouble than any other method of cleaning the troughs. Maple-sugar as made in the mountains may be black in color and diversified with many strong flavors, but the people have a pretty way of running it into empty eggshells, where it hardens, and can then be handed about and carried in the pocket with more regard to cleanliness than is apparent in any other part of its history.

The stately wild cherry, or "mahogany," of the mountains, like the black walnut, has all but vanished, its virtues being its undoing. Of the trees, unknown to the North, that one finds here, the most notable is thc magnolia that lights up the woods in springtime with great ivory-white chalices brimmed with cloying fragrance. Walking in the forest you smell a penetrating, sweet odor that causes you to stand still and search the woods with your eyes until you see the white flowers shining in the distance. There are several varieties of these "cucumber" and "umbrella" trees, as the people call them. Their large, light-green leaves placed in a circle at the ends of the twigs have something of a tropical appearance, and there is also clinging to them that mysterious romance of the East, for although there are some fifteen or more species of this genus in the world, all of them belong to eastern Asia and the eastern United States, some four or five species being common in our Southern mountains.

Another tree which is found only in the Orient and the eastern part of the New World is the sour-gum, pepperidge, or tupelo, whose dark, close-ridged bark and twisted crown, weather-beaten attitude, and somewhat scanty foliage give it an air of individuality that could not be dispensed with in the sentiment of the forest. Its wood is so tough that it soon dulls an axe, and lazy negroes were put to chopping it in slavery times, so the people say.

The sweet-gum, or liquidambar, also abundant here, is not related to the sour-gum, but belongs to the romantic witch-hazel family, which perhaps is why its juices are so aromatic—the tree exuding copal at the slightest incision—and why its bark is so curiously ridged.

Fortunately the larger gum trees, both sweet and sour, are apt to be hollow at the base, otherwise where would the mountaineer get his "bee-gums"? And what could replace in the landscape those rows of cylindrical hives, roofed with a board-end or a flat stone, that stand about wherever the owner takes a notion to set them? Could any honey go so well on hot corn-bread, that came not out of a bee-gum?

It would be impossible within reasonable limits to do justice to the trees here, yet one could not dismiss them without a word concerning that beguiling shape with the unfair name—the sourwood or *Oxydendrum arboreum,* which means the same as sourwood, but sounds better. This ladylike little tree is the most charming thing in the woods when its exquisite young leaves come out in the spring, and again in early summer when it is covered with drooping, handlike sprays of white flowers that look like lilies-of-the-valley, and give forth a fragrance delicate yet so penetrating that one can easily smell his way through the woods to a blossoming tree, where he will find the honey bees ahead of him. For in addition to its other virtues the sourwood yields the finest honey in the mountains, clear, delicate, white, and delicious.

The botany tells us that this *Oxydendrum* is the only species of its genus, and that it is found only in southeastern North America; which is suspicious, since it has recently been discovered that almost if not all of our plants hitherto classed as monotypic have species in the Far East. So undoubtedly our pretty sourwood has an Asiatic sister who sits smiling in some corner of the Flowery Kingdom or the land of the Dragon or looks out over some fair Himalayan height. It is a pity it should suffer from such a name as "sourwood" just because its leaves are sour!—why could it not have been named from its lovely flowers as the silver-bell tree was named from its? Why not call it "honey," as the negroes do those whom they love?

The Southern Appalachian National Park

Since the easiest way for the mountaineer to clear the land is to girdle the trees and let nature do the rest, we everywhere see those dreary openings in the forest known as "deadenings," where spectral dead trunks stand among the growing corn. These "deadenings" are made and abandoned one after another as the thin soil wears out, which on the poorer slopes happens in a year or two. Hence, while the mountains are yet covered with forests, the clearings are everywhere apparent, and in these later days are increasing with alarming rapidity.

Long ago the Southern Appalachians rose clad with trees above a tree-clad world. The Indian roamed the dense primeval forests, cultivating the valley bottoms and hunting in the woods. He did not destroy the trees—and thus the balance between man and the forests was kept. Then came the white man, and wherever he set his foot the tree retired. Wide fields of cotton and corn covered the lowlands, gardens and towns sprang up as by magic. But on the slopes of the mountains the forest undisturbed fulfilled its old-time office of calling the rains and holding the rivers in leash. In time the newcomer reached the mountains and made his clearings on the slopes. He also burned the woods each spring to clear away the pine needles, and thus help the grasses and tender herbs to spring up as food for his cattle. For these reasons the young trees were killed, and the heavy growth of virgin timber in time gave place to the present open woods. Yet the forest was not destroyed; it contended bravely with this strange new foe.

As generations passed, the clearings grew larger and more numerous. Denuded slopes appeared, became gullied and washed, the streams thickened, they grew shallower and lost their crystal clearness as soon as they got to the settled country. The balance between man and the forest was being disturbed.

But the forest yet contended bravely with the destroyer, and there was always that background of inaccessible high mountains, the birth-chambers of the streams, where the forests fulfilled their saving mission without hindrance.

Then came the lumberman with his portable sawmill, entering into the very heart of the forest excepting the highest and wildest places, taking the largest trees, but leaving the top branches and half the trunk to cumber the ground and offer food to the fires that invariably broke out, fires immeasurably hotter and more destructive than the ordinary forest fire. Deeper and deeper into the wilderness pushed the lumberman, taking a small fraction of the forest and killing the rest. Nature gave quick warning. Fertile valley bottoms were overflowed, and the work of man's hands was often destroyed. After seasons of flood came seasons of low water, when the rivers refused their help and the mills shut down. "Why is this?" the people asked; "such things never happened before." Had they looked to the mountains they would have seen the torn, bare slopes, the sun burning the dry earth where once lay water-soaked carpets of moss. The forest that once covered the mountains as with a garment, giving to man not only its wood, but what one might call its spiritual force of adjustment, was rapidly passing away.

What slowly happened in these mountains took place more quickly in other regions until the whole country suddenly awakened to the fact that in a generation or two the wonderful forests of the New World would be no more. The prosperity of a nation depends also upon its forests. To lose them is a calamity too great to be borne, as nearly every one of the European nations has discovered through sad experience—Spain in her mountains of bare rock reflecting the sun, but not condensing the moisture that causes the rains to fall, France in destructive floods, Germany in lack of wood, all in one or usually many ways feeling the cessation of the beneficent work of the forests.

As the population of the world grew denser and man discovered his relation to the trees, and that the performance of their primal duty had been fatally interfered with, he began to bring back the forests, a Herculean task now being performed over the whole of the Old World. What has happened to Europe is beginning to happen to us. Already the cry of the farmer is heard and the complaint of the manufacturer. Man has menaced the existence of the forests without stopping to consider the consequences.

The debt that we of the New World owe to our forests is apparent when we remember that the products of the tree alone occupy the fourth place as a source of wealth to the nation, to say nothing of the many and invaluable uses of forested land. As civilization advances and all the secrets of the earth are opened up, as new discoveries are made and new forces harnessed and put to work, the tree becomes more necessary instead of less. Its wood enters into everything, or if it is displaced in one industry it becomes more necessary in another, one of the latest discoveries causing the destruction of such enormous quantities of wood that one stands aghast before the facts: for the worst menace to our forests today is the all-consuming paper-pulp mill, the most reckless timber-cutting known to history being done in its service. This danger, which threatened the extinction of our forests with frightful rapidity, is now to an extent being met by the manufacturers themselves, some of whom, realizing the extremity to which they will soon be brought under existing conditions, are beginning to provide for their own future by reforesting the cut-over lands. But even at the best the tremendous demands of the pulp-mills are believed to be a menace to the forests of the nation, and we should be made more unhappy at the prospect ahead if it were not for our experience with other threatened dangers, bogies like the diminishing supply of nitrates, mineral fuel, and phosphates which darkly haunted the imagination a short time ago only to vanish before the searchlight of science. Even now the form of the giant bamboo is hovering on the horizon, and if the stately Oriental or our own cornstalks do not feed to repletion the voracious maw of the paper-mill, hope assures us that something else will arrive to do it before our grand forests have sent their last sigh over the valleys and mountains of the New World. Which distant hope does not lessen our present responsibility; and it is consoling to know that the whole country is waking up to the need of preserving our forests before it is too late, vigorous and effective means having in many places already been taken to that effect, state law and the growing intelligence of private owners combining to place large tracts of woodland under the care of trained foresters.

How many of us realize that well within a generation there have been created more than one hundred and fifty national forests in the United States, embracing over one hundred and ninety million acres? Besides this a dozen states have already adopted the policy of creating state forests, and as proof of the vital interest taken in the subject, more than a score of universities and colleges are now providing courses in forestry. The public schools are also beginning to give instruction in the underlying principles of forestry, thus preparing the future citizens of the nation. Indeed, who today can escape knowing the meaning and value of the forests? Even the Southern mountaineer is seeing a new light. The appearance of gullies that ruin his land, the washing-away of his soil, the drowning of his valleys, the drying-up of his life-giving springs, these things he is beginning to notice with consternation and to ask the reason why, so that the race will soon have passed to which belongs the man who recently declared that in his opinion the people would be better off if there was not a tree on the mountains. Of course what he saw in imagination was a land covered with grain-fields, but he is discovering that the destruction of the trees is not followed by fertile acres; in short, that his beloved mountains were not designed by nature for grain-fields.

The inaccessibility of the Southern mountains long saved them, and now, thanks to the new impulse, the Southern Appalachians will escape, to an extent, at least, the most serious dangers of lumbering, though they can no longer escape the lumberman, who is swinging his axe on the most "inaccessible" coves and peaks of the Great Smokies themselves, "the largest lumber company in the world" having recently purchased an enormous tract of two hundred and fifty thousand acres of virgin forest in the North Carolina mountains, forests containing, besides spruce and hemlock, some of the finest hardwood trees ever grown here, notable among which are tulip and cherry, the latter having long since been removed from the more accessible forests. But fortunately this lumber company, in its methods of handling the trees, belongs to the new era. Under its administration there will be no waste. Those great piles of sawdust left by the old-time sawmill, as well as all other remainders, will be converted at a central station into electric power to run all the mills and factories from which the waste is produced, besides leaving some to help run the enormous pulp-mill recently erected in the Pigeon River Valley, a few miles west of Asheville. The use of electricity in running the machinery vastly reduces the danger from fire, as does also cleaning up the waste in the woods, while yet more to diminish the danger the cutover forests are to be under the care of a fire guard.

While the new conscience is thus working in private ways, the people as a whole have become alive to the importance of saving certain parts of the long Appalachian watershed from the possibility of denudation; hence there has grown up so urgent a demand for a national forest in the East, comparable to those forests with which the West for various reasons is so amply provided, that a bill has finally passed through the United States Congress making the foundation of such a domain possible. This, the Weeks Bill, became a law March 1, 1911, and now there is in process of construction a great forest reservation, part of which is to be in the White Mountains of New Hampshire, part in the mountains of Maryland, West Virginia, Virginia, Tennessee, North Carolina, South Carolina, and Georgia, and whose function shall be forever to protect the cradles of the great rivers that are born on the slopes of these mountains.

The largest and most important part of the southern division of the new national forest will lie in the mountains of North Carolina, since from them are thrown off as from a common center the principal feeders to many of the great rivers that cross the southern plains to the Atlantic on the east, and run to the Ohio and the Gulf of Mexico east of the Mississippi River on the west.

The first purchase made after the passing of the Weeks Bill was in North Carolina, where in December of 1911, eighteen thousand, five hundred acres of land in the district of Mount Mitchell on the watershed of the Catawba River became the nucleus of the Southern Appalachian National Park, for the immediate further extension of which lands are under consideration in the Nantahala, Mount Mitchell, and Pisgah areas.

The coming of the national park means more than the preservation of the forests; it means the opening of a glorious pleasure-ground in the eastern part of our continent, how glorious a pleasure-ground no one can know who has not climbed these flowery slopes so exquisitely warmed by the sun and cooled by the wind. The more stupendous aspects of nature are wanting here. Those majestic snow-clad peaks, those abysmal gorges, those rocks of blazing hue, those geysers and natural bridges, those strange geological formations and petrified forests—all those marvels of a younger age that call the world to our Western parks—no longer any of them exist here, for these ancient mountains, the oldest in the country, perhaps in the world, have passed through the wonder stages of geological youth and moved on into the calm old age of mountain life.

But the older mountains have beauties of their own, and our new park can offer attractions that the parks of the West, where nature has wrought in so dramatic and expansive a mood, cannot offer. For one thing, nowhere else is nature so friendly. The world is beautiful, with here and there touches of grandeur, and one may traverse the fragrant forests alone and without fear. Nor is it necessary to make long and extensive preparations to explore these ancient heights: it is enough to start out with a tiny

A Road in the Woods

knapsack and walk away, sure of a welcome wherever night overtakes you. There are great free spaces of forest, mountains, and sky, but at intervals there is always the clearing and the home of the settler, the most hospitable of created beings, and to the student of human nature one of the most interesting. Even in the widest reaches of the park, the home of the mountaineer will be found in some intruding cove or little valley, while there are no sweeter camping-grounds in all the world than those offered by this exquisite country of flowers, fragrances, cold springs, and cool summer nights, not only to the robust hunter and fisherman, but as well to frailer lovers of nature.

But the new park, large as it doubtless is destined to be, after all will cover but a small portion of the mountain region, and finally it is the people themselves who must keep the country beautiful. And this the canny mountaineer will do as soon as he recovers from his ancient fear of the forest and learns the new value of the tree. Among the most ardent workers for the passing of the Weeks Bill and for the Appalachian Park appropriation have been natives of these mountains, men of intellect and culture who have thrown all their strength into the contest, and who are still working for the good of the forests.

The primeval forests must go. The older trees continually go anyway, for, excepting those marvels of our Far West, the trees grow old, die, and fall. But they need not go all at once, and under intelligent care new forests may take the place of the old so continually and so skillfully that we need not be conscious of the passing of the ancient groves. Every one owning land in these mountains should remember that it is also the sacred and inalienable right of the tree to bestow beauty on the landscape, and that the law reads: "Blessed is he who saves a noble tree or preserves a grove on the mountain-top."

The lumberman, upon coming to a monarch of the forest so placed that it could survive the removal of the trees about it, should look at it with the eye of prophecy and pass by, leaving it to delight those who are on their way to the mountains, that vast army of pleasure-seekers whose coming will open up every beauty spot in the wilderness and also bring to the inhabitants of these noble heights a material wealth vying with that in the forests themselves. In these days of fast-moving events every feller of trees in the North Carolina mountains ought also to exercise the functions of a landscape gardener. No one asks that great tracts of primeval forest be kept for sentiment, but one does ask that certain portions of exceptionally beautiful tracts lying along the most frequented routes of travel be hedged about by some protecting power.

Moreover, on the slopes of those ridges that stand at imposing or beautiful points of view, the trees should be kept to preserve those picturesque skylines so characteristic of these mountains and which are disappearing with startling rapidity. It is asking too much that we wait a hundred years for the trees to grow again before we can enjoy the pictures that have made the mountains in their early days so enchanting, and the destruction of which brings, comparatively speaking, so small a return. It is easy to cut a big tree, but we must wait a century or two to get it back again, and who of us can afford that?

The genius of man has overcome the uttermost defenses of nature, and today the triumphant sawmill shrieks and devours in every stronghold of the mountains. The high places, the birth-chambers of the rivers, have struck their colors before the advance of the enemy. The sceptre has long since fallen from the hand of the red man. His successor roams the forest for pleasure, and also puts it to a thousand uses the aborigine did not so much as dream of; but the wisdom of the invader is such that he can if he will use the forest and yet preserve it, strengthen it, enhance its beauty, and increase its efficiency while even curtailing its area, and he will, let us hope, transform our Southern mountains with the intelligence of his higher reason, supplanting the charm of wildness with the grace of beauty. Thus the triumphant forests will continue to fold these ancient heights in their protecting mantle, they will beckon the rains to come, and steady the long rivers that flow to the sea.

Lovely, indeed, are the forests.

How Spring Comes in the Southern Mountains

It comes slowly, which is its unique charm. In the North the spring holds back, then comes with a rush, tumbles its treasures in a heap at your feet, and is gone. Here the spirit of the South prevails, and the spring gradually unfolds for three months, rising in a strong, slow tide that finally breaks over the land in a tremendous flood of color and fragrance and song.

As early as February the alders wake up and shake out their tassels. Small, dark-purple violets peep out from the dead leaves of the woods. The delicious fragrance that comes and goes you quickly trace to the clumps of brown-capped, purple little flowers of the Carolina pine-sap that are pushing up everywhere in the woods. The tops of the maple trees kindle to fire, and the colors of the leafless twigs everywhere begin to brighten.

As March draws near, that illusive spring feeling gets into the air, and that odor of spring that so powerfully exhales from nothing in particular. The peeping of frogs is heard, and up the wind come the voices of the people unconsciously singing the universal hymn of spring.

The trees are suddenly alive with birds. They, too, have felt that monition of spring in the air, and are on their way from the Far South to the Far North. Flocks of robins and bluebirds appear as by magic, then, along with other flocks that have spent the winter with us, they vanish, off, no doubt, to build their nests in more northern climes.

The chickadee, the titmouse, the nuthatch, the junco, the pine warbler, and many another lovely guest that has fed from our porch railing all winter, now share with flocks of migrants that remain with us a few days at a time. Birds on all sides are ecstatically singing. What marvelous outpourings come from that most joyful of songsters, the Carolina wren! Suddenly a new note is heard in the chorus that has broken out everywhere, the veery has discovered the coming of spring. A flock of song sparrows alighting in a budding tree-top all begin to sing at once, until it seems as though the tree had suddenly blossomed out in a bouquet of song. New life thrills the cardinal bird, who pours forth love-notes as he flashes, a streak of fire, through the air. Finches, tanagers, creepers, chats, woodpeckers—birds, red, yellow, blue, and green, show like flowers among the trees, some to pass on, some to remain with us through the summer.

The peach trees have burst into bloom, and on the ground in the woods you find clusters of pink-tipped buds and a few white blossoms peeping out from the evergreen leaves of the arbutus that carpets the woods in places. This is the beginning of a procession of flowers that might bewilder one in a more hasty climate, but here there is also opulence in the matter of time. There is no hurry. The "pretties," as the children here call all flowers, will linger day after day, week after week. Anemones, trilliums, ginger, eyebrights, violets, adder's-tongue, blood-root, hepaticas, all one's old friends have suddenly appeared as well as many a lovely stranger. All one's old friends would still be here if one came from the South instead of the North, for these mountains are a center for the flora of the different sections of the country.

There are certain flowers whose coming marks an era in spring itself, not because of their size or brilliancy, but because of some inherent quality that charms. Such a flower is the *Iris verna.* One thinks of the irises as inhabiting wet places, but not so this one, which grows everywhere in the dry woods, so charming a thing that having seen it one ever after associates it with the beauty of these forest floors. You watch as eagerly for the first iris as for the first arbutus. It is only three or four inches high, its color a clear amethyst blue, and besides being so lovely to look at, it is perfumed like a hothouse violet; that is to say, the variety with a touch of orange-yellow near the center is so perfumed. There is one with a white center, more delicate in color and contour than the other, a dream of beauty as one looks across gardens of it on some mountain-side, but it has no fragrance.

With the *Iris verna* appears the bird's-foot violet, also in the dry woods and pale violet-blue in color. Poised on a long stem with its lovely face held up to the sky, this large calm violet lends peculiar charm to the woods among the grays and delicate young greens of the forest floor.

While the irises and violets are yet in bloom the heavy buds of the pink azaleas slowly expand, the scales open, and airy flowers emerge in bright clusters that light up shady corners in the woods and brim the forest with their faint, refreshing fragrance. Like all the rest they linger long. There is no hurry.

About the time that the pink azaleas begin to open, the earliest of the rhododendrons—those that tapestry the damp walls of the ravines with patterns of twisted limbs and thick evergreen leaves—become embroidered with clusters of blush-rose and cream-white blossoms.

But there are other signs of spring than the coming of birds and flowers. As the season advances, the dark tracery of the trees becomes intermingled with many colors as young leaves bud out of the stiff twigs and rival the flowers in beauty. As you now look off at the mountains, new colors appear among the dark pine trees. Pale green creeps daintily up the ravines proclaiming the awakening of the tulip-trees. Budding hardwood trees everywhere mingle delicate shades of pink and yellow and silver-white, soft greens, and bronze-reds, with the dark green of the pines. The forest is transformed, it gives the impression of one wreathed in smiles. The tide of life is rising strongly though yet slowly.

The mountains, most of the time enveloped in a soft haze, seem far away and unreal. The air is saturated with odors distilled from the earth and the tree-tops; fragrance streams as it were from the pores of things, and the aroma of the budding forest ascends like incense from the earth.

Although the early spring is so ethereal in its beauty, shortly after the blossoming of the peach trees a remarkable change takes place in the general coloring of the landscape. The first delicacy and tenderness are for a time replaced by emerald green and other greens so strongly tinted with yellow as to need all the weight of the darker pines and the more sombre of the hardwood trees to tone down the vividness of the coloring. Pictures made at this time are laughed at and called impossible by those who have not been here to see how much gayer the reality is than any brush could paint. Yet above all this riot, the forest, serene and enchanting, smiles like a sedate mother at the gay spirits of her children. In course of time these brilliant hues tone down and blend together.

As the season advances, the earth puts forth blossoms more and more freely. Those banks of snow that fill whole ravines, those white ghosts that glimmer in the woods, are the white-flowering dogwood trees in bloom. Those rifts of rosy red along the ravines and on the slopes are the close-set blossoms of the Judas-tree or red-bud that open at just this moment as though to heighten the effect of the snowy dogwood. The pines wake up with the other growths. They are always green, it is true, but they have something in reserve for spring, every plume becoming tipped with fresh color as the petalless flowers, and later the groups of young needles, push out to the light. With the severe forms of the pines thus wreathed in garlands of spring, the transformation of the woods is complete.

Throughout this enticing season it is impossible to stay indoors. Household cares by some divine alchemy are transmuted into unimportant details of the real life. Urgent business, it is discovered, can just as well wait until tomorrow. There is no hurry. The real duty of the moment is to walk abroad, or drive, or ride a gentle horse through the mazes of the awakening world. Wherever one goes flowers greet the eye, violets, pinks, saxifrages, columbines—flowers familiar and flowers new. Gay butterflies are dancing about them like flowers with wings, and bright birds are singing everywhere.

You climb the mountains to look for orchids and lilies and

other rare blossoms. And many a time you traverse the lovely Pacolet Valley at the foot of Tryon Mountain, not only to see the flowers, but because of the delicate beauty that crowns it as a whole. For with its gentle, inclosing mountains, with the wonderful light filling it to the brim, with the exquisite colors that in the early morning and towards night, and at certain times even at midday, seem to convert the solid substance of the earth into an enchanting dream fabric, it is one of those creations of nature that have given us our poetic fancies of super-earthly beauty. And it was here, in the valley at Lynn, that Sidney Lanier, who sang with inspired soul of the dawn he so loved, of the trees, the marshes, the sky—it was here in the beautiful valley that America's most tuneful poet "waited for the dawn" through that last night of pain on earth.

As you go about in the season of flowers, you can trace the water-courses by the white foam of the silver-bell tree standing close-ranked, every twig and branch fringed with delicate white bells. And when you approach a ford or a stream you may see the earth hidden under the dainty little shrub yellow-root with its charming foliage and its lacework of small purple-brown flowers, a plant whose decorative value is well known to the landscape gardener, who masses it along his roadways and under his trees, but which perhaps he may not always know is a monotypic genus, its only species being found along the eastern side of the New World—according to the botanies, though the wiseacres will shake their heads at this, and point a prophetic finger across the globe to the Celestial Empire that today is so fast giving up its many hoarded secrets.

That waft of refreshing fragrance comes from the fringe-bush whose loose clusters of lacy white flowers you see on the opposite bank. What is more significant than this dainty and exquisite thing growing securely on the wild mountain-side? And how came it here when all other members of its family live in that remote Chinese Empire so mysteriously connected with us through the life of the plants? What was the bond that united us in past geologic ages? And what tore those tender flowers asunder, separating them by continents and vast seas?

When blossom the blackberry bushes that crowd into every cleared spot and border the paths and the roads, it is worth while going out just to see them, though it would be impossible to go out without seeing them, for the hedgerows everywhere are white like banks of snow. At their blooming-time in April or early May comes a cold storm called the "blackberry-blossom storm," as a similar spell of bad weather in the North when the apple trees are out is called the "apple-blossom storm."

About Traumfest the blackberry has a rival in the Japanese honeysuckle, that, having escaped from the gardens, densely covers banks and open places. Red clay evidently suits it. It buries a stone wall or a fence in a year or two, blossoms tremendously, and loads the air with its delicious perfume. But out in the woods you will find a wild honeysuckle as lovely and as fragrant as its Japanese cousin and with blossoms greatly resembling it, reminding us of that mysterious relationship between the plants of the East and the West; only it is less importunate than its imported relative, it does not smother the earth, but twines about the bushes in a modest manner, and its beautiful white flowers have richer tones of yellow and are sometimes flushed with pink. The red trumpet honeysuckle, loved by every child, also twines about the bushes on the mountain-side in company with other beautiful and fragrant members of the same family.

The heavy curtains of leucothoë that hang over the water-courses have become embroidered with long white flower spikes. And walking at higher levels you will come across the little umbrella-leaf with its uplifted head of white flowers. You might not notice it among the wealth of more striking blossoms all about you, but you will never pass it unheeding when you remember that there is only one other known species of its family, and that that one opens its flowers in far-away Japan.

If interested in these curious relationships, you will find on these mountains many a modest flower whose genealogy is inextricably intertwined with the flowers of the Orient. In this mysterious sisterhood is the wisteria that so often adorns our homes and which is most closely connected in our thoughts with Japan, which we imagine ever wreathed in wisteria blossoms, as we see them twining about the screens and the drawings that come from that far land to us. It is the Japanese wisteria we cultivate and with which we are familiar, though we ourselves have one member of this very ornamental family. You will come upon our wisteria sometime in your wanderings in the lower mountains, where it will be seen climbing the trees and covering them with its mantle of leaves and its myriads of close bunches of purple-blue flowers, a charming thing whose day among the petted darlings of the garden doubtless yet will come.

Of course, growing everywhere over the mountains, though more abundantly and of larger size in the higher mountains, is the highly prized galax, whose silky round leaves, green in summer, and rich wine-red in winter and spring, have taken the fancy of the city florist, sometimes to the discomfiture of the collector, who gets large orders for wine-red leaves in the summer from haughty florists who cannot be induced to believe that red galax leaves, like red currants, have their season. One can have no idea what a really charming thing the galax is until one sees it thickly carpeting the woods. And what one never discovers, from seeing it in the stiff circles with which it surrounds the city nosegay, is that in the early summer it sends up all over the forest floor dainty white flower spikes. It, too, has its mystery and its romance, for who can doubt, learning that it is classed as a monotypic genus of eastern North America, that it has its kinsfolk across the earth, beckoning us to recognize the relationship between the races we look upon as our antipodes?

Huckleberries soon begin to blossom, but prettier than the flowers are the little bright red leaves that add so much to the color of the forest floor in early spring. And there is the sparkleberry, whose pale-green, neat-looking bushes are all a-dangle with little snow-white bells crowded as close as can be on their slender, swinging stems, precursors of the pale-green berries that make a great show because there are so many of them. The people sometimes make jelly of these berries, amazing jelly as bitter as gall.

Important and beautiful as are all these flowers and budding leaves, the woods do not quite belong to you until you have found something in them to chew. Then they are yours in an intimate and peculiar manner. This desire to taste is doubtless a survival of the child in us that we never quite outgrow. When we go into the woods we in a sense revert to a more primitive state, and the sight of sassafras excites the gustatory nerve. Sassafras is abundant. It blossoms like a burst of sunshine along the edges of the yet leafless woods, each of its bare branches terminating in a pretty amber ball of delicately fragrant and fringe-like flowers. There is nothing prettier than sassafras with the sun behind its blossoming twigs. One recalls a sassafras grove on a mountain slope that seemed to have been purposely planted, the trees were so regular in size and position, but the poor soul who owned it said it was a potato-field, and that the harder he tried to root out the sassafras the better it grew. We who do not depend upon sassafras-land for our potatoes love the aromatic plant whose roots, stems, leaves, and flowers yield a pleasant fragrance as well as a pleasant flavor to those who have not outgrown their youthful habit of browsing in the woods; and whose history has also its finer flavor of romance, since the sassafras exists as a single species in the eastern part of the New World, while one other species has been found in China.

With the sassafras one often finds its near relative the spice-bush, whose botanical name is *Benzoin*, because of its fragrance, and whose pungent, camphor-flavored bark is also pleasant to the taste. There are seven known species of the spice-bush, two in the eastern United States, the others in Asia. Another shrub that belongs to us and eastern Asia and that tempts one to nibble is what the people here call "sweet bubbies." It appears in old-fashioned Northern gardens under the name of sweet-scented or flowering or strawberry shrub, but every child who has warmed the stiff, maroon-colored flowers in his hand—and what child has not?—will tell you instantly that "sweet bubbies" is the preferable and proper name. The mountain children warm the sweet bubbies in their hands, but they do not have to go to a favored corner of some garden to find one. They can pick a bushel of them along the roadside within a stone's throw of the house. Like the sassafras, the sweet bubby is spicy to the core; leaf, root, and branch possessing an agreeable flavor.

"Horse sugar," the only North American member of its family, which otherwise lives in South America, Asia, and Australasia, is another early blossoming shrub whose flower clusters of little close-set balls of yellow fringe are fragrant and whose bark is aromatic. Its sweetish leaves, which the people say horses like to eat, have given it its popular name, but the botany, scorning frivolity, christens it *Symplocos tinctoria.*

Of course sap that has exuded from the pine tree, when it hardens to just the right consistency, affords never-failing solace to children of all ages who belong to the woods. Then there are the tips of the pine twigs that leave such a clean and pleasant flavor in the mouth. We wanderers of the earth enjoy the forest with all our senses, and with its fragrance, its colors, its sounds, and its sweet juices we seem also to imbibe something of its freshness and its greatness.

The Carnival

The early flowers are only the prelude in the floral drama that reaches its climax when the mountain laurel, the flame-colored azaleas, and the rhododendrons come upon the scene. Their appearance converts the earth into a spectacle difficult to imagine, and although the outburst is so prodigious, there is no hurry, it is sustained, hanging suspended as it were in almost equal intensity for a month or more. It takes place in the lower mountains in May, in the higher ones, in June and July.

One gets the first hint of what is coming when, driving up a certain mountain near Traumfest, one sees the snowy drifts of the dogwood through a veil of bright red-bud in the misty ravines; that mountain from whose side one looks down to where beyond the hills the lowlands spread, reaching like a summer sea to the far horizon—the lowlands that wherever visible give an illusion of the sea that is sometimes wonderfully real, distance lending a misty blue to the level landscape out of which roll lines of hills like breakers white-crested with smoke or mist or "deadenings." A log cabin shaded by a large weeping willow rests in a hollow on the mountain. Fig trees and rose-bushes grow about it, and a spring of cold water gushes out of the ground. From the back door a winding path leads across a tiny "branch," across a hillside and across a hollow. Here while the dogwood is yet in bloom, one gets a glimpse of the flames that are presently to set the mountains ablaze. This first sight of flame-colored azaleas can never be forgotten. You come suddenly upon great clusters of flowers that blaze forth in a splendor that quickens the pulse. It seems incredible that anything could come to such perfection of beauty in the rude environment of the mountainside where so many plants struggle together for life. Even the celebrated azaleas of Ghent, the pride of the hothouse, pale before the marvelous beauty of these wild growths.

All flowers are imprisoned sunshine in a figurative sense, but of no others does that seem so literally true as of these. They appeal to the imagination as delicate flames incarnate. Each bush has its own colors. Before you stands one whose blossoms are the color of flames, beyond it is a bush clad in crimson bloom, and there behind the bright-green leaves of young trees one sees a blaze of scarlet. Orange-yellow shading to pale flame glows on the edge of the hollow; a regal bush blossoming with the gold of ripe lemons stands a little apart; as you look up the near hillside, your eye is caught by wonderful bronze tints, by shades of pink, and elusive pale-rose tints. In this arras of exquisitely blended colors, soft shadows lying on the petals yet more mingle their hues together.

You feel as if something important had happened as you turn away from this your first view of the flame-colored azaleas in their native soil. You have a sense of possession and gratitude to the generosity that thus presents to you, not a laboriously cultivated plant in a pot, or even a great bed in a country garden, but a mountain-side of incomparable flowers as free as the air.

The road up Rocky Spur at the time of the carnival of flowers is a succession of pictures where blossoming bushes are grouped at every turn. Over the slopes above you and the slopes below, between the straight tree-trunks and the leafy boughs, wherever the eyes rest, glow these flames of the azaleas. When you reach the central ridge, the high knife-edge top of the mountain where you can look off both sides, you see not only the landscape of mountain and valley immersed in the soft light, those far blue spaces and that near mingling of green foliage, but you have at your feet rolling down the southern slope of the mountain such a wave of bloom that suddenly seen makes you catch your breath. This is the end of the road, and leaving the carriage you go down the mountain-side into the sunny chambers of the forest luminous with blossoms that inclose and embrace you. Above your head hang clouds of gold, at your knee press billows of flame, all about you are great globe-like clusters of these incomparable flowers.

You look towards the mountains that lie to the south, height upon height, the near ones green above with intense blue shadows towards their bases, the more distant ones a sweet, mystical blue, and you know that on all those slopes far and near are blazing the same fires that illumine the earth about you. Being thus close to the flowers, you cannot help noticing the exquisite texture of the petals, their great size, the symmetry of each flower and of the large clusters, as well as the ornamental shape of the bushes with the young leaves piercing through the bloom here and there in green points. It is the texture of the flowers and their width—some of them are almost round—that gives them that charmingly expansive, one might say luscious, effect. The petals are so delicate that the light seems almost to shine through them. These wild azaleas of the Southern mountains lack the somewhat dense effect of the well-known cultivated plants, and when transplanted to parks and gardens they lose something of their sumptuousness, their wonderful clearness and richness of coloring, and to an extent their exquisite texture. They lose their aspect of dainty wildness and become as it were citified.

To see the perfect fire of the azaleas you must come to their mountains. They may be found from southern New York to Georgia, but only in the high parts of the Southern mountains do they attain perfection. Although the azaleas are so widespread as a family, why is it that this species with fire in its veins lives only here and in the Far East? The Himalaya Mountains, like the mountains of Carolina, have their slopes adorned with these tremendously glowing flowers that gave to the gardens of Europe their choicest azaleas long before these of the New World were known.

To find these azaleas one must ascend the mountains, for they do not grow as low down even as Traumfest. When they are in bloom, we visit the Warriors for certain hollows, we go up Tryon Mountain because of certain slopes, we frequent the wild heights of Hogback and Rocky Spur. We warm our senses for a month in the fire of the flowers, and then if we like we can go higher up—and enjoy it all over again. In the higher mountains the azaleas are more abundant than here, though they are no more beautiful, for that would be impossible. When those noble heights beyond the Blue Ridge wreathe themselves in flowers, one finds whole mountainsides aglow, for where the trees have been cut off, fiery azaleas oftentimes cover the wounded earth. The open spaces are resplendent beyond words, one sees acres of flower-flames ablaze on the slopes. These close-crowding bushes in the cleared places are low, laying a stunning carpet of color over the mountainside, but in the woods they grow tall, and you see them on all sides glowing in the shadows and burning in the sunlight. The outbreak of color is almost overwhelming, and one is grateful for those intervening spaces where are no flowers. From a world of exciting colors one passes into the cool and peaceful green of the forest, presently to turn a curve in the road and find the slopes again on all sides in furious bloom.

Thus for a season the earth is transfigured, the mountains on all sides are burning with flames that do not destroy. The spectacle is on a grand scale; one can wander over thousands of square miles encompassed by flowers—beyond the limits of North Carolina these unconsuming flames have spread over hundreds of miles of the ridges and spurs of the Southern Appalachians, so that one seems to get lost even in thinking of it. The people call these azaleas "yellow honeysuckles," and get tired of them. The azaleas flaming throughout the forest are like great music, great poetry, great pictures; they strike too high a note for the lives of the people. Such fervor wearies their unaccustomed nerves, and they turn for consolation to a calmer expression of the great renewal.

For the flame-colored azaleas, marvelous as they are, form but a part of the flood of bloom that rolls over the mountains. About the time they appear, the fair and restful *Kalmia latifolia,* or mountain laurel, begins to open. The mountains here are green with kalmia—or laurel, as one prefers to call it—as the hills of the

North are green with grass. When the forest is burned over, the mountain laurel rushes in and competes with young pine trees for the soil. It grows in impenetrable jungles in the ravines and along the water-courses. Where grown in the open and safe from fire, it attains great size, there being laurel trees about Highlands and elsewhere as large as ordinary apple trees. Generally, however, it appears as bushes from three to fifteen feet high that, annually covering themselves with bloom, light up the mountains from end to end. Standing waist-high on a level of low-growing laurel, the bushes concealed by the heavy billowing masses of bloom, you seem to be afloat on a sea of flowers.

The laurel freely covers the lower as well as the higher mountains. It wraps Traumfest as in a mantle. Who does not know the "laurel path" that winds through an otherwise impenetrable thicket? Over this path in the blossoming season you wade, as it were, through a flowery labyrinth that opens to let you pass and closes behind you as you follow the winding way. Masses of bloom lightly touch your check, or graze your shoulder, tall bushes loaded with blossoms close over your head—you pass under an arch composed of flowers. You look through an opening in the bushes that surround you, and the slope below you is covered with a carpet of rosy-white bloom. In Traumfest some of us go out to see the laurel as the people of Japan go out to see the cherry blossoms. You climb Melrose to be buried in laurel bloom. You ascend heights that you may look down upon the earth hidden under flowers. Again you drive along the upper edge of a ravine that runs for miles bank full of laurel blossoms.

The air is pervaded by the bitter-sweet smell of the flowers. The ground is white where the cups have begun to fall—or perhaps it is red, for there are bushes that bloom year after year as red as a rose, and others that clothe themselves in a garment of delicate pink. There are also those whose bloom is as white as snow, the crisp and upright cups scarcely pricked with the red dot that marks the anther pockets so conspicuous in some of the laurel.

Nothing is more charming than a laurel cup with the anthers

on its recurved filaments still hidden in the little pink pits that indent the inside of the corolla in a circle. These curved and captured stamens, pretty traps to force invading insects to bear away pollen on their wings, at the slightest touch spring back and curl up at the center of the flower dusting the intruder, and you, passing among the laurel, are sure to be dusted with little pellets of pollen bombarding you on all sides. And the cups themselves! Scalloped on the edges, shaped and decorated like tiny afternoon-tea cups, who does not know and love them! There is something familiar and homelike about laurel, and it is easy to understand why the people prefer it to the azaleas. Like the New Englander they call it "calico-bush," a comfortable name suggesting Sunday starch and fresh young girls. And here, as in New England, the laurel is also known as "ivy," the name laurel being here bestowed upon the lordly rhododendron.

The mountain-laurel and the flame-colored azaleas, though both so abundant, do not interfere with each other. There is room on the vast surface of the mountains for both. And while a zone of flowering azaleas belts the mountains, just below it or interrupting it or claiming intruding ravines is the tremendous calm sea of the blossoming laurel.

As though the marvelous outbreak of the azaleas and laurel were not enough to express the joy of life animating the earth, the rhododendrons open their regal buds. No one would think of calling the rhododendron a "calico-bush"! It belongs by every line of its stately foliage and more stately blossoms to the aristocracy of plant life. Its thick, glossy, evergreen leaves, much larger than those of the laurel and darker in color, its tall growth and crooked stems make it a noticeable and very decorative presence even when not in bloom. At the elevation of Traumfest the greater rhododendrons do not grow, only those smaller, early blossoming ones whose more delicate forms and exquisite pale-pink or white blossoms grace many a ravine and roadside bank. But on the higher mountains the slopes and ravines are often impassable because of the dense growths of rhododendrons, the king of

A LAUREL PATH

which is the *Rhododendron maximum,* that sometimes becomes a tree forty feet high, though more often it is a large shrub.

Smaller than this, seldom reaching a height of twenty feet, and very abundant on many of the mountains, is the *Rhododendron Catawbiense,* or mountain rose-bay, blooming earlier than the other, its large clusters of lilac or purple or sometimes rose-red flowers making one of the most showy spectacles of the carnival season, particularly as it chooses open places and the summits of the mountains to display its colors. How many mountain scenes one recalls made glorious by this splendid shrub, and perhaps nowhere does it give more pleasure to the eye than where it stands in groups on the long and beautiful slopes of the Grandfather Mountain, those southern slopes sweeping down and down into the foothills of the John's River Valley. One of the finest roads in the mountains crosses this southern front of the Grandfather, winding through the forest and over the open places, keeping for many miles an elevation of about four thousand feet. It is in every sense a high place. The air is clean and cool and fragrant; in the distant spaces lie fair valleys and noble mountains, while close about you the mountain rose-bay enchantingly colors the earth. The effect of these masses of bloom on the grassy slopes against the blue sky is lovely.

The color of these flowers varies a good deal, all the way from rich purple-red to a clear, sweet rose color. Some people condemn the flowers as "magenta," seeing only that among all the colors they assume. But there are occasions when even this despised color can ravish the senses. Up near the top of the Grandfather Mountain, for instance, one should see the purple rose-bay against the blue-gray rocks in the quivering blue atmosphere of a summer day to find out how glorious a thing a magenta flower in its right setting can be.

As the mountain rose-bay passes, the great waxlike flowers of the *Rhododendron maximum* come forth out of the heavy bud clusters. The *Rhododendron maximum* generally grows in ravines or along damp slopes, where it makes jungles of tropical luxuriance. Its large flowers, which are usually white or a delicate peachy pink, grow in clusters like the flowers of the other rhododendrons, and though the *Rhododendron maximum* does not bloom so profusely as the laurel, the sight of the high wall of a ravine tapestried with its large dark-green leaves, in which the great flower clusters gleam out, is something to remember. The regal *Rhododendron maximum* is not so exciting as the flaming azalea, not so home-like as the laurel, nor so theatrical as the mountain rose-bay, but it possesses a degree of dignity and elegance belonging to it alone and that distinguishes it among all the forest growths.

There are several species of the rhododendron found in different parts of the mountains, among them the charming little *Rhododendron Vaseyii* that, unlike the other rhododendrons, sheds its leaves in the fall. It was said at one time to be extinct, but this is not true, as any one knows who, early in the season, has seen the cliffs on the north side of the Grandfather Mountain brightly colored with its rosy bloom.

The azaleas, laurels, and rhododendrons, although so abundant in the Southern mountains, are by no means confined to them, some species being found throughout the whole Appalachian system from Canada to Georgia. One recalls certain New England pastures that are mantled in laurel, while the *Rhododendron maximum* occurs locally as far north as New Hampshire. The red-blooming mountain rose-bay begins its course in Virginia, making a wonderful show in the Cumberland Mountains, as all will recall with pleasure who have passed through the Cumberland Gap in its blooming season. And the flame-colored azaleas, as has been said, light their fires as far north as Southern New York, though they do not burn with the brilliancy and variety of color anywhere else as here where they so wonderfully set the slopes of the mountains ablaze.

To the mountaineer all things are admissible that serve his ends, and one is horrified upon first coming to find him burning rhododendron and laurel wood because, he says, they make a hot fire good for cooking. Think of cutting down for such a purpose a rhododendron or a laurel tree with a trunk thick enough to be split into four sticks of wood! Familiarity with the country, however, modifies this horror. When there is rhododendron enough to get lost in, one can afford to burn a little now and then.

With the passing of the azaleas, the laurel, and the rhododendrons, the fervor of the blooming season here subsides, and it is then that one being in Traumfest often goes down to a certain stream over which a bridge unites two cornfields. At either end of this bridge on the edge of the water grow large azalea bushes different from the others. These now begin to put forth, not pink nor flame-colored azaleas, but snowy white blossoms with a strong and spicy fragrance that carries one back to certain New England swamps where one learned to love and watch for these fragrant things. These are the last of the azaleas down below and the only white ones. But there is a species of white azalea up on Toxaway Mountain and elsewhere, closely resembling this of the brookside, though it grows on the dry slopes, yielding the same delicious fragrance. It may be said in passing that sweet-fern, dear to the heart of every one familiar with New England pastures, also grows on Toxaway, Pisgah, and other of the high mountains. What a turn it gives one to see it here unexpectedly and to smell its incomparable odor, an odor that more than any other revives slumbering memories.

But these fragrant white azaleas are like the epilogue at the end of the play. When the gleaming petals of the *Rhododendron maximum* fall away, the curtain has dropped on the Carnival of the Flowers, and spring moves on into summer and fruitage.

Summer in the Mountains

After the reckless profusion of spring, what is left for summer in the matter of flowers? There is indeed nothing to match the early display, yet the summer is not flowerless, and it has a beauty of its own in the fruitage that overwhelms one for a time.

One notices how vines are everywhere twining and climbing—festooning the trees, overlaying the bushes, tying the tall weeds together, clematis here, woodbine there, smilax, trumpet-vine, so many vetches, so many pretty vines whose names one does not know—how they cling and climb and riot in luxuriant life! Everywhere along the ravines the forest trees are hung with the strong cables of the grapevine, whose foliage mingles inextricably with that of the tree it mantles, and whose delicious fragrance loads the air about the time the little white urns of the persimmon tree fall to the ground brimmed with delicate perfume.

We find six kinds of morning-glories choking up our vegetable garden in August. We have given up all hope of vegetables, but we go out in the morning to rejoice in the glory of the usurper. Those vines with star-shaped leaves that run over garden and fields, fairly carpeting the earth in places, are passion-flower vines, as you would know from the wonderful flowers that cover them. Think of red earth numbering among its weeds the great blue disks of the passion-flower. Your garden is a riot of blooming weeds, so that you cannot see anything else. Everything except the vegetables has grown as though possessed.

Not that all this marvelous growth even of weeds is without its difficulties. There are caterpillars. Besides these, many other hungry insect guests of the summer appear as if on purpose to cut short the mad career of the plants—sometimes with ludicrous abruptness. But these incursions seem generally to take place after the plant has accomplished the maturing of seeds enough to weed down the earth another year.

Now from the depths of the woods comes the voice of the "moaning dove," as the negroes call it, whose frequently uttered *coo—oooo—oo* in the hot, still, summer days fills the heart with an indescribable sadness and longing, and the wood thrush yet heralds and closes the day with its ringing notes. At the faintest hint of dawn one hears a clear, soft refrain. Like the morning prayer of the Arab that passes from tower to tower, the song of the thrush is caught up by bird after bird until the air throbs with song. This lasts until the sun is shining, when the ecstatic hymn to the dawn ceases.

Yet silence does not reign when the birds stop, for the insect chorus, that began in the spring with weak chirps and trills, has swelled to a deafening shout that ascends as the sun goes down, stops suddenly before dawn, only to be renewed, though less vociferously, by other insects during the day. Cicadas spring their rattles and whirr past in startling proximity to your face, and when the "seventeen-year locusts" swarm out on Tryon Mountain, you must needs shout into the ear of your companion as you drive through the forest vibrating with their shrill voices. It is almost as noisy as a storm at sea, and it is hard to understand how these hordes happen to have their seventeen-yearly anniversary so often.

But excepting for the locusts on Tryon Mountain, the turmoil of the day is nothing to that of the night. One wonders who they all are, those strident-voiced myriads hidden under the leaves. Above everything else rise the insistent cries of the katydids, while out of the woods come all kinds of purrings, and squeakings, and trillings. Those little meteors that trail through the bushes are fireflys, as are also the rapidly moving constellations of stars that gem the treetops.

Always in summer a voice rings out as the sun goes down, and continues chanting its wild refrain all night and every night, until stilled by the cold of winter. *Whip-poor-will! whip-poor-will!*—sometimes you will hear half a dozen of these tireless vocalists performing at once.

Another voice of the night is the soft, tremulous call that comes down the aisles of the forest when the sun sets and the little downy owls come forth. The owl, it is said, puts the night to evil uses, catching and eating the birds and despoiling their nests of eggs and young; but whoever has heard the many sweet cadences, the crooning, caressing tones of these fluffy, nocturnal revelers, will be convinced that the chief occupation of the owl at night is the pursuit of happiness. Sometimes far away, deep-toned, and mysterious comes the *hoo—ooo—ooo, hoo—oo* of the great horned owl, and you, listening, can easily believe that he at least is up to mischief. You do not often see the owls, but sometimes walking in the woods at dusk a shape will float past noiseless as a disembodied spirit.

In the higher mountains there are no mosquitoes, and there used to be none at Traumfest in those good old days before the stranger had begun to "improve" the place. The summers of Traumfest are sweet beyond words to express and the thermometer goes no higher here than in the North—not so high very often—and the nights are cool; but the hot season lasts longer, so that those accustomed to five or six weeks of midsummer heat sometimes grumble when they get four months of it. But no one who has not spent a summer here can hope to know what these woods are capable of in the way of sweet smells.

All the mountaineer does these days is to "work the corn" with a cultivator, if he happens to have one with the necessary adjunct of a mule; or otherwise with a slow hoe. Sometimes he does not work it, and complains of the result. The corn crop looks like a joke to the newcomer accustomed to corn in other regions. "What are you doing?" was asked of a boy busy in a field of young corn so sparse as to excite mirth. The boy looked up, and cheerily replied, "Oh, I am thinning the corn." And so he was! When the corn has been properly thinned, you will find but one stalk to a hill and the hills far apart, excepting in the river bottoms where the showing is better. Man ploughs the corn, but woman often hoes it, she and the children. The children begin to hoe at the age of eight, and you will often see them busy in the fields, both boys and girls—but it is not necessary to pity them, for they like it.

The cornfield is ever present in the landscape, not only covering the valley bottoms, but lying precariously on the steepest slopes surrounded by the forest. Beans are often planted with the corn, where they climb the convenient stalks, but it is the corn one sees, and the corn which gives that odd domestic touch to the wild scenery of the Southern mountains. For corn is not only the principal food of the mountaineer, but supplies as well that important beverage, variously known as "corn-juice," "moonshine," "mountain-dew," "blockade," "brush whiskey," and in the outer world, "corn-whiskey," which is extracted from the grain and surreptitiously distributed.

Fortunately this important crop is able to defy the rigors of the summer and conquer, with man's help, the overwhelming army of weeds—or flowers; for many of these wild growths could be called "weeds" only by a soulless farmer regardless of everything but crops.

As summer advances, the compositæ begin to carpet the fields with cloth-of-gold, and tapestry the hedges with gay colors, but the summer flowers are as nothing compared to the procession of fruits that, beginning in the spring with strawberries, lasts throughout the hot season. Strawberries at Traumfest are ripe in May, and so are cherries—what there are, for the cherry does not flourish here; and no sooner does the fruit turn red on the few trees lovingly watched by their owners than there appear upon the scene a large and happy flock of cedar waxwings, for no slight reason named "cherry-birds."

When the procession of fruits is fairly started, you will have hard work to keep up with it for a few weeks. About Traumfest plums, peaches, peaches, peaches, berries, the most delicious of grapes—Traumfest is noted for its grapes—apples—such as they are—figs—and melons! Wagonloads of watermelons stand about waiting, not in vain, for customers. You know the approach of the melon season from the vanguard of empty rinds lying along

In Summer Time

the roadside. There is no trouble getting at a melon. All you need do is to "bust it open," root into the crisp, pink, and juicy interior with your hands, and go ahead. This the negro children do, lacking a knife, and you will see them, tears of pure delight, as it were, streaming from the corners of their happy mouths. The Southern watermelon! What other fruit ever bestowed such joy on humankind. To see a Carolina negro camped down before a big watermelon is to see what the philosophers try to make us believe does not exist—a perfectly happy mortal.

How we do revel in ripe fruit! And then—all of a sudden—the procession has passed. The seemingly endless abundance stops short. You realize with a sort of anger that it has gone. Why did you not eat more? Why did you not pickle, preserve, can all those vanished blessings tenfold more than you did? It seemed as though such abundance could never end—and now!

But it is not quite ended. If you look over those fields where, in spite of the efforts of the farmer, the great blue passion-flowers bloomed all summer, you will see leathery-skinned fruits as large as a goose egg lying about by the basketful. These are maypops. If you break open a thoroughly ripe one, you will be assailed by an aroma that makes you think of tropical fruits, of perfumed bowers, of Arabian Nights banquets, of fairy gardens, and strange tropical flowers. Inside, the maypop resembles a pomegranate, but the patrician pomegranate has no such heavenly flavor as has this wild and worthless maypop. What our fruit-makers are thinking of not to cultivate the maypop, one cannot imagine. It offers possibilities that ought to tempt them beyond the power of resistance. In some parts of the mountains the people call the maypops "apricots" and eat them, though they belong principally to the age of childhood. These strange, exquisite, good-for-nothing fruits are the product of the passion-flower vine.

Later than the cultivated grapes, about the time of the maypops, come the wild grapes, among them the large sweet muscadines that the country children bring in by the bushel. These come on the edge of autumn, but before the summer is over there is yet a unique and gorgeous display in the plant world that cannot be ignored. It is not flowers this time, though as the summer nears its end, the ground blossoms out in the most extraordinary manner. What are those large gold plates lying in the woods? Those exquisitely yellow, or orange, or pink or purple disks, those masses of coral, red, yellow, or ivory-white? Those pearly or snowy caps? Those enormous frills and those smoky little buttons? Ah, yes, they are the mushrooms! How many shapes and sizes and colors spring up in a night! Sometimes they are beautiful and sometimes they are not. But they are always amusing, as though trying to tell us to take all this fuss and fury of the fruits and flowers calmly, or even somewhat as a jest. "After all, what matters it?" they seem to say; "they are gone and here are we, just as gay and twice as funny"; and they roll up or straighten out into all sorts of shapes. They break the spell of the flowers and fruits, as it were, and put one in mood for the next great event, the vivid and most tender splendor of the autumn.

AUTUMN

Slowly Autumn kindles her torch. Here and there a yellow leaf shows among the green. Then comes a premonitory softening of the whole landscape. Then colors, almost as dainty as those of spring, creep over the earth, so slowly that time and again you decide there is to be no great display this year, when, some warm November day, you look out to find the world transfigured.

The difference between the autumn coloring of the North and of the South is that there it is brilliant, while here it is tender. There the hardwood trees blaze, here they glow. The reds that here so wonderfully emblazon the book of nature have a peculiar delicacy and softness of tone that give a character of its own to the landscape. As the oak leaves deepen to wine-red, the dogwoods turn exquisite shades of old-rose and pink, and the sourwood adds its ruby splendor. The tall pyramidal forms of the sweet-gum, mantled in dark purple or deep reds touched with orange, add depth to the color-tone of the forest, or its leaves turn yellow—and sometimes all these colors mingle together on the same tree. A sweet-gum in autumn dress with the sun through it fairly takes one's breath. Sassafras points the woods with thrilling spots of scarlet, orange, and red. Sumac burns in the hedges, while huckleberry and other bushes crimson the ground.

Mingling with the reds, or apart by themselves, are the clean yellows characteristic of this region. Tall tulip-trees stand in the hollows and along the ravines with crowns of gold. Hickories and beeches add their yellows and browns, and the chestnut oak, when other oaks are red, keeps up the pretense and turns golden-brown, the color of fading chestnut leaves.

The whole world is at times immersed in a light that strangely enhances its beauty. Is it smoke that makes those intensely blue spaces under the trees? The forests have not yet begun to burn, only the people are burning brush here and there. The color seems to be in the air itself. The very tree-trunks often look blue, the delicate, mystical blue of the Blue Ridge Mountains.

One wakens day after day to transports of color. Out of each window a new scene constantly unfolds. The sun shines in to you through a tent of red and yellow leaves that incloses the house, and the mountains seen through them take on intenser tones of rose-color and blue, of purple and peacock green. The mountain slopes far and near at this time seem hung with an arras from some enchanted loom. The splendid colors of the hardwood trees are interwoven with the sunny plumes of the pines, while here and there the twisted crown of an ancient pine tree is drawn in strong lines against the glowing background, while golden sunlight sifts and quivers through it all.

Slowly the autumn draws on, and slowly it passes, lingering as lingered the coming of spring, sometimes sustaining its flames well into December. Indeed, there are splashes of crimson remaining all winter, for which one has to thank the horse-brier, the most exasperating plant that grows, but to see it in midwinter festooning the young trees and the bushes with its trailing wreaths of fire is to forgive it everything. If you go down to the brookside in November, supposing the flowers are gone and the winter at hand, you will meet with a pleasant surprise. Those deep blue spindles standing upright among the fallen leaves are closed gentians, more graceful and of a deeper, purer blue than the closed gentians of the North.

When the leaves are taking on their autumn colors, the cornfields turn to gold, and men, women, and children go out to "pull fodder," an occupation that in the meadowless regions, and to an extent all through the mountains, takes the place of haying, and, consistently, is less arduous. The stripped-off leaves and the cut-off tassels are hung up to dry on the yet standing stalk in the crotch made by the ear of corn, or sometimes in the crotch of a convenient tree. And that is all there is to it.

When the fodder-pullers have finished their work and the dried fodder has been "toted" home, the cornfield for a time presents the most extraordinary appearance in its history. It suggests a company of pygmies, each standing erect with his pack over his shoulder, for the heavy ears of corn turn down and are all that is left on the stripped and beheaded stalks. Throughout the mountains these absurd cornfields are a feature of the autumn landscape, lying on the slopes, covering the valley bottoms, and appearing without warning in the midst of an otherwise unbroken forest. The Northern visitor sometimes compares them, to their disadvantage, with other cornfields of his acquaintance, where noble stacks stand in even rows, great golden pumpkins scattered over the ground between. But what he does not consider is that such a cornfield would be out of place here, and the golden pumpkin might strike a false note. Pumpkins there are, it is true, but they are pink, thus failing in one of the most important functions of a pumpkin. A pink pumpkin! But it would do very well if called by some other name; that is, as an ornament, for you can by no means make good pies out of a pink pumpkin, "pumpkin pie" remaining the unchallenged treasure of the North.

In course of time the ear of corn also disappears from the bereft stalk, it is "toted" home and husked, then a part is shelled and the white and wrinkled kernels ground into the sweetest meal in the world, between the slow stones of little mills that stand along the water-courses. If a man is successful in life and owns "right smart of corn-land," he will likely have his own mill, though it may be no larger than a good-sized chicken coop, with perhaps a wooden wheel, taller than itself, on the outside, a wheel that turns slowly and with dignity, the silver water dropping from the broad paddles in a miniature cascade. The miller in the smaller mills is sometimes a woman in a sunbonnet, but running the mill is not very hard work, since it often consists in pouring the corn into the hopper, then going away for a few hours or all day, and coming back in the fullness of time to take the sweet meal from the box below the leisurely stones.

Besides the cornfields there are those frequent fields of something that "imitates corn a right smart," as the people say, but which is only sorghum, from which in the fall the mountaineer extracts molasses for home consumption. Sorghum is a picturesque crop from first to last. When the slender stalks have been cut, the juice is expressed from them in sugar-mills simpler even than the corn-mills. Between two cogged wheels the long canes are fed by a patient man sitting on a log, while the wheels are turned by a patient mule at the end of a long beam, walking forever round and round and going nowhere. During this process the family is generally grouped about the mill, while the vat into which the sweet juice runs is the scene of tragic deaths, as into it crowd bees, flies, and wasps greedy for a share of the harvest. Near the cane-mill, and like it standing in the open air, is a large pan under which a fire is built and in which the juice is boiled—bees and all. Standing over the caldron is a man enveloped in clouds of steam as with a long pole he stirs the bubbling sweet. In a short time "them molasses" is done. Sorghum cannot be reduced to sugar, or, if it can be, it never is here in the mountains. It is put into jugs and provides the principal "sweetening" of the family.

Man is so close to the soil here that he recognizes the relationship. He sees his bread—and molasses—come directly from the earth. He loves the land, and the ambition of every youth is to possess a little farm of his own. In the wild forest he clears a place, plants the corn, cultivates it, watches it grow, gathers in the harvest, grinds the meal and makes the bread, most of these things being done in the open air. And there is no hurry. He feels the sun and the wind, he looks into the forest and is not afraid, neither is he unhappy. The cornfield is almost the boundary of his desires. He sells corn, or its equivalent in "blockade," for money with which to supply his needs. He fattens his pigs on corn and with it feeds the poultry. The mule and the horse eat corn, knowing no other grain. It is fed to them on the cob, since shelling corn for an animal able to shell it for himself would be a waste of time.

The Sorghum Cutter

Although the corn is the hope of the farmer, one sees an occasional oat-field, and sometimes a field of wheat or rye, but these seem to have been sown for the purpose of beautifying the landscape, the red soil showing through the scattering blue or green stalks with pleasing effect. In some valleys of the higher mountains these grains may be raised with profit, but on the eastern slopes of the Blue Ridge corn is the safer crop; although the people have a beautiful faith in the possibilities of their land, one farmer proudly saying of his venture in wheat, "There never was no better-headed wheat on earth, what there was of it—but there wa'n't none." And these fortunate people are as cheerful under failure as they are hopeful of success in impossible conditions. "What you doin' up there, Dicky?" your driver calls out one day derisively to a man gathering an almost invisible crop from a hillside. "Nigh about nothin'," Dicky cheerfully responds.

Autumn is not wholly devoid of fruits, though about Traumfest summer claims the greater share of those that elsewhere belong to the later season; maypops linger on, and when their time is past there comes the triumphant harvest of the autumn, which harvest also belongs to winter. Persimmons are ripe!—a crop that never fails. When the autumn woods are in their glory, the persimmon tree is covered with a glory of its own, every twig being loaded with little flattened globes, salmon pink in color and covered with a bloom that in the shadows is deep blue. But be careful of these tricksy fruits, for pretty as they are, they may not yet be perfectly ripe, and until they are, nobody—not even the most longing negro—shakes a tree, for the pucker of a green persimmon is such as to set even the teeth of memory on edge. When ripe they begin to fall, and when you find a treeful of good ones, for there is great choice in persimmons, you will know why the negro loves them so.

Inseparably connected with the persimmon in one's mind is the 'possum. For the 'possum loves the 'simmon as the nightingale loves the rose. Of a dark night he may be found sitting in the tree among the ripe fruit. He gets fat on 'simmons, and acquires that peculiarly rich and delicate flavor so highly appreciated by the negro. All through the hunting season you are wakened by the excited bark of the 'possum dog, accompanied by the wild yells of the negroes and an occasional gunshot. The 'possum dog, like the poet, is born, not made. You can never know what dog will develop genius in this direction, excepting that you may be sure it will be one of pure mongrel strain. The 'possum dog is no beauty, but he is worth his weight in 'possums, which is the same as saying he is a very valuable dog.

There is no denying that fat 'possum is a dish for the gods. If you live in the South you will doubtless some day bake a fat 'possum, that is to say, you will bake it, figuratively speaking, for the actual task must be performed by a generous, genial black cook who loves 'possum. She bakes it *con amore*, and with sweet potatoes. The memory of one's first 'possum dinner lingers like a happy dream. After eating it, one does not wonder at or blame the negro for spending night after night in the woods—to the detriment of his day's work—in hilarious quest of the fat 'possum sitting among the persimmons—the fatiguing, happy, and exciting hunt to have the sequel of "baked 'possum and sweet taters."

Baked 'possum is the Christmas goose of the epicurean negro, and as the season moves on, the voice of the 'possum dog is heard in the woods assisting in the preparations for that season of high living and neglect of work which is the negro's perquisite, inherited by him from the days of slavery. "Christmas" about Traumfest does not mean a niggardly twenty-fifth of December; it means that, and all the days following, until sunset of New Year's Day. To be fair, however, one must add that in these modern, trying times, the week-long holiday is very much interrupted by daily labor. It is a fiction more than a fact, yet it no doubt adds a certain feeling of festivity to the day's work, a feeling that one is somehow having an extra good time, though it might be hard to tell just where to put your finger on it.

Is It Winter?

It is winter, according to the almanac, and the dates on the Northern newspapers that come regularly and too often. For the newspaper is a sort of inverted anachronism here where life is a good half-century behind the times. Why waste the golden hours reading things that by the time we catch up with the world will have been happily forgotten by everybody? The leaves have fallen, but it does not look like winter, the laurel is so green on the slopes and the pine trees are so sunny, while the uninvited mistletoe burdens the oaks with its pale-green form. Birds are singing—the wren always believes it will be summer tomorrow, and comports himself accordingly. The air acquires a sparkling quality, without wholly losing its softness.

The native people speak of the coming of winter as a calamity, and you, too, half dread the cold that is to pinch, and yet does not come. But one day it does come. The wind howls, the air is icy, and your blood chills. You fill the fireplace with logs, and resign yourself to the inevitable. But in three days you are out without a hat. How warm the sun, how delicious the air! And was there ever such color on the mountains! One has a rare surprise in this color of the winter mountains. They remain so warm and tender. They are drowned in light, and assume the marvelous pale blue which is unlike the blue of other mountains. But sometimes they are lilac, and blue in the shadows, or they are white and blue. They sometimes look white through the trees, a pure gleaming white with intense blue spaces, though there is no snow on them, only a shimmering light as though they were giving back the sunshine absorbed by them through the long summer. It is in the winter months that one gets that glow on the mountains, so tempting and so illusive to the painter's brush, when towards night you often see the southern slopes tinged with the pink of the wild rose, again warm lilac or deep red, while the sky and the earth that inclose them are sympathetic shades of blue and gray. It is nearing Christmas and Christmas berries are blazing in the thickets. Down the Pacolet Valley rustling canebrakes are green and gold, while golden sedge-grass spreads over slope after slope, its silky white plumes trembling in the breeze.

In our drives about the country we soon discover why the people dread the winter. It does not take very cold weather to make one shiver over an open fire, when the house walls are open to every breeze that blows and one's clothes are not winter-proof. One never sees a winter wood-pile in this country, and as to "filling the cellar," with the ant-like thrift of the New Englander, it is undreamed of. There are no cellars, neither the quality of the land nor the climate lending itself favorably to cellars: one reason, perhaps, for dreading the winter. Corn-pone, dried beans, and salt pork must get somewhat monotonous, even to those who love them. Storehouses are almost as rare as cellars, and is one to deprecate or envy a state of mind that enables people cheerfully to sell their corn in the autumn at thirty cents a bushel, with the certainty that they will have to buy it in the spring at eighty cents?

We take advantage of each soft and sunny day, as though it were to be the last. It is yet December, so the calendar says, but along the roadside one sees a maze of sunny, yellow petals, the witch-hazel defying the season. Gay red berries are falling from the trees, and little bushes are crowded with coral beads. The holly tree, decked with scarlet, stands with its toes in the rippling brook. Jack-oak leaves glow tremendously, and crimson horse-brier makes gay splashes against the evergreen pines.

When Christmas comes, the people celebrate with firecrackers, and sometimes they have fireworks at night—rockets, pinwheels, Roman candles. But in the remoter places there is no Christmas. Santa Claus has not been discovered, and the day passes without notice.

Days come at last when you resign yourself to endless cold, but presently the sun bursts out in a fury, and your blood seems to feel a thrill of spring. This is premature, however, January is not spring; and we are smartly reminded of that when, one day amidst howling winds, the air is filled with snow. The ground now is white. How cold we are! How exasperating these tumultuously blazing open fires that roast you on one side while you freeze on the other! One resigns one's self with as good a grace as possible to the cold of a Southern winter, against which one is so defenseless, when you discover that a change has come. The snow is all gone. You are a little surprised, and crestfallen, to find that the extreme cold you grumbled so about has lasted just three days. Sometimes there comes a day of witchery, when the flakes are large and soft, and there is no wind. Softly, swiftly, the white mantle covers the earth, shrouds the trees, the green bushes, and the tall, brown weeds. How lovely is the pine forest at such a time! Enjoy it while you can, for by night fairyland will have vanished.

Thus the snow comes and goes. In the high mountains, it comes earlier, and stays longer, but you will not find any noticeable preparation for winter. Even the sleds you sometimes see are used to haul wood in summer.

Days of fury are followed by days of sweetness and warmth, when walking leisurely about you wonder at the size of the laurel and azalea buds and the buttons on the dogwood trees. These things keep on growing as though they did not really believe in winter—and what is that? A large gauzy-winged grasshopper leaps up and sails away at your approach. As you watch the light on the wings of these insects that dart up one by one before you, as you look over the green forest shining in the warm sun, you forget where you are; for a moment you think it is summer. The wren has evidently made the same mistake. There is hardly a winter day severe enough to still his happy song. And whenever there come those frequent warm days that cause the sap to stir in twigs and hearts alike, you hear the joyful outpourings of other birds, those wintering here, or those belonging here. It is only January, but the red-bird has begun to whistle—indeed, there is not a month in the year when some

Sunday Morning

bird is not singing a joyous song; and when February comes no bird holds back any longer.

When the ground freezes, or snow comes, the birds confidently draw near to the houses, and at many of them they find a table always spread. Over on her ridge the dear lady from C. beckons you to come on tiptoe to the window, and see the hermit thrush in the food-box—and there he is, whether you can believe such a thing or not. Another bird-lover, whose back door opens into beautiful spaces bounded by the not too distant form of Tryon Mountain, has also persuaded the hermit to conquer his shyness, and feed from her stores.

Birds that, according to the books, do not belong in this part of the world, are frequently seen and recorded by eyes always on the watch. Thus are captured—in the records—many a stray wight.

There is one bird, however, here that never comes near the houses. One sees him drawing marvelous lines in the sky, rising and floating, circling about and about in the vast spaces of the air on apparently motionless pinions. What is it that thus sustains the incredible flight of the buzzard? What is the secret of the illimitable wing of this lonely spirit of the sky, whose companions are the clouds? As you sit on a log, some winter day, absorbed in watching the buzzard wheeling in the sky, you become conscious of something moving on the ground, and look down in time to see a striped chipmunk whisk behind a stump. Again, your unsuspected companion may be a gray squirrel who betrays himself by a quick motion, as he flirts his bushy tail around a tree trunk to get out of sight. Squirrels are no longer abundant here, they have been hunted so remorselessly, but in the fall the gray squirrel comes in companies to harvest the nuts of your trees—or, may it be, only for a little excursion out into the world? The shy little red squirrel who hides in the depths of the woods is known as the "mountain boomer," a name also derisively applied to the mountaineer by his low-country neighbors, whose own title, equally descriptive one supposes, is "tar-heel."

Another rodent, abundant but seldom molested, is the pretty little flying-squirrel, whose form may sometimes be seen at dusk bridging the space between one tree-top and another, like a miniature aëroplane. He is a gentle little creature, but a sad rascal, who hides by day and chases up and down between your walls at night, coming into the house and gnawing to pieces whatever excites his admiration, though he never deigns to taste your food. Although a nuisance, he is better than rats, which, the people say, never come to a house occupied by flying-squirrels. Of course the common rat is here as elsewhere, but he is not very abundant, and his place is sometimes taken by the comical wood-rat, whose curious habits are not destructive to anything but your nerves, until you find out the cause of those eerie noises that render the night uneasy.

The chipmunk is all too easily tamed, but, what we plume ourselves upon as a rare occurrence, we once had a family of woodchucks living under our porch. They came out at dawn, like so many little bears, and we watched their clumsy yet sinuous movements through the flowers, and we saw them sit up and with their hands draw down our best pinks and eat off all the blossoms.

If gray squirrels are not abundant, rabbits are. Hunting does not seem to thin their ranks. You often see a bright round eye turned square upon you, as you are walking through the woods. It belongs to Molly Cottontail, sitting under a bush, as still as a mouse, with that great eye sentinel over a dangerous world. If you pause or leave the path, she is off, a vanishing mist of gray fur. There are rabbit paths everywhere in the bushes, so that one must needs be careful, and not stray away into these curious highways of the furry folk that go nowhere that man, or dog, can follow, but lead the unwary into thickets of bushes tied together by prickly vines. Close to the ground the little path tunnels its way, but one would need be as small as the rabbit to follow it.

There are places where one, watching quietly at night, can see the rabbits at play. And when snow is on the ground, who but they make those double tracks that everywhere line the woods, usually accompanied by the prints of a dog's foot, the dog himself visible to your mind's eye in frantic but useless pursuit! How ridiculous Molly Cottontail can make poor doggy appear! In the woods you hear him barking excitedly as he runs—then across an open space drifts a fluff of fur. After it, some distance behind, comes the dog, not resembling in the least a fluff of fur, and not drifting. The contrast between the desperate efforts of the jointed dog, and the fleet farewell of the little vision floating off ahead, apparently without effort, makes one laugh in delight. All winter you can hear the whining cry of the hounds as they course about, hunting for their own amusement or accompanied by a man with a gun. Other tracks in the snow are made by the birds—here has passed quite a flock of quails, and here has gone hopping along—a robin, perhaps.

You are still in a state of defense, waiting for and dreading the winter that comes, and yet does not come, when one day you find the alders in bloom! And then, walking in the woods, there comes a sudden, cinnamon-like fragrance, sweet, spicy, and clean. You would say flowers were blooming somewhere near. And there, indeed, under the trees is a little bunch of brown-capped, rosy blossoms—the Carolina pine-sap that scents the winter woods like a breath of spring.

After this there will undoubtedly be cold days and cold storms that will drive you into the chimney corner, but between these short, cold spells how hot the sun!—and who can believe in winter, seeing the alders in bloom! Besides, the birds, one might say, are also in bloom. You thought they sang all winter, but when you hear them now—well, you need no further assurance that the winter is over and gone.

Yes, the winter is behind you, and you suddenly realize that you have spent nearly all of it out of doors, and, although a Northerner and a skeptic, you begin to believe in the sun.

Cæsar's Head and Chimney Rock

There are two places on the eastern side of the Blue Ridge that one, being at Traumfest, should visit: Cæsar's Head, that grand promontory of the Blue Ridge that at one commanding point holds back the tumultuous sea of foothills beating against its base, and Chimney Rock, one of the gentlest and most charming little valleys one could wish to know. Each lies a long day's drive from Traumfest, one to the south, the other to the north.

The way to Chimney Rock lies through valleys of corn and along sunny slopes where the cotton grows, for one of the advantages of Traumfest is that from it you can step down into the cotton country that begins at the foot of the Blue Ridge. The Northerner, whose eye has never swept a cotton-field during the changing seasons, imagines that its only moment of interest is when the picturesque negro is gathering the harvest. He does not know that the cotton, like the peach, is a flower as well as a crop, the starry leaved plant bearing large lemon-yellow and rosy red hibiscus-like flowers; and of course when the great pods burst and the fields are whitened with the snow of the harvest, it is worth one's while to take a run down into the cotton country. On the lower slopes of the Blue Ridge the cotton resembles the corn in its sparse growth. The red soil shows through even at maturity, and as summer advances the mellow reds, yellows, and bronzes of the leaves and stems cover the cotton-fields with a rich brocade of colors.

When we descend to the cotton country in quest of Cæsar's Head, we cross into South Carolina and follow well-known and very red roads beneath the eastern front of Hogback and the line of low, rounded forms that lie beyond it, and that end in the abrupt and shining cliffs of Glassy Mountain. Now, the real cause for a pilgrimage to Cæsar's Head is the view you get of the lowlands that lie spread, three thousand feet below you, a magical sea of light and color as far as the eye can reach. For whatever else the high mountains may offer, you must come to some favored crest of the Blue Ridge for these thrilling views of the Southern lowlands.

From Glassy Rock, on the top of Glassy Mountain, there is an outlook rivaling that from Cæsar's Head, and here some day you will go, up over a road so execrable that you will finally leave the carriage and walk, or else you will perhaps ride horseback the whole distance. Upon ascending Glassy, one's first full view of the lowlands is from a sharp turn in the road, whence on a clear day you see them quivering below you, reaching away and away until they enter the sky at the far horizon. Then glimpses of them come and go, caught through a green veil of pine trees that wonderfully intensifies the blues of the nearer spaces. It is the magical light, the transforming vast sunshine of the South drenching the plain and the air, mingling as it were the sky and the earth, that transfigures the scene. To say that the lowlands are blue gives but a hint of the truth. They are like an inverted sky meeting the real sky at the horizon.

As you follow the steep way, you come again and again to some open place whence you can look off over the plains, and when the corn is ripe, and you look abroad through the golden screen it makes, the wide reach of the lowlands and the distant blue heights become so intense in color as almost to pain the senses. There are lonely cabins with flowers about them at long intervals all the way up Glassy, and if you come in the spring, you will see the blue sky above and the blue sea below through a veil of peach blossoms, which is wonderful.

We cannot see Glassy from Traumfest, as it lies behind Hogback. It belongs to that indefinite and mysterious region known as the "Dark Corners," and the people tell us of wild deeds done here in bygone days. But there is no hint of anything ugly, as one ascends its rough road on a fair day, and looks out through those openings across the azure sea. The road leads to an unpainted church on the top of the mountain where on "preaching-day" the women assemble in their best black sunbonnets and the men in their Sunday clothes. From the lonely little "church-house" a path guides you to the top of Glassy Rock, whose steep front shines like glass when wet—which is much of the time. The top of the rock is covered with those crisp and aromatic growths that belong to mountain-tops, and which are so pleasant to rest upon. Moreover, all sorts of dainty little wild flowers peep out from the crevices; and from it one gets an unobstructed view out over that ineffable sea of color, losing itself in ineffable sky spaces, of which one has caught glimpses while ascending the mountain. But from here there is a wider horizon and one sees the long and lovely line of mountains lying like islands in the dreamy sea, those charming ridges where the mountains come to an end.

As we sit here one day, a mountaineer approaches, and, pointing to a man crossing a field on muleback far below, laconically remarks, "That gentleman's pa was killed at Glassy Mounting church." Then he tells how the people were waiting for the preacher to come one Sunday, when suddenly shots were heard, and two men of the congregation fell dead. The cause of this ghastly deed was the usual one, a quarrel between two moonshiners; and the method of revenge was characteristic, one of the men having warned the other that if he went to church next preaching-day, he would have him arrested. Of course he went. Worse things than this have happened on Glassy Mountain, notwithstanding the enchanting light in which it is now immersed. Glassy, on its western side, has many a wild ravine for those who wish to hide.

If bound for Cæsar's Head, one passes the Glassy Mountain road without turning in, traverses cultivated valleys and a long reach of wild forest, until finally the road climbs in long curves up the side of the Blue Ridge itself to where the settlement of Cæsar's Head lies, nested in the sunshine.

There is a change of climate at Cæsar's Head, for it is four thousand feet high. One sees grass, and the air is cooler and more stimulating than at Traumfest, but you have no idea where you really are until you follow the path under the trees to the top of the terrible cliff, where, looking to the east, one sees radiant mountains rising rank above rank, while to the west the eye plunges into an abyss floored by the glowing sea of the lowlands.

Perhaps the most impressive view of the lowlands is from a point below the top of the cliff, where, past the sharp edge of near and substantial rock, the eye leaps, as it were, out into space. On the edge of the cliff, nature has sculptured the rude outlines of a human face, from which we are told this commanding spot got its name. The cliff itself, towering above those vast spaces, does honor to Cæsar, whatever may be said of the ape-like profile.

From the cliff one also looks directly down into the "Dismal" at its foot, beyond which rises the smooth and forbidding stone front of Table Rock. The Dismal is impressive enough at any time, and it may give you one of the grand spectacular moments of your life if you are fortunate enough to stand over it after a storm at sunset, when down from the mountains roll rivers of mist, to enter the abyss of the Dismal and fill it with glory. Below, you will see surging, lifting and falling, soft thunderheads of gold, of bronze, of copper, and purple. The Dismal seems a wizard's gulf, swallowing the hues of the heavens, which one imagines it will in time cast forth again to sweep over the sky. And walking back towards the hotel in the twilight one may look through an open space at Hogback and Glassy Mountains against a calm and radiant background, and above them the whole Saluda Range, beautifully outlined.

Besides the views offered by the position of Cæsar's Head, just below it passes one of the few roads that cross the barrier of the Blue Ridge to the upper mountains, this one leading to the renowned valley of the French Broad River.

Early spring is a good time to visit either Cæsar's Head or Chimney Rock, and perhaps you will turn towards Chimney Rock before nature has begun to cover her red soil with summer verdure. The road leads down and around the end of Tryon

Mountain and between the hills that lie to the north of it. The grain in places is well started; here and there you see a glowing hillside sparsely covered with pale-blue rye or bright-green wheat. The red soil is furrowed in concentric lines, curves and counter-curves; rows of beans are visible, and young corn-blades are up. Nature, never weary, is gayly beginning her perennial task of feeding the world. In some of the fields cotton is lifting up its head, and about the houses fruit trees are in bloom.

You keep the "main leading wagon-road" as directed, cross the once dreaded torrent of Green River, not now through the dangerous ford, but over a safe, new bridge. The Green River—so green as you cross it on the train up in the mountains beyond Saluda, and so charming in the "cove" below Saluda, where water and banks are so very, very green, the trees reaching over and forbidding the sun to shine too brightly in the cool solitude—the Green River down here is also green, though it has already begun to lose a little of its mountain freshness.

The "main leading wagon-road" finally leads you down the pretty valley of Cane Creek to the wide Hickorynut Gap Road, on its way to Rutherfordton, a state road, if one is not mistaken. Entering it, you turn to the left and follow it up the Broad River Valley and close to the water that comes in jumps and tumbles, darting and whirling down from its sources in the high springs of the mountains. Large trees border the valley, beeches and oaks and tulip-trees, with straight dark pines for color balance. Looking up it, you see one of those happy arrangements of mountains that make a valley something more than mere solid earth and running water. It is these overlapping, down-reaching mountains that give this region its characteristic charm. For the Broad River Valley is noted for its beauty, although it has no high mountains, nor any remarkable grandeur of scenery.

Crossing a charming, though somewhat deep and rocky ford of the Broad River, you continue on up the beautiful valley, the mountains draw in about you, and you are at "Logan's," a large, old-fashioned farmhouse which was converted to the uses of a wayside inn when the road went through to Rutherfordton, connecting the mountains above here with the low country. Logan's is "in the scenery," so they tell you a good many times while there—and unquestionably it is. A beautiful cultivated valley lies about the house enchantingly surrounded by mountains. The mountains of this region, although so individual in form, so picturesque, or so beautiful, are, according to General Logan, worth about a cent apiece, there is so little soil on them.

Close to us is the Old Rumbling Bald, high up on whose rocky top is what appears to be a cabin, but which is such only in seeming—from some trick of the shadows against the broken rock. This is pointed out to the visitor as "Esmeralda's cabin," so named because here at Logan's the author of "Esmeralda" wrote her play in the presence of the Old Rumbling Bald. The Old Rumbling Bald is, perhaps, the most noted of any mountain in this part of the world. Up to 1878, he was just the "Old Bald," but then he began to rumble and shake the earth, and thereby attained a distinction that set him apart from all the other mountains of the Blue Ridge. Whatever else the others were or did, none of them "rumbled." From '78 to '80 the Old Bald kept the people wondering, and those near him apprehensive. What was he rumbling about? Why was he shaking the earth? And what would he do next? He rumbled his last rumble in '85, we were told, since when he has been as quiet as of old.

To look at the rocky wall of the mountain and see the clean, new granite gives one an intimation of what has happened. Great slabs and cliffs have split off and settled down, no doubt "rumbling" as they went, and the crack that suddenly appeared on top has grown to a chasm ten feet wide, one hundred feet deep, and three or four hundred yards long. Curiosity prompts you to approach the Old Rumbling Bald over a pleasant path where one passes a lonely cabin that might be a child of the old gray mountain, and out of which comes a lovely little girl with glorious blue eyes, her face framed in a wideruffled pink sunbonnet. In one hand she carries a pretty basket of green things, and in the other a great bunch of roses and snowballs. We climbed Old Bald's rocky front, stopping for a long draught of icy water from a spring that comes out of the rocks, and to admire the thrifty appearance of the peach trees in an orchard on the stony slope. We were told that these bore peaches of exceptionally fine quality, after which we were not at all surprised to learn that they were in the thermal belt!

At last we get to a great crack in the mountain—not the chasm on top, but a crack lower down, that makes a series of caves, from the threshold of which one looks out between massive walls of granite far down the valley, over the tops of the near mountains, and across to the blue line of the horizon against which stands outlined the beautiful King's Mountain, "where we whipped Ferguson," our guide reminds us. It is a commanding view down over the lowlands, for the Old Rumbling Bald is the last of the mountains in this direction, its mighty form standing like a sentinel above the lower country, at the gateway that passes between it and Chimney Rock Mountain, just across the valley.

Then we go into the cool caverns reached by narrow halls and partly by ladder, and whose walls are of freshly exposed granite, where great slabs and splinters look ready to fall at the slightest rumble. There is an opening to the sky at the far end, but inaccessible. But there is a "window" that lets in light, and out of which one can look past massive casements of solid rock, and across the valley to Chimney Rock Mountain and Sugarloaf, and between other and lower mountains down into the hot, quivering blue plains of the lowlands. It is delightfully cool in the caves, and as one looks around at the fresh granite walls, one has a sense of being present at the creation of the earth.

If you follow up the Broad River Valley as far as the settlement of Bat Cave, you will find another mountain with similar cavernous openings, and some one will guide you to the largest of these, Bat Cave. But more beautiful than Bat Cave is the Broad River Valley on a smiling May day, with its gentle scenery, its fresh growths, and its lovely mountains, and in it, with a perfectly justified name, is the

Mountain View Hotel, and—of course—Esmeralda Inn.

All through the mountains "faults" in the rock occur, usually on a small scale, and landslides in some sections are frequent; while at Hot Springs the water comes forth ready-heated from some internal caldron, as though to keep us in mind that the earth we live on is yet in the making, even these ancient mountains continually changing their shapes.

Being at Bat Cave, we can continue along the good road over the watershed that separates the Broad River from Hickorynut Creek, and down the Hickorynut Creek Valley, on, over the plateau of the Blue Ridge, even as far as to Asheville. For the Broad River, which has its sources on the eastern slopes of the Blue Ridge, has no connection whatever with the more famous French Broad, which runs in the opposite direction.

But one must not leave Logan's yet, not before taking that delightful walk up the creek to the Pools, a series of large, round, fabulously deep pot-holes. There are three of them, and, according to the people, one of them has no bottom, while another is one hundred feet deep, and the third, eighty feet deep. Aside from their invisible depths, the pools are worth a visit because of the visible and charming manner in which Pool Creek comes sliding over smooth rock faces, finally to leap in a cascade into pool after pool, striking with force and whirling around the smooth stone wall of the basin. Pool Creek has many cascades; and it is shaded by tall trees, and bordered by the beautiful growths of the region, and beset with wild flowers, in their season. So, even were its pools of commonplace depths, one would look back with pleasure to a walk up the enchanting stream.

The Chimney Rock region is quite noted for its waterfalls, most of the streams that come from that part of the mountains making their escape to the levels below by long leaps down the walls. And the Broad River Valley might be called the "Valley of Many Waters," with its long cascades and its rushing streams.

Chimney Rock itself, an uphill walk of an hour or more from Logan's, and from which the place is named, is a great pillar of solid rock, separated from the main wall of the near mountain and rounded by the elements. To its right is by far a nobler stone battlement, but the distinction of Chimney Rock is in its total separation from the main mass of the mountain, which here rises in sheer, bare walls, a characteristic of the mountains of this region, many of which are wooded on top and at the base, with a broad girdle of bare cliffs between. For a long time Chimney Rock was inaccessible, but now anybody can get on the top of it, simply by climbing a stairway and crossing a timber bridge that has brazenly connected the lonely summit with the common world.

On the rocky top three or four dwarfed and twisted pine trees have managed to grow. At the base of the rock and of the mountain, the small pink rhododendron was everywhere in bloom, and, as we ascended, a delicious fragrance became more and more perceptible, until we discovered, growing above us on the ledges of the main mountain, great airy masses of blossoming fringe-trees that hung over the edges of the cliffs and shone white in the deep woods behind. The sparkleberry bushes were also swinging their snowy bells, and the wild gooseberries were trying to rival them in prodigality of bloom. These gooseberries, common at a certain elevation, are very wild, indeed, becoming, as they develop, closely covered with long prickles, which, however, does not prevent one from eating them when ripe.

The view from the top of Chimney Rock up the Broad River Valley might be described as that of grand scenery in miniature. It is the atmosphere that makes the mountains here so charming, for, seen near at hand, they are rather forbidding with their stern, bare rocks. They are frequently finished on one side into rounded turrets. One can imagine that there might be times when this part of the country would appear less seductive than it appears on a fair spring day.

Because of the natural phenomena, so abundant about Chimney Rock, the rumbling mountain, the caves, the isolated "chimney," it is not surprising that a number of strange legends have collected about it, in which ghostly visitants play their part, although as a rule the mountain people are not superstitious. They go fearlessly through the wilderness alone, even "lying out" with their herds, or for other reasons, with no apprehension of seeing anything more terrifying than a bear or a wildcat, an encounter with either of which would be regarded by the mountain man as a most fortunate adventure.

The High Mountains

The long, curving wall of the Blue Ridge, rising from the foothills like a rampart, guards the mountain region that lies beyond it so well that it is difficult to find an entrance through. But this charming wall, so abrupt on its eastern side, all but disappears when looked at from the west, for on that side it is often no higher than the plateau of which it forms the eastern boundary, although it rises here and there in notable peaks such as the Grandfather, the Pinnacle, Graybeard, and Standing Indian Mountains.

The plateau! One ascends a thousand feet above Traumfest to find, not a flat tableland, but a new world of mountains, mountains that might have seated themselves aloft for the delectation of mankind, so cool and fresh and yet so gracious do they appear to one coming up among them through some enchanted gate in the wall of the Blue Ridge. This plateau, which is about two hundred miles long, is bordered on the east by the long, irregular, unbroken, and winding wall of the Blue Ridge, and on the west by the parallel and more regular line of high and massive mountains known as the Unaka Range. The Unaka, unlike the Blue Ridge, is divided by deep gorges into several sections, one of these being the Great Smoky Mountains familiar to all through the stories of Charles Egbert Craddock, where they are so truly and charmingly portrayed.

The plateau, narrower and higher in the north and gradually lowering as it runs southward, is crossed by a number of short high ranges. At its narrowest point just north of the Grandfather Mountain, it is only about fifteen miles across, and all this northern portion has a general elevation of about four thousand feet, that is to say, its larger valleys lie at that elevation surrounded by mountains. South of the Grandfather the plateau widens out to about sixty-five miles across and drops until its larger valleys lie at a general elevation of from two to three thousand feet. But while the valleys here are lower, the mountains are higher, there being in this region many of the highest and grandest mountains of the whole Appalachian uplift.

Along the crest of the Unaka runs the boundary line between North Carolina and Tennessee. On this line or close to it, now on one side and now on the other, lie some of the highest mountains of the region, although the most remarkable uplift is perhaps the short Black Mountain Range, in North Carolina, well away from the Tennessee border, and where, although the range is only fifteen miles long, there are more than a dozen summits above six thousand feet in elevation, one of these, Mount Mitchell, 6711 feet high, being the highest point east of the Rockies.

It is not very long since the geographies taught us that Mount Washington in New Hampshire, with an elevation of 6293 feet, was the highest mountain in the East. But since then the surveyors have been at work in the Southern mountains, to find in the Great Smokies, the Blacks, and the Balsams over twenty peaks higher than Mount Washington. A North Carolina government report, after giving a list of altitudes of the principal mountains, concludes thus: "In all, forty-three peaks of six thousand feet and upwards. And there are eighty-two mountains which exceed in height five thousand feet, and closely approximate six thousand, and the number which exceed four thousand, and approximate five thousand are innumerable."

The principal mountains between the two bordering chains are placed in a somewhat orderly manner in short ranges that for the most part lie nearly parallel one to another, crossing the plateau in a generally northwesterly direction. The most northerly of these, however, the beautiful dome-shaped Black Mountains lying to the north of Asheville, is not parallel with the others, but runs almost north from the point where it leaves the Blue Ridge.

Southwest from the Blacks and to the south of Asheville rises the range of the Newfound Mountains, and south of that the charming Pisgah Range that takes a northeasterly direction. Next

A "Bald"

in order, and nearly parallel to the Newfound Mountains, is the high Balsam Range containing some fifteen summits exceeding six thousand feet. Then comes the wild Cowee Range, then the bold and beautiful line of the Nantahala, beyond which the mountain country sinks to lower levels in Georgia.

A knowledge of this regularity in the position of the more important mountains is helpful to the explorer, though it is by no means apparent to the casual observer, who, coming up among them, sees mountains on all sides, some rising close at hand in ridges, summits, and walls of foliage, and between these and over their heads others that show forth delicate, spirit-like forms against the sky.

Although the mountains are so generally covered with hardwood and pine forests, the upper parts of the higher ones are clad in a dark, unbroken mantle of spruce and balsam fir, and many have "bald" summits that, covered with grass, make natural pastures, sometimes many hundred of acres in extent.

One ascending to the plateau finds, as it were, the beautiful world on the slopes of the Blue Ridge lifted skyward with its fragrance, its flooding sunlight, and its marvelous colors unimpaired. The dreamy Unaka Range, with its superb group of the Great Smokies, takes the place of the Blue Ridge in the landscape, but it is more broken in contour, rising in massive domes and lovely rounded peaks. It is like the fabric of a dream as one sees it in the distance. Through the gorges that cleave its stupendous walls and add grandeur to the scenery, rush the rivers of the plateau to enter the Mississippi by way of the Tennessee and Ohio—only one river breaking through the wall of the Blue Ridge to find its way eastward to the Atlantic, for the plateau slants to the west throwing the waters towards the higher Unaka Mountains. Thus the Blue Ridge, in spite of its lower elevation, is the watershed of the mountain region.

This portion of the Appalachian system where the high mountains lie, although a part of the long uplift reaching from Canada to Alabama, and in which is no geological break, is nevertheless dissociated from the northern part by its higher elevation and lower latitude, these differences isolating it and bestowing upon it its rich dower of beauty. For although there are higher precipices and deeper ravines here than in the North, these mountains never convey the same impression of sternness—the everywhere present vegetation that rounds the outlines and the soft atmosphere combining to give the landscape a gentle expression. Perhaps the difference between the Northern and the Southern mountains can be expressed by saying that those are grand and these are lovely. In the magical atmosphere of the South you see the Great Smokies like wraiths against the western sky, the Nantahalas in the distance swimming in a sea of glory, the stern Balsams, the fir-crowned Blacks, all immersed in a light that transforms them.

Between the mountains lie enchanting valleys, and everywhere bright streams are running. The brooks or "branches" racing down the slopes, the rivers rushing along, the numberless waterfalls and the ice-cold springs everywhere gushing out of the earth, give freshness and life to the mountains. But while the running waters are so abundant, one soon notices the complete absence of natural lakes. Here are none of those beautiful basins that so enhance the charm of our Northern mountain regions.

The reason for this difference lies far back in the millenniums when the great ice cap that lay over the northern part of the earth, quite covering Mount Washington and all that region where the New England and Canadian lakes now lie, stopped short of the Southern mountains. Since the glaciers that scooped out or dammed up the lake beds of the North never reached these delectable heights, it happened that while the Northern mountains were being scraped bare to the bone by relentless ice, the Southern mountains were accumulating that soil out of which has been woven the wonderful mantle of trees that clothes them from top to bottom.

Also, because the glaciers did not reach them, these mountains were able to weather slowly through the ages, which has produced their beautiful, rounded contours, although there are some very rugged cliffs among them. For the same reason the best soil is often found near the top of the mountains, which accounts for the curious appearance of cornfields hung up like wind-blown banners on the steepest slopes.

It is largely due to the ancient glaciers that the Northern mountains are yet so bare and stony towards the top. And because the Northern mountains are so cold and barren, the people live down below and look up to them. Here the people live among the mountains themselves. They love them, and are afraid to go down to the country that lies level below, because, they say, if you go out of the mountains you die. And truth to tell very likely you do.

One of the pleasures of being in the North Carolina mountains is the presence of the simple and kindly people scattered everywhere over them, this great wilderness containing some two hundred thousand inhabitants, among whom may be found men and women who even yet have never ridden on a railway train, seen an automobile, or heard of an aëroplane. Shut up within the barriers of the mountains and isolated from contact with the rest of the world, the mountain whites, like people cast upon an island in mid-ocean, have developed customs and a dialect of their own. With their quaint speech and their primitive life they form perhaps the last link left in this country between the complex present and that simple past when man satisfied his wants from the bosom of the earth, and was content to do so. All over the mountains is a network of paths and each path leads to the door of a friend. One need not fear to walk alone from village to village, from "settlement" to "settlement," to wander at will in this vast sweet forest, where every man, woman, and child is glad to see you and ready to help you get what you want.

Thoroughly to enjoy the mountains, however, you must walk, or ride horseback. There are roads everywhere, but too often to drive over them assumes the nature of an adventure. The one drawback to walking is the crossing of the waters, for the mountains are so closely veined with streams that you cannot go a mile without having to cross at least one, generally on a "footway" the sight of which fills the novice with dismay. They are often very picturesque, these foot-logs, but one is apt to lose sight of that in the imminence of having to walk over one. Some of the bridges are good, sound tree-trunks leveled on the upper side and supplied with a hand-rail, but this is luxury. His wildest currents the mountaineer prefers to span with the smallest pole that can bear his weight, and his wide rivers he crosses on a "bench."

You will be likely to remember your first bench. Imagine long-legged saw-horses driven into the bed of the river the length of a long plank apart—two saw-horses placed tandem at each junction. Now imagine a plank reaching from the river-bank to the first saw-horse, and supported by it some four feet above the water. A short gap is succeeded by another plank extending between the second and third sawhorse and so on until the river is crossed. Such is the bench. A good recipe for crossing your first

Crossing the River

bench is to imagine that somebody is looking as you step up on it. This helps you to assume an easy attitude, as though you were there for the scenery. Then edge along a step, sideways, and again stop and thoughtfully regard the beauties of nature; thus, edging along and stopping every step or two for a long and reassuring look at the distant tree-tops, you will get to the first saw-horse. At this point it will be well to use your own judgment.

But one loving a walk need not refrain because of the bridges. You soon become used to them, and a long stick is so great a help as to rob any ordinary foot-log of more than half its terrors. The foot-log, indeed, soon becomes one of the pleasures in a mountain-walk, for it seems naturally to choose the most picturesque place on the stream, generally beginning and ending at the foot of a large tree. To stand mid-stream on a broad, squared log thrown across from bank to bank and guarded by a rail on one side, to stand there and watch the lights glinting through the forest foliage on the swift, rippling water, to look into the deep shadows under the clustering laurel and rhododendron bushes and the arching tree branches both up and down the stream—to do this is to get from the mountain bridge enough to balance other moments when perchance a three-cornered fence-rail thrown across the top of a waterfall offers the only avenue of approach to the other bank of the stream.

Flat Rock Community, an Ideal of the Past

The easiest though least romantic way for us of Traumfest to scale the rampart of the Blue Ridge, and storm the magical heights beyond, is to take the train that goes to Asheville. Out of the gorge of the Pacolet, that in the season of flowers and in the right light is a fitting gateway to the imagined world above, the train climbs with the help of two engines, and reaches Saluda, cool and breezy—a favorite summer resort for the Southerners of the low country, although it has none of those large estates and signs of a courtly past that so charmingly distinguish Flat Rock that lies farther along the way. The village of Saluda lies at the end of the Saluda Mountains, on whose slopes are born the headwaters of the Saluda River that follows down a little valley back of Hogback and Rocky Spur, and whose name, Saluda, or Salutah, means "river of corn," the valley of the Saluda for many miles being, indeed, that most charming of nature's fancies—a river of corn.

Just beyond Saluda the train crosses the becomingly named Green River, and then on, around, and about it goes till the Blue Ridge is fairly surmounted and we are on top of it, as well as on the widest stretch of plateau in the whole mountain region. One gets glimpses of blue heights through the pine trees, and the air one breathes is not the air of Traumfest, for we have ascended a thousand feet, and to the softness of the Southern air is added a fine, keen quality that wakes one up. In time the train reaches Flat Rock, one of the oldest and most interesting places in the mountains, although one can see nothing of it from the railway station.

Long before a train had surmounted the barrier wall of the Blue Ridge, the beauty, and salubrity of the high mountains had called up from the eastern lowlands people of wealth and refinement to make here and there their summer homes. The first and most important of these patrician settlements was at Flat Rock, the people coming from Charleston, the center of civilization in the Far South, and choosing Flat Rock because of its accessibility, and because the level nature of the country offered opportunity for the development of beautiful estates and the making of pleasure roads through the primeval forest that in those days had not been disturbed. Into the great, sweet wilderness, now quite safe from Indians, these children of fortune brought their servants and their laborers, and selecting the finest sites, whence were extensive views of the not too distant mountains, surrounded by the charming growths of the region, in a land emblazoned and carpeted with flowers, built their homes of refuge from the burning heat and the equally burning mosquitoes of the coast land.

The train comes from the seacoast today, but half a century ago it was much more of an undertaking to go to Flat Rock from Charleston than it now is to go to Europe, and much more romantic, for Flat Rock, more than two weeks' journey distant, had to be reached by way of the country roads over which the people drove in their own carriages, accompanied by a retinue of servants and provision wagons.

At the west side of Hogback, there comes up from the lowlands a road that, crossing a gap in the mountains, makes its way over and about and between them, passing Flat Rock on its way to Asheville. This is the old Buncombe Pike, or rather what is left of it, for since the war it has been allowed to fall into disrepair, only parts of it here and there hinting at any period of prosperity. From the opening of its first tollgate, in 1827, this road became the great artery of passage between the rich Southern lands and the new and prodigiously fertile West. Over it passed droves of horses, cattle, sheep, and hogs, as well as whatever produce the mountains and the lands beyond them might have to exchange for the products of the more civilized East, products that in their turn came up and over the mountains to the people of the West. To the romance of this old road was added a charming touch when, with the spring flowers, there came every year that migration from Charleston, like a flock of birds winging their way over the blue mountains in search of their summer homes.

One can imagine these processions of young and old starting out for the two weeks' picnic along the road, a picnic to the young people at least, who one can well believe looked forward to it undaunted by any thought of the possible storms that might put the rivers in flood, and convert the roads, even the best of them, in places, into bottomless sloughs of red and liquid mud, a procession that makes one think of the stories of far-away times, when queens and princesses traveled from one city to another over roads as bad as these. This procession up the mountains had fewer trappings on the horses and less gayly attired escort than did those of the olden time; but we may be sure that the carriages of the gentlefolk of the nineteenth century were pleasanter conveyances than the mule litters of the Middle Ages, and we may also be sure that no lovelier faces looked out from the gorgeous retinue on its way across the hills of the past than could be seen in the carriages where sat the ladies of the New World, with their patrician beauty and their gracious manners. And although the escort of the New World travelers did not number a thousand gayly dressed cavaliers, it consisted of a retinue of those ebony children of the sun, who loved the pleasant journey, and loved their gentle lords and ladies—for all this happened in those halcyon days "before the war" when the angel of wrath had not yet righted the wrong of holding even a black man in subjection to the will of another, and when the real "quality" cherished their slaves and were greatly loved by them.

It must have been like coming to Arcadia, up from the heated plains, in those days before the forests had been hurt by man, when every stream was full of fish, and the surrounding forests were full of game. Flat Rock, at first consisting of only a few families, soon grew into a good-sized community of delightful homes, and there is still an air of elegance and seclusion about its old estates, with their mansions of a by-gone day set back behind the trees, and there are yet living a few who remember with tenderness and regret the old days when life at

Flat Rock was a joyous round of visits and merrymakings, among which costume balls for the young people, and dinner-parties for their elders, are recalled with retrospective pleasure, while the boulevard of the time, the Little River Road, was thronged with carriages and riders, all enjoying themselves in the wonderful air—exchanging greetings and making a gay scene in the midst of the wild nature that surrounded them.

One of the most charming of these old places, "The Lodge," with its broad views, its avenues of big trees, its formal garden, its old-fashioned kitchen and commodious outbuildings, was owned and laid out by one of the English Barings, of banking fame, and here, following a certain path that leads through the grounds towards the road, one comes to a gate that appears to be closed by short bars, but when you touch one of these bars, down it falls and all the rest with it, allowing you to pass, when it closes again. It is a "tumble-down stile" like the one near Stratford-on-Avon, which your driver assures you is the very one where Will Shakespeare, poacher, was caught trying to get through with a deer on his shoulders.

One cannot help noticing, when wandering about the winding roads of Flat Rock, the white pines and hemlocks there, and that the soil is gray. White pines and hemlocks are the right trees for such a place, where one looks over broad meadows and into apple orchards, and where trees and shrubbery are grouped to please the eye, the native rhododendrons giving a fine patrician touch to the effect of the whole. The box hedges and the shrubberies, the high fences along the roadside at Flat Rock, speak of another civilization than that of the mountains, as does the picturesque church of St. John-in-the-Wilderness behind its screening trees, and it is very pleasant to pause a little in this corner of the great wilderness, set apart and beautified by the "quality" of a past generation.

It was the builder of the Lodge, Mr. Charles Baring, with three or four others, who founded the community of Flat Rock, to which were quickly added the homes of many of the most distinguished men in the history of their state. Among the names of these pioneers in the forest of Arcadia, we find Rutledge, Lowndes, Elliott, Pinckney, Middleton, and many others. Coming somewhat later, as friends of Mr. Baring, were Mr. Molyneux, British Consul at Savannah, and Count de Choiseuil, French Consul at the same place, the beautiful homes of these distinguished foreigners still gracing Flat Rock.

Perhaps the most cherished name in this mountain settlement was that of the Rev. John G. Drayton, for many years rector of St. John-in-the-Wilderness, and to whom the dignified and noble estate of Ravenswood at Flat Rock owes its origin, as well as those wonderful magnolia gardens on the Ashley River near Charleston, gardens where one wanders away into a dreamland of flowers unlike any other dreamland in the world.

Then there was the Secretary of the Treasury of the Confederate States, Mr. G. C. Memminger, loved for his generosity and public spirit, who also had a home in the fortunate land of flowers and fresh air.

And always, when talking to any of the old residents of Flat Rock, comes forth the name of Dr. Mitchell C. King, who, for more than half a century, was the greatly loved physician of the community, and who, while a student at the University of Göttingen, formed so warm a friendship with a fellow student, known as Otto von Bismarck, that, for many years after, a regular correspondence was carried on between the greatest statesman Germany has ever known and the genial and kindly physician of the little mountain settlement, these letters being carefully preserved by the descendants of the doctor.

The estates at Flat Rock have changed hands with the passing of time, yet many of them retain their original form, and new estates have been added by the "quality" of today; also new roads, beautifully planned, and beautifully bordered with the choicest growths of the mountains, have been built, giving promise of a renaissance that shall surpass in beauty the accomplishment of the older civilization of Flat Rock, and give direction, let us hope, to the future development of all that beautiful region.

Asheville

A short distance beyond Flat Rock, the train stops at Hendersonville, a gay garden of buildings as seen in the distance, and where upon arriving one is dismayed to hear the *pouf! pouf!* of an automobile. For Hendersonville has recently grown into a place of importance where summer visitors congregate, and it would also like you to know it is a railway center. At least, besides the main line running through it, there is that branch line crossing over into the French Broad Valley and proceeding up past Brevard and on over the mountains into the Sapphire Country, that enchanting region where, besides silver cascades and blue mountains, one finds sumptuous hotels, artificial lakes, and the ways of the world.

Beyond Hendersonville the train continues across the plateau some sixteen miles to Asheville, villages, from each of which one gets beautiful views, growing closer together. These villages in the forest, not visible from the train, make pleasant summer resorts for the increasing numbers of those who come up to escape the heat of the plains. Each of them, of course, is destined to a great future, and the youngest and smallest, the one that bears the name of Tuxedo, must perforce bear more than this, for the trainmen in calling out the station prick the bubble of ambition by putting the accent on the last syllable, when they do not put it on the first.

Two miles before reaching Asheville, the train stops at a place which might cause the bewildered traveler, if unprepared, to wonder where he is. A corner out of some village of old England seems to have been set down bodily in the heart of the New World wilderness. It is the village of Biltmore, lying in full view from the train on a perfectly level space, a charming collection of houses surrounded by smooth lawns, wreathed in vines, shaded by trees, and grouped about a square and along winding streets.

A church, Early Gothic in style, with a strong square central tower, is the natural and dignified center of the village. The beauty of the interior of the church is enhanced by a number of fine stained-glass windows, one of which was placed there to the memory of Frederick Law Olmsted, America's greatest landscape gardener, who laid out the grounds of Biltmore, and another as a memorial to Richard M. Hunt, who designed the church as well as Biltmore House, the residence of Mr. Vanderbilt, which, standing three miles away, is not visible from the train.

Coming suddenly upon Biltmore out of the surrounding forest, one has a prophetic sense of the change that is about to overwhelm these so long changeless mountains, and at Biltmore one must stop and become acquainted with the very interesting development that has there taken place. First, however, Asheville, the oldest, largest, and best-known town in the mountains, must be considered, since some knowledge of its history is necessary in order to understand the history of the mountains, including Biltmore.

Leaving Biltmore the train soon reaches the city, for Asheville really is a city, with a population falling a little short of twenty thousand. It lies in the valley of the French Broad River, which is far too narrow to hold it, so that the town has spread out over the surrounding hills, many of its houses, like those of Traumfest, standing with their lower regions on the slope beneath, and their front door decorously opening at street level. The history of Asheville, though not hoary with age, is yet interesting. Clearly to comprehend it one must retire to the year 1663, at which time Charles the Second of England gave "Carolina" so munificently to the lords proprietary, the territory thus summarily disposed of reaching from Virginia to Florida, and from the Atlantic to the Pacific. This tract was subsequently divided into several large states, one of them being North Carolina, or the "Old North State," as the people fondly called it.

The Old North State, a territory larger than New York, the Empire State of the North, became the goal of so varied an emigration that in 1754 a public document declares its population to be composed of almost all the nations of Europe, and so fast did it grow that, at the time of the Revolution, North Carolina ranked fourth in population among the thirteen colonies. As the people increased in numbers, the bolder and more independent spirits among them pressed farther into the wilderness, finally reaching the mountains where their energies found vent in fishing, trapping, and fighting the Indians. The people of the Old North State from the mountains to the sea have always been noted for their fearlessness and independence, these qualities in no degree decreasing as the pioneer element of the early settlers pressed towards the dangerous mountain wilderness.

Beyond the Blue Ridge, in the very center of the vast unbroken forest that covered the high unknown mountains, Buncombe County was erected in 1791, so large in area that its people proudly called it the "State of Buncombe," but which in course of time shrank to its present dimensions of about four hundred square miles, keeping, however, its most precious gem, Asheville, as well as the noblest of its scenery, its ancient pride, and its name, which latter has made it the best-known and most exploited county in the mountains, in the state, and indeed in the country at large, a county name seldom reaching the fame of Buncombe.

Asheville, if not actually old, is at least old relatively, for here stood the first settlement of white people in the mountains west of the Blue Ridge. This settlement was started soon after the Revolutionary War, as prior to that time the Indians had not learned to respect their neighbors' scalps sufficiently to make life among them agreeable, and only trappers and hunters ventured into this hazardous region, then swarming with game.

The little group of log houses, at first called Morristown, later, by the desire of the people, was named Asheville, in honor of Samuel Ashe, the well-loved governor of the state, and one of a family of gentlemen and heroes who loyally defended their adopted country against British rule, there being no less than five officers serving at one time from this family during the Revolutionary War. The origin of the name of the town explains the indignation felt by the people when careless strangers spell the first syllable without the letter *e*.

The stories of the early settlement of the South are as thrilling as stories of settlement in any part of the New World; there was the same reckless bravery, the same opposition to oppression, the same spirit of adventure, the same encounters with Indians, the same defiance of hardship and overcoming of difficulties, that afforded such stirring material to early writers in the North.

The little hamlet up in the mountain wilderness that thus honored the name of Ashe consisted at first of less than a dozen log cabins, but those cabins had been put there by the kind of men who see a city when they look at a forest, and who regard an obstacle, including hostile Indians, as a happy chance to do something. Since they were made of the stuff that takes an axe and goes confidently into the woods to hew out a nation, they were also prophets, as witness the case of Zebulon Baird, a zealous promoter of the interests of the community, who, pleading most eloquently in the general assembly for an appropriation for a wagon-road over the mountains, uttered the wild prophecy that his children would live to see the day when a stage-coach with four horses would be seen in the west, and the driver's horn would wake the echoes of the mountains! The road was granted, and came up from the eastern foothills of North Carolina some miles north of the railroad that now runs from Saluda through the Pacolet Valley to Asheville. It crossed the Swannanoa Gap at the present "long tunnel" on the Southern Railroad, a few miles above Old Fort, where as early as 1770 a small fort had been built to keep back the Indians who frequently poured down from the gap upon the settlers below the mountains, and which today is a small village with a railroad station. This road followed down the Swannanoa Valley to the present site of Biltmore, crossed where Asheville now stands, and continued down the beautiful French

Broad as far as Hot Springs, connecting the mountains with the western wilderness of Tennessee as well as with the better-settled eastern foothills. The first wagon passed from North Carolina to Tennessee in 1795, and the making of this, the first road in the mountains, is recorded as marking an epoch in the development of the country, and if the prophecy of Zebulon Baird was not fulfilled to the letter, as it probably was, one has only to look at the railway trains now passing many times daily over the route, broadly speaking, of that first wagon-road, to know that the prophecy was fulfilled in spirit. Zebulon Baird, besides being a prophet and a legislator, was an enterprising business man, he and another man being the first merchants of Buncombe County. To be a merchant in Buncombe in those days, when produce had to be obtained, guarded, and carried on muleback, or over the new wagon-road—which, judging from the conduct of wagon-roads in the mountains today, must often have been a feat in itself—called for the same kind of courage and skill necessary to a general in an army. And that Zebulon Baird did not neglect the æsthetic needs of the human heart is proved by the fact that it was he who introduced the jew's-harp into the mountains, that dulcet instrument which has remained to this day enshrined in the hearts of the people. The life of the pioneer develops those quaint, humorous, or sterling characters that make easy the path of the novelist; and the imagination lingers with pleasure over the picture of George Swain, postmaster, who for twenty years, it is said, was never absent on arrival of the mail, and who distributed every letter with his own hands! The Asheville Post-office, that in 1806 became the distributing center for Tennessee, Georgia, North Carolina, and South Carolina, probably did not receive letters enough to overtax the powers of a strong man, and one can see the zealous postmaster eagerly awaiting the arrival of the mail that was to be consigned by him, and him alone, to the inhabitants of the, to him, known world.

The sterling qualities of the postmaster were inherited by his gifted son, David Lowrey Swain, one of the most honored names not only of the mountains but of the State of North Carolina. He was born in a log cabin at Beaver Dam, near Asheville, at the foot of Elk Mountain, in 1801, and was educated at "Newton Academy," along with all the ambitious boys of that day, who came from far and near to profit by the instruction of the Rev. George Newton, who, as early as 1797, started a classical school at a place a mile south of Asheville. From the log school-house in the mountains David went to the University of North Carolina that had recently been established at Chapel Hill, near Raleigh, then to Raleigh, where at the age of twenty-two he was admitted to the bar. From that time all the honors within the gift of the people were heaped upon him. Before he was thirty he had been elected five times to the legislature as well as entrusted with other important public functions, including his election as judge of the supreme court, which office he resigned after two years, upon being elected, when only thirty-one years old, governor of the state. While governor he was elected a member of the convention to revise the constitution, and in the same year was proffered the presidency of the University of North Carolina, which important position he occupied for more than twenty-five years. Swain County, taken from Buncombe, was named after him, and his name is still cherished in the hearts of his loyal countrymen.

The founders of Asheville chose the strategic position of the mountains for their settlement, which lay on the natural line of travel between the fertile plains of the new West and the lowlands of the South, and which took an important step towards fame and fortune when, in 1880, a turnpike road, the famous Buncombe Pike, was chartered to pass from Paint Rock on the Tennessee line across the mountains to Greenville, South Carolina, by way of Saluda Gap, Paint Rock lying on the French Broad River a few miles below Hot Springs, the terminus of that first road whose course has already been indicated. It is one thing to charter a road in the mountain wilderness, another to build it, and not until more than a quarter of a century later was this great thoroughfare between the South and the West opened.

Meantime, Asheville had not been standing still, as is shown by the fact that in 1814 there was built within her borders—a frame house. A great event this, you can imagine, in a country where the sawmill had not begun its triumphant career. This first frame house was built by James Patton, whose name is on the honor list of the settlers of this part of the country, and after whom the principal street of Asheville, Patton Avenue, was named. He had come up into the mountains from the lowlands in 1792, at the age of thirty-six, and taken a large tract of land on the Swannanoa River. By birth an Irishman and by trade a weaver, he came to the New World, like so many others, to make a place for himself, and by the untrammeled use of his natural gifts he succeeded. A man of sterling worth and honorable methods he developed the resources within his reach, finally becoming one of the foremost merchants in the little community where the merchant was the man of importance. We are told that "traffic over the new road was immense, vast droves of horses, mules, cattle, and hogs being driven from the rich pasture lands of Tennessee and Kentucky to South Carolina and Georgia," in consequence of which "a large trade grew up at Asheville." At that time the present site of the city was owned entirely by James Patton and James M. Smith, the latter distinguished as being the first white child born in North Carolina west of the Blue Ridge. Only the site was there, however, not the city, for though we are assured that between 1805 and 1844 Asheville had nearly doubled in size, we know that even so it contained less than a score of buildings, notable among which was a frame store building on South Main Street, owned by Mr. Montreville Patton.

The older frame house, built by the elder Patton, was not to be eclipsed, however, for it became enlarged into the once famous "Eagle Hotel," with the distinction of being the first three-story building erected in that county so dear to the early settlers, and whose name was to give a new word to the dictionary, and a new phrase to the political and literary worlds. For although the county was named after Colonel Edward Buncombe, a brave officer in the American army, its notoriety is due to one of its own unique children, by name Felix Walker, whose fluency of speech had earned for him the popular title of "the old oil jug." Being patriotic as well as fluent, Mr. Walker sang praises of Buncombe County in season and out of season, and, having been sent as first Member of Congress from that district, he arose to address the House. Here was his chance, and although he had nothing of importance to say, he ambled on until many members left the hall, when he kindly told the survivors that they might go too if they liked, as he would speak for some time longer, apologetically explaining that "he was only talking for Buncombe."

The new road not only gave a great impetus to the commercial development of Asheville, but brought to the mountains the wealthy aristocrats of the lowlands, who came each summer to enjoy the climate and scenery of the mountains on the estates they acquired and beautified in that lovely land, the greatest number and the finest of these estates lying, as we know, at Flat Rock. But while the city visitors came in pomp up the mountains in the enchanting spring and went back in the glorious autumn, the merchants of Asheville and the other mountain settlements went down in the late fall on horseback, their wives and daughters accompanying them in carriages, a train of loaded wagons bearing the produce of the mountains to be exchanged for the luxuries of the city. While the men attended to business, the other members of the family enjoyed a few weeks in the delights of city life, when all went back home again. These visits to the great world were confined, of course, to those who had been able to profit by the advantages of the situation in the mountains, where life was yet primitive and most men poor.

But Asheville was moving on, and in 1835, we are told, Dr. Samuel Dickson established there the first young ladies' seminary, so admirable an institution that there came to it not only the girls of the region, but also many from the low country. This school was held in the first brick building in Asheville, described as a handsome colonial residence on South Main Street.

Both the Newton Academy and the Young Ladies' Seminary were established and taught by Presbyterian ministers, and the first church was Presbyterian, a large and comfortable brick building, we are told, having been built on a beautiful site presented by James Patton and Samuel Chunn, where the Presbyterian church now stands. The Methodists began in a wooden school-house on the site of the present Methodist Episcopal Church. The Episcopalians made a small beginning, but in 1849 were able to build their church on land given them by James W. Patton, where the present church now stands.

The Baptists had the hardest time of all at first, but the unflagging efforts of the Rev. Thomas Stradley, an Englishman who for many years was almost the sole representative of the Baptists in this region, were finally crowned with success, and he got both congregation and church. But if the Baptists had difficulty in getting started, their turn came later, for their doctrine so appealed to the people outside the town, or their zeal was so great, that in a few years practically the whole rural population was Baptist, or "babdist" as the country people always say.

From 1840 to 1860 was the golden period, as we are told, of Buncombe's history, when comfort reigned and hospitality was the rule. Big state-coaches ran daily from Asheville to the three nearest railroad points, sixty miles away, for the railroads of those days stopped when they encountered the bulwarks of the mountains. Then came the Civil War, when the old order passed away and the whole South was prostrated for a time. Deserters from both sides took refuge in the mountains. Desperadoes of the worst sort lived in caves and raided the country. Nevertheless, by 1870 Asheville had grown to fifteen hundred inhabitants, with eight or ten stores, and that influx of Northern travel had begun which was to give it its next wave of prosperity.

In 1876 the first railroad triumphantly scaled the Blue Ridge, coming up from Spartanburg, South Carolina, ascending at the south of Tryon Mountain by way of the Pacolet Valley. But this feat so exhausted its resources that it was ten years before it got from Hendersonville to Asheville. Meantime, the state of North Carolina, in 1881, built a railroad that, approaching the mountains from Salisbury by way of Morgantown, followed the course of the first turnpike past Old Fort, surmounted the troublesome Blue Ridge in a series of curves and spirals and windings that was a feat of engineering, finally tunneling through the mountain and continuing down the Swannanoa Valley to Biltmore, where, turning westward, it went on to Asheville, whence, in 1882, the line was completed to Paint Rock. The town now grew so rapidly that, in 1887, it proudly boasted of eight thousand inhabitants, and of having become one of the leading resorts of the South, thousands of tourists coming there from nearly every state and territory in the Union, while banks, hotels, clubs, schools, and churches appeared as by magic. About this time, also, the estate of Biltmore was purchased by Mr. Vanderbilt, the development of which was destined to play an important part in the civilization of the mountains.

Then did the prophets again raise their voices, the guidebook of the day predicting within a decade or two a city of from twenty to thirty thousand permanent residents, with new railroads, half a score of fine hotels, hills and valleys dotted with villas, and river-banks lined with manufacturing establishments of various kinds giving employment to thousands of operatives. Two decades have passed since then, and the prophecy has been fulfilled with a few extras thrown in in the way of costly waterworks, electric lights, street-cars, and automobiles.

But the prosperity was not unbroken. For a number of years Asheville was a noted asylum for tuberculosis patients; then its transient population began to wane, its beautiful climate was declared not suited to the disease in its more advanced stages, rivals grew up in various parts of the country, the sick deserted, and the well were afraid to come because so many invalids had been harbored there. But this reversal of fortune was short-lived, and Asheville, marked for a bigger destiny than that of a mere health resort, is beginning a new era with a fast increasing population whose interests are centered there. The prophets who cast roseate lights over the future are again predicting, and the only mistake these soaring souls are likely to make is that they may fly too low. For besides the suddenly awakened lumber industry, already representing millions of dollars, and the many new mining operations that are starting, the fine water-power is attracting manufacturers to the mountains, of which Asheville is, and always must be, the center.

That Buncombe yet exerts her old power over those who fall under the spell of her magic is shown by the presence of the Vance Monument in Pack Square, erected to the memory of Zebulon B. Vance, of Buncombe, governor and senator, but given by the people of today, largely assisted by Mr. George W. Pack, after whom the square is named, for though not a native of Buncombe Mr. Pack has enhanced the beauty and advanced the interests of the county with the greatest generosity.

New men are coming, and new names are being added to the long list of enthusiasts who have worked and talked "for Buncombe," but the names of those early settlers, only a few of which have here been given, are preserved in the streams and valleys about Asheville, every name redolent of the history of the past. Crossing Davidson's River near Brevard, for instance, you will recall that the first county court was held at the log house of William Davidson at the "Gum Spring" on the Swannanoa River. And hurrying down the beautiful gorge of the French Broad on the railroad you pass Alexander, the principal trading station in those old days when traffic went on four legs, and was so heavy that Captain Alexander sometimes stood dealing out corn three days and nights in succession without time to go to his meals.

Today Asheville takes itself seriously as a city, and you are tempted to grant the assumption when you see automobiles driving through the streets as unconcernedly as in New York or Washington. Street-cars come from various directions to a sociable gathering in Pack Square, the heart of the city. These same cars take you to the confines of town, or up over neighboring mountain slopes to commanding viewpoints. You go to Asheville to do your shopping and to see the world. There are imposing castle-like hotels there, modern and handsome houses on the residence streets, a great many small houses, and outlying districts where the cottages are occupied by colonies of negroes. Yet you can never make the mistake of supposing yourself in a real city when in Asheville, for you have only to lift your eyes to see the vast green forest pressing close about you and the mountains rolling away, peak after peak, to the far horizon. Besides, in spite of its urban airs there is the ever-conquering sun, shining on Asheville and drowning the mountains in its sweet Southern haze, there is the balmy languor of the South and the mellow voice of the negro, to make you feel yourself in some secluded haven of rest, some happy escape from the turmoil and strife of a city, and this in spite of the census and the convenience of streetcars.

But to the native mountaineer Asheville is not only a city, it is *the* city. Deep in the wilderness the people may never have heard of London or Paris, and but vaguely of New York, but Asheville is a reality. It is the true center of civilization. Happening one day to speak to a man, living near Roan Mountain, of the World's Fair that had been recently held in some, to him, unknown city, he showed a great deal of interest, but thought the location of the fair a mistake. "Why didn't they have it where everybody could go?" he complained; "why didn't they have it in Asheville?"

The hills of Asheville lie at an elevation of about two thousand feet, and are surrounded by mountains that stretch away in summits and ranges in whatever direction one may look. That beautiful form with the dome-like top, southwest of Asheville, is Mount Pisgah, and that ridge, a little lower and to the left of the summit, is the Rat. "Pisgah and the Rat!"—the two names inexorably yoked together because the two shapes make one group, and the lower of them has a form so suggestive that there is no escape for it. They are so near Asheville as to attract immediate attention from the newcomer, who, according to his temperament, is shocked or amused at his first introduction to "Pisgah and the Rat."

It is Asheville's position which has made it so long a favorite with those seeking these mountains for their pleasure. From its hills one looks away to peaks and ranges not too near and not too far, and one feels to the full that sense of elevation and of great sky expanse, which is so notable a part of the landscape of this region that the name, "Land of the Sky," once felicitously bestowed upon it, has clung to it ever since.

It would be tiresome to enumerate the mountains visible from the various hills of Asheville, one looks out upon so many, from the grand chain of the near Balsams on the west to the distant Craggy and Black Mountains towards the north, but one never gets tired of looking at them, and in these later days good roads lead away to parks and viewpoints, to the near and some of the distant villages, and to the artificial lakes now being made in increasing numbers to supply scenery and mosquitoes to the tourist; for the pleasure-seeking tourist has found the mountains, there is no escaping that momentous fact, and the mountaineer is everywhere waking up from his long slumber and beginning as it were to look about him.

There is so much that is interesting in Asheville and the country roundabout that it is easy to understand what Mr. Walker felt, for, like him, having once started, it is hard, even for a stranger, to stop "talking for Buncombe."

The Early Settlers

The history of Asheville tells in part the story of the people, and in part answers two questions always asked by the newcomer, Who are the "Mountain Whites," and how did they get here? The foot-hills, as we know, were settled early in the history of the state, and there was a sparse population on the eastern slopes of the Blue Ridge long before any one ventured to establish a home in the mountains that lay beyond that barrier, the first permanent settlers west of the Blue Ridge not appearing until after the Revolutionary War, in the course of which the Indians were partly subdued. As time passed, the restless drifting of those people who came to the New World in search of homes brought one and another to the mountain country, fabled for its beauty, healthfulness, and possibilities; and while some of these wanderers drifted away again, others settled down and raised families who clung to the land of their birth, where their descendants are yet to be found.

Since North Carolina was settled from "almost all the nations of Europe," one looks to find traces of this motley assembly among the present inhabitants of the mountains; and there are traces in the names and the features of the people, although the population in course of time became homogeneous for several reasons. For one thing, it was similar qualities and tastes that first drew the people to the mountains and afterwards kept them there; also, by far the greater number of these emigrants came from the British Isles; and finally, the conditions of life in the mountains was such as still further to leaven all society to the same consistency.

The early settlers came in that youth of the nation when land was free and hopes were high, younger sons sometimes, and business men of small property who had a dream of possessing a landed estate and "founding a family" in the New World, the fabled western mountains powerfully attracting these seekers for fame and fortune, most of whom in course of time were doomed to discover that owning a tract of land was not the only requisite to success. Nobody got rich in the mountains, excepting the fortunate few who had placed themselves in the line of traffic that, in course of time, was established between the South and West; the poor soil was an insuperable obstacle, as were the social conditions induced by slavery. The settlers in the mountains did not realize their ambitions, but many of them found a home and peace and plenty, according to the modest standards of those days.

Besides those well-to-do settlers who came to found a family, and formed the "quality" of the mountains—who are not to be confounded with the "quality" of Charleston, which was quite another matter—there were others who, for various reasons and at different times, drifted in from the eastern lowlands as well as down from the North. Most of the writers tell us rather loosely that the Southern mountains were originally peopled with refugees of one sort and another, among whom were criminals exported to the New World from England, which, they might as well add, was the case with the whole of the newly discovered continent, America being the open door of refuge for the world's oppressed. Hither fled dissenters from all sorts of established form, from French Hugenots to convicts, a company of seekers who, for the most part, were to fulfill a high destiny in the making of a nation.

The popular writers, in speaking of the origin of the "Mountain Whites," rather insist upon the criminals, perhaps because of their sensational value, but one can find no evidence that these malefactors, many of them "indentured servants" sent over for the use of the colonies, made a practice of coming to the mountains when their term of servitude expired. And knowing the manner in which many of these white slaves, wretched precursors of the black slaves, were procured, without any other fault of theirs than their helplessness, one need not tremble with fear at thought of them.

The truth is, the same people who occupied Virginia and the eastern part of the Carolinas peopled the western mountains, English predominating, and in course of time there drifted down from Virginia large numbers of Scotch-Irish, who, after the events of 1730, fled in such numbers to the New World, and good Scotch Highlanders, who came after 1745. In fact, so many of these stanch Northerners came to the North Carolina mountains that they have given the dominant note to the character of the mountaineer, remembering which may help the puzzled stranger to understand the peculiarities of the people he finds here today. The Celtic element has also strongly impressed a love of nature upon the people, as shown in their care of flowers and their pleasure in the beauties of the wilderness. They can tell you where to go for the finest views, and they know any peculiarity of rock or tree that may occur in their neighborhood.

Emigration to the mountains, at one time considerable, practically ceased when the great West was opened up and the people flocked thither, no longer drawn to the less exciting region of the Southern mountains. The more enterprising of the North Carolina mountaineers also went West, we are told, thus leaving behind the conservative element, another fact rich in explanation of the people here today, and leaving also the less ambitious natures, as well as the weaker ones. The easy conditions of life here doubtless appealed to many who had not been endowed with the kind of strength required to wrest success from active life in the New World, some of them seekers after better things than they could hope for at home, gentle souls who were not tempted by the glittering prizes to be struggled for in more favored parts of the then unexplored continent. The rapid growth of slavery no doubt discouraged many, who, unable to succeed in the slave states, were crowded to the mountains, or else became the "Poor White" of the South, who must not for a moment be confounded with the "Mountain White," the latter having brought some of the best blood of his native land to those blue heights. He brought into the mountains, and there nourished, the stern virtues of his race, including the strictest honesty, an old-fashioned self-respect, and an old-fashioned speech, all of which he yet retains, as well as a certain pride, which causes him to flare up instantly at any suspicion of being treated with condescension, this pride being one of the most baffling things to the stranger, who never knows when he is going to run up against it.

That the people are, for the most part, of English, Scotch, and Irish descent, their names show. And what good names some of them are, names that are crowned with honor out in the big world—Hampton, Rogers, McClure, Morgan, Rhodes, Foster, Bradley, and dozens more; and to those fortunate ones, who out in the big world have gained fame and fortune, these Highlanders are undoubtedly related. The same blood flows in their veins, although they are here, and living back in the eighteenth century.

Why have they remained in the mountains all these generations? The answer may be found, partly, at least, in the fact that in the beginning it was too easy for them to make a living, that is, such a living as contented them. Game was abundant, and their flocks and herds supplied their own wants upon the mountain "ranges" for practically eight months of the year. The reason for their remaining after the easy conditions of pioneer life had passed are, first, because those who remained were not those who came, but their descendants, born and raised in the wilderness, inured to its life of want and of freedom, and with no knowledge of any different life. And then, they were imprisoned in their mountain fastnesses because of lack of means of communication, in part the result of obstacles presented by the slave states that surrounded them like an unnavigable sea; by lack of communication and by the conditions of life in the lowlands where the black man was king as well as slave. As time went on, they were forgotten by the rest of the world, which they in turn forgot.

Excepting in a few places where people came a little while each summer for pleasure, and where the traffic of the mountains passed out, the mountaineer had no contact with the outside world. Even the coming of the summer visitors, who, in the early

An Old-time House

days, brought their own servants in the form of slaves, did not to any extent influence the lives of the natives. To get a living from the poor soil required all their energies, the mild climate indisposing them to exertion beyond that needed to supply the merest necessaries of life. And so it happened that for a hundred years or more most of them were completely lost to the world.

Bad blood there was among them as well as good, and brave men as well as weak ones. The brave as well as the bad blood sometimes worked out its destiny in vendetta and "moonshining," although there never existed in the North Carolina mountains the extensive and bloody feuds that distinguish the annals of Virginia and Kentucky.

For more than a century, then, the mountain people lived as their pioneer forefathers had lived before them, retaining their language and their old customs modified only by the slow growth that comes in a fixed environment, and slowly spreading over the whole mountain region wherever a "cove" or a valley offered hope of sustenance, until today, there are some two hundred thousand of them in the North Carolina mountains alone. Little villages grew up where some natural advantage drew the people together, or near where the people from the lowlands chose to come for their summer outings. So while the rest of the world was advancing in a mad rush toward some unseen goal, the Southern mountaineer was simply living. The stranger who occasionally penetrated into his wilderness was amazed at the simplicity of life there, as well as at the native intelligence and shrewdness of a people so separated from all contact with the world of action.

When a new tide in the affairs of man began to bear people again to the Southern mountains, this time in search of health, retirement, mines, lumber, or "business" of various kinds, the mountaineer appeared as a unique and puzzling personality, more or less difficult to cope with. Cautious, suspicious of newfangled notions, and very suspicious of any attempt to "improve" him or his community, believing that what was good enough for his father was good enough for him, he stood like a bulwark against the advance of new ideas, and particularly against the intrusion of the rich and "bigotty" newcomer, who he imagined looked down on him and his simple ways. Hospitable to a fault among his own, and to the stranger whom he trusted, but resorting at need to more than questionable methods of freeing himself from the presence of an obnoxious neighbor, the Southern mountaineer was an enigma to the well-meaning but impolitic stranger, who, seeking to make for himself a beautiful home in the Southern mountains, was perhaps forced to leave the country before the exactions and the implacable hostility of the native people. If you are friends with the people, all is well, but if you are a mere customer of their commodities or their labor, then you must match not only your wits against theirs, but your ignorance against their knowledge of the mountains, with the odds seldom in your favor.

The mountain people are many of them poor and ignorant, but the ill-clad man, who to the city visitor may look like a vagabond, is not to be treated as such; he knows some things the fine-appearing stranger does not know, and is well aware of the fact. The mountaineer is very old-fashioned, so old-fashioned that he values native shrewdness above what he calls "book-larnin'"; so old-fashioned that he thinks his neighbors as good as himself, and himself as good as his neighbors, irrespective of who has the biggest cornfield; and so old-fashioned that he believes progress to be a menace against his personal freedom, a thing to be combated at every point. His long-continued, almost communal life in a free wilderness, where every one had a right to do what he pleased—hunting, fishing, pasturing, even cutting down trees wherever it happened to suit his convenience—made for him the acceptance of other ideas of property rights peculiarly difficult. He gladly sold his land to the newcomer whose slaughter of the forests he understood, but if the purchaser, instead of destroying, tried to preserve the forest land, prohibiting burning-over, pasturing, and common use of the territory—then there was trouble. Also the inalienable right to hunt and fish when and where he pleased was a part of the faith of the mountaineer, whose long sojourn in the wilderness had ingrained in him primitive ideas which the gradual filling-up of the country did not change, although his methods were rapidly exterminating both fish and game animals.

But while the new pioneer among the settled natives of the Southern mountains had his troubles, the native himself, although it may not have been apparent at first, was changing. He learns slowly, but an idea once established grows and flourishes with astonishing vigor. In course of time the advantages of modern methods, particularly in business, dawn upon him, when, sometimes to the discomfiture of his unconscious teachers, he takes a hand and proves himself a winner in the new game. Indeed, nothing concerning these people is more interesting or more illuminating than the quickness and success with which they adopt the ways of the world when once their interest is aroused. That they are honest, intelligent, and efficient workers has been proved by all who have employed them with discrimination, and nowhere better than in the development of the large estate of Biltmore, which, the first enterprise of great importance to enter the mountains, won its way to success by help of the people, though not without many and unforeseen difficulties, principally in connection with controlling the land purchased.

Biltmore and the New Era

Somewhat more than twenty years ago, before that phenomenal wave of prosperity, which is now sweeping over the South, had started, and while the country people were still living essentially as they lived when the first pioneers came to the mountains, there appeared among them, as if by magic, a perfect illustration of the advanced cultivation of the outer world.

Unlike the transient and self-centered community of Flat Rock, that fell into the wilderness like a jewel, and made about as much impression, Biltmore, its antithesis, expressing the new era, was not inorganic, but living. Its roots were strong and full of sap. It had to grow, and the form of growth it took played an important part in the development of the mountains, a development which though just begun is rapidly changing the life of this region.

What the native people, after living a life of stagnation for so long, most needed was an ideal—a point, as it were, at which to aim, and a knowledge of how to work, and how to care for their lands. These Biltmore gave them. It showed them, not only perfect results and how those results were obtained, but, what was of paramount importance, it made the people themselves the instruments that produced the results. The thirty miles of macadamized road traversing the estate, and the hundreds of miles of dirt road that make accessible all parts of the large forest connected with the estate, were made by the mountain people, the real significance of which lies in the fact that these roads, made in the country where the people themselves live, and in which the grave difficulties of road-making have been overcome by scientific methods, have taught the people of the mountains how to make their roads, as well as something of the advantages of good roads and the necessity of caring systematically for them. Then there was the stock farm where domestic animals were cared for, and where were learned the advantages of modem sanitary methods as well as of high-bred animals; and there were the gardens where new methods and new products were introduced to the workers; and there was the forest where the astonished mountaineer was to discover that a tree is as well worth careful raising as a cabbage.

It was the scale upon which the work was done, more even than the nature of the work itself, that gave it its substantial value; for each year young men from all parts of the mountains were employed at Biltmore, not by tens, or by hundreds, but by thousands. They were put to work and, what was of equal value in their development, they were subjected to an almost military discipline. For the first time in generations they were compelled to be prompt, methodical, and continuous in their efforts. And of this there was no complaint. Scotch blood may succumb to enervating surroundings, but at the first call to battle it is ready. Not only did the men do the manual labor, but, as time went on, the most capable of them became overseers in the various departments, until finally all the directors of this great estate, excepting a few of the highest officials, were drawn from the ranks of the people, who proved themselves so trustworthy and capable that in all these years only three or four of Biltmore's mountaineer employees have had to be dismissed for inefficiency or bad conduct.

Nor was the dissemination of new ideas confined to the people at work on the estate. Milk from Biltmore appeared at Asheville in glass bottles, while Biltmore butter shot a golden ray into the lives of discriminating visitors to Asheville. Today all the milk in Asheville is delivered to the better class of customers in glass bottles, and the country dairies have been remodeled to meet the growing demand for cleanliness; and for it to be said of a dairyman, "He got his training at Biltmore and follows Biltmore methods," is the same as a gold medal from the last World's Congress. When such novelties as spinach and celery appeared in the Asheville market, the mountaineer scorned them until he discovered that people really did buy them, when he began to take interest. In this way gradually came better varieties of all the vegetables, until the Asheville market was transformed. And whether Biltmore really was the mother of every new good thing that came, it at least got the credit for being.

Of the many valuable enterprises of Biltmore, the most important to the mountain people has doubtless been the preservation and administration of the large tract of forest land, more than one hundred thousand acres in extent, connected with the estate, and, because it lies partly on Pisgah Mountain, known as "Pisgah Forest." Not only were the virgin forests of this tract put into trained hands for their perpetuation and improvement, but the cut-over lands belonging to the estate were reforested and cared for according to the best science of the day on the subject. The woodland was not only preserved, it was utilized, supplying at one time quantities of firewood to Asheville, and, as it can bear it, lumber and bark are removed for other uses. The forests are traversed by roads—thus making lumbering easier, more successful, and less harmful to the prosperity of the woods. And what is of utmost importance to the people, the trees are scientifically preserved by mountain men trained for the purpose, these forest rangers thus learning the needs and uses of a North Carolina forest, a drill whose value in this era when the North Carolina forests have suddenly become of vast importance and great value, cannot be overestimated in bringing the mountaineer not only to a knowledge of forest administration, but to a change of mind in regard to the treatment of his own wooded land. The North Carolina highlander may be slow to take an idea, but once firmly lodged in his mind, it is there to stay, and the rapidity with which he acts, when once it dawns upon him that a given action is the thing, fairly takes one's breath, particularly the breath of one who has rested in his midst before enlightenment had disturbed his slumbrous existence. And what an influence must the training of thousands of young men in practical forestry have in educating those who not only have the greater part of the forest land in their keeping, but who will soon be needed to administer and beautify the new national park!

It was at Biltmore that the "Good Roads Movement" was started which has made such wonderful progress in the state for the past few years. Here also was born the idea of the great Southern National Forest which has just become a reality, and here years ago for their education came some of those most deeply interested in the preservation of our natural forests, because Biltmore was at that time the only place in the United States where scientific forestry was practiced on a scale large enough to be of value to them.

Pisgah Forest, besides its other uses, is also a game preserve, so that the red deer once more bounds along its shady aisles, while the wild turkey and ruffed grouse grow and multiply, and flocks of quails fearlessly trot along the road ahead of your horse. What added grace belongs to the forest where the quails are not afraid of us! Not that the wild denizens of Pisgah are wholly undisturbed, or so one infers from the recent phenomenal increase of game in the Asheville market during the open season, and if the venison enjoyed by visitors to Asheville does not always come out of the remote wildernesses of the Balsam or Smoky Mountains, that is a technicality which does not disturb the pleasure the stranger takes in the delicacies that come his way.

Related, in subject at least, to the forests are the nurseries and gardens of Biltmore for the propagation of plants suitable to the region; not only exotics but all those charming growths of the mountains that make the country itself so engaging, and many of which are equally adapted for use in other parts of the world, quantities being shipped to the North as well as to Europe; for the gardens and nurseries of Biltmore, besides supplying materials for the estate itself, also supply large numbers of plants to the outside world. These gardens and nurseries, as well as the greenhouses, are now almost entirely under the care of mountain men, some of whom have developed remarkable ability in working with plants. Besides the natural forests of the estate, and the nurseries and gardens, with their many choice exotics and native growths, a living book for the botanist, there is a botanical library which contains besides books several herbaria, among which latter is the collection of Chapman, author of the "Flora of the Southern United States."

The first question asked when a stranger comes to Asheville, and again when he goes back home, is, "Have you seen Biltmore?"—and if he has not, it is his own fault, for the extensive grounds of the estate, covering some ten thousand acres, are open to the public two or three days every week. Carriages enter from the village of Biltmore, which was so named by Mr. Vanderbilt at the time of the purchase of the estate.

The merely curious visitor may not divine the real charm of the place, may even be disappointed at the lack of display there, to him a large part of the carefully planned grounds seeming in no way different from the rest of the country, excepting the roads, which are perfect. But let the nature-lover or the poet in any other form enter these roads winding through the apparently untouched forest, and he will feel something that he does not feel in the wilderness, something that moves him as a great picture moves a sensitive spirit, and for the same reason. Back of the painted picture throbs the universal soul of man, and in the work of the great landscape artist is felt the aspiration of the human heart. For these grounds were planned and to an extent perfected in detail by America's greatest landscape gardener, whose work in our public parks is a source of national pride.

Just why his surroundings produce so pleasing an effect upon him, the visitor to Biltmore may not know, but if he is an artist he will know, and if he is somewhat acquainted with plant life he will soon add, to the general impression of beauty, another in which his pleasure is increased by discovering, among the apparently wild and untrained growths along the roadside, a tree, a bush, or a plant that blends with the rest, enhancing the effect, but which is not a native of the mountains. Perhaps among these aliens he may note a very rare exotic, but it is not displayed. Perhaps not one in a hundred will recognize or notice it, yet its presence gives the perfect touch to the place it adorns, and even without his knowing it, gives pleasure to the sympathetic passer-by. These beautiful exotics, placed in the right spot to strengthen a group of trees, to emphasize the greens of a mass of foliage, or to add a sudden glow of color, are gems that reward the careful eye of the botanist, though most of the plant life that hedges the drives of Biltmore is the wild life of the forest skillfully persuaded to create a desired impression, without betraying to the most careful observer that its perfections are not wholly due to the beneficence of nature. Look up that charming little valley—why does it bring a smile and a memory of something sweet and dim and poetic? Nobody seems to have touched it, and yet it makes one feel as one never feels in a wild mountain gorge, no matter how well one may love the gorge. The bottom of this valley is smooth and green, its sides as they ascend are clothed first in bushes and low-growing things, then with trees, the largest at the upper edge. You do not see this at first, perhaps you will not analyze it at all, seeing only a lovely valley with rocky, shrubby walls irregularly and charmingly clad with nature's wild growths that seem to reach up into the very sky in noble sweep. It is so sweet, so natural, so sympathetic a part of the landscape that you can scarcely believe it is one of those rude ravines that furrow the mountains, and which, charming as they often are, yet lack the perfection of this apparently wild glen.

At Biltmore one gets ideas of what to do with one's own glorified acre of wild land, to make it yield the highest return in pleasure. With how little labor and how many compensations in happiness might not a thousand small places be converted into dreams of beauty! Nature here is so enchanting when left alone, or even when abused, what might happen if her efforts were helped by loving hands!

With the passing of years, the untiring industry and devotion lavished on Biltmore have produced the result seen here today, a result that money alone could not have produced. And with the passing of time the mountain people have changed, too. They speak with a new note of appreciation of the estate from which so many of them have drawn or still draw sustenance, and from which they have received so abundantly that which is worth infinitely more to them than the week's wages. They are also beginning to understand the new business methods that are now manifesting themselves in so many ways in different parts of the mountains, and for the coming of which Biltmore, in a sense, paved the way.

The grounds and roads of Biltmore are an object lesson, not only to the natives, but to every stranger who comes to these mountains to make himself a home, an object lesson that serves to show what could be done with a small holding as well as with a large one, and with almost any kind of problem the mountains offer, so varied is the contour of this large pleasure-ground.

Biltmore house stands three miles from the entrance gate, on one of those high open places from which one gets that sense of space and sky that has fastened the name, "Land of the Sky," so firmly on this region. It is a large and stately mansion, suggesting a French château, and the terrace upon which it stands is supported by a noble stone wall that reminds one of the impressive rampart at Windsor Castle, or of those great walls that guard the mediœval castles on the hills of Italy; though this is no rampart for defense, and the world about it is neither English nor Italian, the exquisite mountains that stretch away, range above range, belonging distinctively to the New World. And the house, too, has played its part in the development of the people. While the men and boys were learning important lessons out of doors, the young girls were being trained in the same manner indoors. And here, too, the scale upon which the training was given has constituted its far-reaching influence, which is its chief value, hundreds of young girls owing to Biltmore their first preparation for the new life which is so fast coming to the mountains.

Besides, there is the "Biltmore Industries," a school for girls and women as well as for boys, which has also opened the doors of the new era to many a waiting heart, but a consideration of which belongs to another place. In short, Biltmore, appearing upon the scene when the industrial development of the South was about to begin, had the opportunity and the task, in many ways difficult, of giving the people their first training in the ways of the world. But it has done more than this. Besides disciplining the people and giving them an object lesson in the practical development of the natural resources of the country, it has, as we have seen—and this will seem to many its highest value—shown how to beautify the mountains while transforming them.

Of course Biltmore is not the only influence which has been at work transforming the life and work of the people. Every one who has come from the outside world to live in the mountains, and who has employed, or taught, or come in any kind of real contact with the native people, has had a share in their advancement. There are many, too, who have lived and worked directly for them, but there has been no other single influence so large, so varied, and so far-reaching as Biltmore, and none other has dealt so practically and so thoroughly with the all-important subject of forestry.

The large hotels at Toxaway in the "Sapphire Country," with a holding of twenty-eight thousand acres, have employed the mountain people in clearing the land, building the dams, and otherwise preparing for the lakes that were made by flooding valleys. They have also made roads, but on a comparatively small scale, and their forest is held as a game preserve, where deer are plenty, but where no forestry is practiced beyond keeping out fires.

It is the presence of Biltmore, the Toxaway hotels, and the many people of culture who within the last twenty years have come to the mountains to make their homes, that are the hope, one might almost say the prophecy, of the future. For as a consequence of the new prosperity of the South, throngs of people are pouring into the mountains. The bewildering rapidity with which cotton-mills have sprung up all through the cotton country has directly and indirectly put money into the pockets of thousands of people who never before had been able to spend a summer at the mountains; and it is these people who, but for the check and educating power of other influences, would put upon the new development of the mountains the hopeless stamp of mediocrity which it would take generations to efface. The old-time picturesque house of the mountaineer is bound to go. It cannot be modified to suit the demands of modern comfort. The ugly structure that, among the recently prosperous and ignorant classes, is so prone to succeed it, has already been anticipated by a style of architecture simple, pleasing, and in harmony with the scenery, showing every one that it is as easy to build an attractive house as an ugly one.

It is the highest type of progress that one wishes to see at work in the mountains, the spirit that transforms by enhancing instead of diminishing beauty, the spirit that converts steep, rough, and dangerous roads into winding highways, and that banishes the unnecessary scourge of fever that each summer invades the farthest recesses of the mountains. And this spirit may animate not only the man of millions who comes to build a stately pleasure-house in these enchanting mountains, or place a group of palatial hotels on some choice eminence, but it may equally animate every one who owns a piece of land, be it ever so small.

Nothing can stay the march of progress that has now begun. The old order is passing. Let the new order be better than the old. If the charming hoyden we call Picturesqueness must go, let her nobler sister Beauty take her place. And whatever may be the future history of Biltmore, if the mountains continue to develop in the direction of sanitation, safety, and ever-increasing beauty, the honor belongs to her of having been the guiding star in the difficult passage from the old order to the new. May the prophecy which she seems to hold be fulfilled in the new era which appears, to those looking on, to be approaching these mountains of beauty radiantly, like the rising sun.

The People

To come from the turmoil of city life to these mountains is like taking a journey back into the history of the past. Notwithstanding the changes begun by the recent intrusion of the outside world, life here in many ways is yet primitive. One breathes fresh air and gets down to elemental things.

"Stoves?" said an old man; "I ain't never owned a stove and I don't never aim to. I don't see no use in stoves noway. I wouldn't have one in the house. You can't bake bread in a stove. I don't want nar' thing but meal and water mixed together and baked in the fire. I don't want salt in the bread. I was raised on that bread and it is the best in the world." Imagine a condition where one's physical wants are reduced to corn-meal and water!

Because the people are so obviously untutored, the chance visitor is prone to imagine the whole mountain a favorable missionary field, but finds it a field that contains many disconcerting surprises. A favorite grievance of the average good Samaritan is the "ingratitude" of the people. They take what you do for them as a matter of course, if they take it at all, and do not often say "thank you." What the donors do not understand is, that it takes a good deal of social training to enable any one to say "thank you" gracefully, or to say it at all. "Why do you give me this?" asked a woman, turning the little trinket over in her hand with a pleased and puzzled expression. "Nobody ever made me a present before. I have heard of presents, but I never had one." How could any one with such a narrow range of experience *say* "thank you"?

Frequently well-meant efforts to help the people are proudly resented.

"Why won't you wear the aprons I gave you?" a Northern lady asked the young mountain girl who was living with her, and with whom she had tried her best to make friends.

The girl refused to answer for some time, then said:—

"Well, if you really want to know, I will tell you. I can't afford to buy aprons such as that."

"But I don't want you to buy them; I want to give them to you."

"Well, that's just it. I haven't got anything to give you, and I don't want to take where I can't give."

Another stranger fed a mountain woman, who, having come to town to "trade," stopped at the door tired and hungry, to sell her butter. Next day the woman came back with a chicken.

"Why, no!" said the lady, "I cannot take your chicken. I gave you the dinner."

"Say you did?"

"Yes."

"Say you gave me the dinner?"

"Yes."

"Well, if you can give me a dinner, why can't I give you a chicken?"

The unsanitary condition of the poorer homes which so excites the genteel visitor, although bad enough, is less important than it seems to those accustomed to sewer-drained cities; for natural causes here—the hot sun, the free winds, the wide spaces, and the scattered population—prevent the consequences that follow similar habits in crowded and shut-in places. The people are fairly healthy, though, as a rule with exceptions, not long-lived, and while they are young their mode of life is not felt by them as a hardship, the burden of it falling upon the sick and aged.

The most frequent disorder among them is dyspepsia, for which the pale-green, or saffron-yellow, brown-spotted, ring-streaked and speckled luxury known as "soda biscuits" undoubtedly bears a heavy burden of blame. These wonders of the culinary art are freely eaten by all who can afford to buy white flour, and their odorous presence is often discernible from afar as you approach a house at mealtime. Typhoid fever is another frequent visitant, though the "mountain fever," as it is here called, appears in a light form that seldom results fatally.

When looking at the average highlander with his bent back, his narrow shoulders and lean frame, one suspects that back of everything the people are starving—not so much physically as mentally and spiritually. For it seems to be just as necessary to escape from primitive life as it is necessary to go back to it occasionally for rejuvenation. The unfed mind reacts upon the body. The pretty girls too often become old women at the age of thirty, with a "hurtin' in the breast," that no doctor's stuff can assuage. One suspects the "hurtin'" of being really in the heart. They are generally grandmothers at an age when a New England matron is still discussing the psychological development of her infants at the mothers' club.

The slender lads with their gentle manners and friendly eyes become bent old men when men out in the world are in the prime of life. The forest is filled with divine fragrance. The mountains are dreams of beauty, but the man who looks out has no future. Often he cannot even read. He knows nothing but how to be kind. But he does not know that anything is wanting. He laughs and takes life as he finds it, thinking his lot the common lot of man. Having no conception of a world different from his own, a city to his imagination is a mountain village with a few more houses. A native of the Grandfather region, proudly showing his spring of cold water to a Northern visitor, not long since, said politely, "I reckon you-all have got good springs in Boston, too"; but his tone of voice indicated clearly enough which land he believed to be most highly blessed in its springs.

The mountain home is generally well filled with children, and the grandmother, who is about the age her daughter looks to be, is vastly proud of her numerous descendants, though she sometimes has difficulty in remembering their full names, or even their numbers, and one of them, trying to count up her grandchildren, once said, "It seems like there are fifteen, but I will have to study jest how many."

The children take care of themselves, and where there are so many a few more or less makes no difference, hence orphans are received into an already overflowing home with a cordiality that might put to shame the exclusiveness practiced in some other, and richer, parts of the world. Also illegitimate children are cared for with an affection equal to that bestowed upon their better credentialed brothers and sisters. When a young girl presents her parents with an unaccountable grandchild, the neighbors politely refer to it as an accident. The number of those among the poorer people who have "met up with an accident" is not inconsiderable, which perhaps accounts for the fact that so little importance is attached to it. The girl generally marries later, when her first-born takes his or her place in the family circle on the same footing as the rest, though, of course, among the better class of people, morality is esteemed the same here as elsewhere.

The children share the responsibility and work of the home from the start, and in the remoter and poorer districts are as wild as rabbits. Sometimes half-grown children are unable to pronounce their own names so as to be understood. As a result names have actually been changed, an instance of which is the Madcap family. You naturally inquire into the behavior of a family with such a name, and failing to find anything to justify it in those immediately under observation, you go back a generation, and finally, through much inquiry, find that the name was undoubtedly corrupted from Metcalf, and that Johnny Madcap is not a wild young blade nor in any way to blame for his name. But it must not be supposed that all the Metcalfs have been thus metamorphosed; only those poorer owners of the name who have gone deep into the wilderness, and there lost themselves.

The little children, like flowers in the forest, often have the prettiest and most unusual names. Of course there are John and Mary and Tom, but there are also Mossy Bell, Luna Geneva, Vallerie May, Luranie Carriebel, Pearlamina Alethy Ivadee, and a thousand others like them. Oftentimes the poorer the family the more fanciful the children's names, as though, this being the only inheritance, the parents wished to make it as rich as possible. One wonders where these names come from until one discovers that certain women of the mountains, gifted in this matter, collect the pretty names they hear, or think of, or read in the story papers that fall into their hands, drawing on their stock in behalf of their friends. And is it patriotism or poetry that invest the female members of one family with the charming names of Texas, Missouri, and Indiana? Sometimes a child will have half a dozen of these ornamental names bestowed upon him—or more generally her, as the greatest play of fancy is exercised in the selection of names for the little girls. It is one of the pleasant memories of the mountains, these little human flowers with poetical names, that one finds everywhere in the woods.

The principal recreation of the country people is visiting. They go long distances for the purpose, and the smallest cabin is never too small to welcome home the married sons and daughters who have come with their families to stay awhile with "Mammy" and "Pappy." Nor is the poorest home too poor to welcome with open arms half a dozen or more people appearing quite unannounced from some distant region to stay a few days. The only pig is slaughtered, the bean-pot is filled, and everybody has a delightful time, hosts as well as guests, although the days of "visiting" may consume the provisions for half the winter.

In the villages there are the ordinary amusements of young people: parties, dancing, picnics, "box suppers," where the girls fill the boxes with fried chicken, bread, and cake, and the boys buy them; and of course there is music, the violin and guitar being the most popular instruments. In the remoter districts there are fewer diversions. "Huskin's" are common everywhere, and in some sections there is a form of entertainment known as "candy-breaking," where the boys buy the candy, and everybody eats it.

The country music is oftenest heard in the cool of the evening, when the day's work is done and all sit about the blazing logs of the big fireplace. How pleasantly comes back to memory one such scene! The only light comes from the fireplace, and dark

GOING HOME

shadows steal about the room as the fire flickers. In the glare of the burning logs sits a youth with his violin, rendering with zest the compositions of a local celebrity—"Sourwood Mountain," "Cotton-eyed Joe," "The Huckleberry Bush," "The Blue-eyed

Girl," "Old Uncle Joe," "Aunt Sally Good'in, A pot full of pie, And an oven full of puddin'." With what enthusiasm he plays them, one after the other! And as he plays, coal-black Jim sits in front of him, knee to knee, and "beats straws." The youth cannot keep time without this unique assistance, which is rendered by means of a piece of broom-straw held between the fingers of the right hand and struck against one string at the neck of the violin, while the musician plays. Black Jim also manages to beat time with his feet without disturbing the rhythmical *tang, tang* of the straw, or distracting the player. "Beating straws" seems to be confined to a section on the eastern slope of the Blue Ridge, where, however, it is in common use. After the violin solo, black Jim dances the "stag dance" for us, first retiring to put on his shoes, for though he says he can dance better without them, the splinters of civilization have to be considered, a dirt floor being the original and proper foundation for the dance. He dances very solemnly, oppressed no doubt by the presence of strangers, and in the heat of the fire his face presently shines like polished ebony.

Since the family get up with the sun, or considerably before that, all soon go to rest—the visitors in the parlor where stands the best bed. There is a carpet on the floor, and a round table in the middle of the room holds a lamp and, as ornaments, a dozen oyster shells.

One's ablutions are supposed to be performed in a tin basin standing on a bench on the porch, the family taking turns, but when, unused to the customs of the country, one begs for some water in one's own room, a basinful of it is promptly brought in and set down on the hearth. In the morning the kind hostess appears with a large wooden pail of water, fresh and icy from the spring, a long-handled gourd dipper floating on its sparkling surface. A cold bath with a vengeance!

The women have one consolation which the stranger visiting their beautiful mountains conscientiously deplores, forgetting how short a time it is since his own ancestors of both sexes comforted themselves with snuff, even if kings and queens happened to be numbered among them. In the pocket of many a mountain woman and pretty young girl today hides the snuffbox. It is not a silver ornament beautifully chased or set with jewels, however, but the little tin box in which the snuff is bought. Nor is snuff taken after the manner of former generations of snuff-takers. Here the people "dip," that is to say, a stick chewed into a brush at one end and kept for the purpose is dipped into the snuff and rubbed over the gums and teeth. It is not a pretty practice, but it seems to afford peculiar satisfaction, enormous quantities of snuff being consumed in this manner. When a mountain woman refers to her "toothbrush" the snuff-stick is what she means. She says that to dip snuff preserves the teeth and strengthens the constitution. A young girl scarcely grown out of childhood gravely told how thin and sickly she had been until her father brought her some snuff and ordered her to use it. The child had not wanted to take it, having a natural repugnance to the habit, but her father insisted, and she had no sooner begun its use, so she said, than she began to improve until she finally became strong and plump like the rest of the girls!

The men do not use snuff as a rule, nor do many of them smoke, though they sometimes chew. Tobacco is not raised to any extent in the mountains, and the snuff habit is the one extravagance of the people, who back in the mountains are not ashamed of it, but near the villages they are getting sensitive and hide the snuff-stick when they see you coming. The first step, no doubt, in the passing of the snuffbox. That the habit is not a polite one is recognized even out in the country where you are informed it is the "illest manners" to dip snuff in company. In the villages, although the people may not have "all the modern improvements" in their houses, neither do they, to the same extent, use the snuff-stick, nor follow the more homely manners and habits of the country people, although they closely resemble them in one respect—they show the same spirit of kindliness to each other and to the harmless stranger.

The Speech of the Mountains

Perhaps the first thing a stranger notices upon meeting the people is their quaint speech, for although they speak "English," one cannot talk with them five minutes without hearing something new and strange, their language besides other peculiarities containing many an odd phrase and word that returns us to the language of Shakespeare's day, or even to that of the "Canterbury Tales." Not that these people have remained incarcerated in the mountains from Chaucer's time, but they came across the seas a century and a half or more ago from country places in England, Scotland, and Ireland where the old words were yet strongly intrenched, though nowhere else in this new world has the language of the past survived to the same extent as in the Southern mountains and the adjoining foothills.

Since the mountain people were as a rule separated from contact with the negro, their speech differs, therefore, from that of the Southern lowlanders, and while it is true that the people of the whole mountain region, as well as those of the foothills, have many idioms in common, yet the dialect of the natives of the North Carolina mountains differs from that of the people of the Virginia and Kentucky mountains, and other sections of the highlands, as indeed slight variations occur even in valleys separated by rough mountains, or among people living on opposite sides of the same mountain, so little communication has there been between those thus separated.

Of course, like all who live in the backwoods, the mountaineer is untrammeled by the rules of the grammarian, although he adheres strictly to a few rules of his own, and today his is the most purely "American" of any language in the United States, it having grown from its English source, untouched by contact with a motley world.

"Farwel, for I ne may no longer dwelle," says Chaucer in the "Knight's Tale." "He don't never say farwell if he can holpen it," says the North Carolina mountaineer, using Chaucer's double negative and Chaucer's "farwell" and "holpen" in the same breath.

That "yonder" is in common use you know when you hear a baby lisp out, "yonda comes a cow," another pointing out the interesting fact that "yonda's a hen with a gang of little chickens," and "yon" has not been relegated to the realm of poetry where the child tells you that his cousin lives "yon side the mountain."

In some places the people still go to the "milking gap" to milk the cows. "Least" as a diminutive, and "nary" are in such common use that one soon ceases to notice them. "I've made a kiverlid for each of my daughters but the least one, and I ain't made her nar'," says a woman you know. "I've suffered three years in that house," another who is moving her household goods will tell you, but in your sympathetic inquiries as the cause of her misery you learn that she had simply been waiting there until her own house was built. "Some people seem to have a sleight at it and can chop good," says a woman discoursing upon the subject of firewood, while animals "use" certain places when they frequent them or live in them, as you learn when told that "there's a rat using in that hole," or "a bear uses on that mountain."

A universal anachronism is the use of the personal pronoun "hit," instead of "it." The baby, for instance, is "hit," from one end of the mountains to the other. Shall one ever forget the dissertation on infants given by a young person of four to the visitor who suddenly dropped into her home one day! She sat on the edge of the bed swinging her legs, her round black eyes shining with excitement as she described the advent of her baby brother. "Hit was the b-l-ack-est, me-an-est lookin' little thing you ever see, and," with unutterable scorn, "hit was a boy! And," with, if possible, yet deeper disapproval, "hit is a boy *yet!*" "Hit" is sometimes used until the child is several years old, particularly if there is no newcomer to usurp the title and "Babe," applied as a temporary provision pending the finding of a suitable name, often clings to the youngest son for life.

It is not necessary to go into the remoter fastnesses of the mountains to hear quaint expressions. The speech of a people is the last thing to yield to new customs, and in all the villages, even in Asheville, one constantly hears unfamiliar and interesting words and phrases. If you do not know what is meant when a mountaineer selling you peaches asks for a "poke" to put them in, the fault is in the times. Your English ancestors, several generations back, would have known and at once produce—not a "paper poke" in those days, but a sack of some sort.

"Peart" is a survivor from bygone times when its use was perfectly proper, and "tolerable" in the form of "tollable" almost usurps the place of "fairly" or "rather" as an adverb. "She's tollable peart," you are told when inquiring after the health of an absent member of the family. It is seldom that any one admits to being "stout," "jest tollable" being the polite limit of health. "Tollable by grace" is sometimes heard, and when a woman tells you she is "poorly, thank God," you feel that piety can go no farther.

"Ill" retains the old meaning that survives with us only in the proverb of the ill wind, and it is compared, some snakes being iller than others and the king snake the illest of all. We have "moonshiny nights" in the mountains just as they had in England in Addison's time, and as they doubtless have in the country there today. Relatives are "kin" here, those closely related being "nigh kin," "nigh" as a rule everywhere taking the place of "near" or "nearly." When the ground is slippery it is "slick." A calf frisking along the roadside you hear referred to as an "antic calf." "It is big enough to hold quite a content," one is told of a parcel concerning which the speaker is speculating. "Yes, I've a nice chance of flowers," a woman modestly admits when you admire her little garden. Here we "aim" to do a thing, and "claim" that we have done it.

When you hear one of your friends spoken of by a highlander as being "common" you are puzzled, to say the least, until you learn that the word is the most complimentary possible, retaining its original meaning as understood when we speak of the "common people," the "common good." The "commoner," you are, that is, the more you treat the people as though you were one of them, the better they like you. And to be called "homely" is also a fine compliment, in a land where the expression means that the homely one makes people feel at home, takes good care of the home, is, in short, what old-fashioned people of the outside world sometimes call "a home body."

Children "favor" their parents, though a peculiar form of the word appears when you are told that a certain young girl is "the likliest favored person that ever came down from the North." But "favor" in this sense is often replaced by the modern and more graphic "imitate"; to be told that a child "imitates" his father meaning that he resembles him in appearance.

"We laid my pappy away yesterday, he was bedfast six weeks," a young girl tells you.

One often hears the cow or mule referred to as a "beastie," though the cow is also known as a "brute," and sometimes as a "cow-brute"; while we are told of a certain cat that it was "afraid of a manperson." Bread that does not rise is "sad," while an old or ill-kept horse is "sorry." "That's good enough for a hireling," the woman says of the coat she gives the hired boy. And one frequently hears the expression, "I'm no hireling." When you ask a man who is driving a stake in the ground what he is doing, he may tell you that he is "jest pounding in a stob," and one looking for a boundary line was heard to say, "There ought to be a little old stob somewhere here."

The old plural form of words ending in *st* yet survives in the mountains, where the people speak of the "nestes" of the hens, the "postes" of the fence, the "waistes" of the dresses, pronouncing the words in two syllables. It may be said in passing that the word "waist" is generally replaced by "body," while the skirt of the dress is the "tail"—and one can imagine the agitated feelings of the newly arrived New England lady to whom a mountain man came, asking if she could not sell him a "body" for his wife, as she already had a "tail," and wanted to go to church. But this is a diversion, and returning to the more serious subject of antiquated speech one finds that "done" expressing past action, as a supplement to the auxiliary "have," is universally used. "He's done gone," "he's done hooked up the horse [to the wagon]," "he's done filled the water-bucket," "she's done baked the bread"; one hears it all the time, and upon occasion one is informed, of a completed action, that "he's done done it."

One could go on indefinitely gathering together old words and phrases that bind us to the past. But there are other peculiarities of speech equally interesting which have been acquired and crystallized in the speech of the people during their sojourn in the New World, and one is delighted to meet a well-known proverb in the following guise,—"You kin carry a mule to the branch, but you can't make him drink." "Branch" means any stream of water smaller than a river, and when a stream or a road forks, the two divisions are "prongs." To be advised to take the right-hand prong of a road is amusing at first, but when you think of it, it is at least consistent.

The mountaineer's rules of grammar are few but rigid. Whatever ends in *s* is plural, hence one finds such words as "molasses" preceded by a plural particle, but when the singular is used, as it sometimes is, the grammatical plural termination is discarded and the word consistently and deliciously becomes "molass." In course of time one gets used to "them molasses" and the assertion that "they make a good many molasses"; as one also does to the word "several" applied to quantity. To be told that a man has raised, or, as he says, made, "several potatoes," soon goes without notice, though it always comes with a pleasant kind of shock to be informed that he has "made several molasses." The mountaineer, it may be said in passing, sells his molasses by the bushel. Since a noun ending in the sound of *s* is naturally regarded as plural, we have "fuse," to the people a new word introduced with blasting, supplied with the convenient singular "fu."

"Oxen" is singular, and the plural of course is "oxes." The men still wear "galluses"— as they did in New England a generation ago.

The efforts of the people to comprehend the subtleties of grammar is well illustrated by one of them who, anxious to speak correctly, asked whether, when a piece of work was all finished, it was better to say it was "done done" or "plumb done"; and another, in an effort to be exact, explained, of something that you thought ought to be, "Oh, it's ben a bein' a long time."

The usual illiterate transformations have taken place in the use of verbs, adjectives, and adverbs. "Reckon you'll have wood enough to do you until tomorrow?" the boy inquires. "John, did you give me out?" a woman asks her husband whom she has kept waiting. People here do not "carry," they "tote"; and they "reckon" instead of "think," though when they think hard, they "study." Instead of saying you must do a thing, you say you are "obliged" to do it. "I'm obliged to go home and get the dinner," the woman with whom you have been talking says apologetically as she leaves you. That the "moon fulls tonight" is an interesting fact, for soon, that is, on the "dark of the moon," you can plant your corn.

"Gwine" in some places takes the place of "go," and you freely hear such expressions as "gwine to gwine," "done gwine," and even "done done gwine," although this is not common in the higher mountains. "Mighty," "powerful," and "plumb" universally take the place of "very." When you find the road all but impassable, you may be informed that the recent rains "undermined it mightily." "I can't hear mighty good," one woman says, while another, whose little chickens you are admiring, informs you that the hawks catch them "powerfully." Again you are told that "you-all will have a powerful hunt to find any blackberries now," while one neighbor says of another that he is "a reg'lar wash-foot Babdist, the powerfulest you ever saw in the world." "Now the truth's the truth," says a woman apologetically of her worn calico dress. "This is all I've got but what's so hot it plumb swelters me to death."

Without the various forms of "mighty," "powerful," and "plumb," the speech of the mountaineer would be "powerful" weak, and illy could be spared the convenient "smart" and "right smart" that so freely adorns his remarks. "He holp her a right smart," some one says, joining the discarded form of yesterday to the invention of today. "Is it far?" you ask. "Yes, a right smart," is the reply. The variety of uses to which "right smart" can be put is both bewildering and wonderful.

"Trick" is also of general application. "That's a right smart of a trick," a mountain woman says admiringly of your opera-glass. "They've got a plumb cute little trick over yonder," a woman tells you of a neighbor's baby. But perhaps the best thing we ever heard about a mountain baby, or any other, was told us by a woman of her sister's child,—"You never did see a prettier big baby in your life—hit's as pleasant as the flowers are made."

"He has a very glib team," we are told of one whose horses have made a hard journey in a short time. And of a neighbor suddenly fallen ill one is informed as the cause that "he has taken on too many apples." "It's not doin' much good noway," a disappointed farmer says of his corn crop, or again you will be informed that the land is so good that two or three acres of it will "eat a family," which does not mean what it says.

There are no "stones" in the mountains—only "rocks." The boys "rock" each other when they get angry, they "rock" the cows, and we found a little girl "rocking" a hen that persisted in sitting on some round "rocks." "Air ye lookin' fer rocks, stranger?" is a common question in the regions of valuable minerals. Neither are there "hives" in the mountains, only "bee-gums," which the bees fill with "right smart of honey."

Perhaps the most immediately noticeable peculiarity of speech is the universal use of "you-all" in the singular. "How are you-all today?" by no means applies to the health of the family. "We-all" and "they-all" are good form, though not so often heard. One imagines the genesis of "you-all" to have been in those early days when people lived so far apart that meeting with one member of the family necessitated inquiring concerning the health and welfare of all, and when an invitation for the same reason necessarily included every member of the family.

"Howdy" is the usual form of salutation, and the people have the friendly habit, in common with the rustic communities of all civilized countries, of courteously greeting the stranger they may meet. You must make your bow and say your "howdy" to every man, woman, and child you pass, a custom that links people together and removes the instinctive fear the city-bred traveler has of meeting a stranger on a lonely road. Even in the larger villages the stranger receives a polite bow from any native citizen whose eye he meets.

The voices of the people are low and pleasant, expressing the kindly nature of the speakers, and also one imagines the friendly quality of the landscape and the climate. And their speech, although quaint and archaic, is not coarse or rude: one never hears offensive talk or low epithets, slang is unknown, and profanity in most parts of the North Carolina mountains is looked upon as a grave offense.

'Light and Come In

The best way to see the people as well as the mountains is to walk. This one can do because "a mountaineer never meets a stranger," as a native philosopher explained, adding, "The people round here give the kind hand to everybody, they haven't learned better, they have never traveled"; but one desiring to explore the mountains without either walking or riding can gain much by driving in a leisurely manner over such roads as are passable.

One winds slowly along, it may be on a perfect summer day, the radiant Southern sky seen between overhanging branches, with now and then an opening in the forest through which the mountains show intensely blue, or like pale wraiths in the distance. Along the way cold springs come gushing out like joyous living things from under the roots of a tree or under a fern-draped bank—the waters purified by how many miles of groping through intricate dark passages in the heart of the mountains, springs not always visible from the road, but whose presence the knowing eye detects by the hard-beaten path winding down from the roadside. Crossing the cool, swift streams your horse stops knee-deep to drink, or to make believe drink, in order to stand there awhile.

The road winds along, now hidden among trees, now emerging to ascend some open height where mountains come to view, near, green, and dark-shadowed, or distant, azure, and dreamlike; again it makes its way around the end of a damp ravine where a stream jumps down in bright cascades, and the banks are smothered under ferns, leucothoë, and laurel. Through the vistas that open, pleasant pictures come and go—a farmhouse in a hollow, a log cabin surrounded by cornfields ripening into gold, the invincible, sunny forest pressing down upon it on all sides. And then, turning a curve in the road, directly before you stands an old house shaded

A Mountaineer's Home

by ancient oaks, a spinning-wheel on the porch—or, if you happen to be in the right valley, a hand-loom may be there.

This house that you approach, wherever it may be, seems to be expecting you, at least you have a friendly sense of knowing it, although you have never seen it before. As you draw near in the sweet summer stillness a friendly dog comes wagging to meet you, and some one, man or woman, comes out and hails you, "Howdy, 'light and come in." This is the universal salutation. Or if you are walking, as you come within earshot you are greeted with a pleasant and expectant, "Howdy, stranger, come in and rest yourself." Often, the moment you come in sight a chair is set ready on the porch, and the family assemble and seat themselves in expectation of your arrival. They greet you with a warmth that makes you feel as though you had known them always, and they insist upon your spending the day with them. Truth to tell, one enjoys a sense of very genuine welcome where the eyes of the hostess look into those of the unexpected guest, undimmed by a thought of what she is to have for dinner. It is no doubt the extreme simplicity of the food, and the fact that everybody, rich and poor alike, have the same, that give the people their gracious gift of hospitality and their feeling of equality. The knowledge that everybody serves the same dinner in the same way must go far towards leveling social distinctions.

As you go about the mountains, you will come to many an old-time log house, the pictorial survivor of an age when the log house was the only house built. Those of better class, made of hewn logs and built by the "quality" of former generations, are large and substantial with a stone chimney at either end, from the depths of whose vast fireplaces one can still in imagination smell the banquets prepared in the "ovens" that stood in the ashes, and in the pots that hung suspended from the wrought-iron cranes.

Oftener than the large log house, you come upon the smaller one of only two or three rooms, or the cabin of but a single room, yet each and every one has its big stone chimney, and most of them have the porch wreathed in vines, while one yet sees roofs covered

Getting Dinner

with hand-made shingles. The outside chimney standing against one end of the house gives the finishing touch to the appearance of the log cabin, but its picturesqueness is its chief virtue. The flames that go roaring up it in such splendid spendthrift fashion may warm the imagination, but they produce comparatively little effect upon the temperature of the room, and in these undegenerate days the open fireplace is often flanked by a modern cooking-stove that, however useful, is not at all ornamental.

The interior of a cabin, needless to say, is as simple and oftentimes as picturesque as the outside. The great fireplace with its generous flames is the center of attraction, and one may believe has something to do with the genial nature of the people reared about it. A large open fire expands the heart of man. The iron crane from which swing the pots, the circular "ovens" standing in the ashes, the red heart of the fire, the human forms played over by the flickering light, awaken strange emotions of a shadowy memory from out some past existence. Next in importance to the fireplace are the beds, several of which often stand in one room, and even in the larger houses it is customary to find at least one bed in the parlor.

Oftentimes a bench along the wall supplies seats at one side of the narrow table, and sometimes there is a bench on both sides, chairs being few, straight-backed, and narrow, for the furniture is generally home-made. Somewhere in a remote cove you will come across the man who makes the chairs, but who is always too busy doing something else to fill an order in less than a year. But what does that matter? In course of time and somehow the people get their chairs, strong, honest things made with special reference to bearing a man's weight when tilted against the wall on their back legs—this being the mountaineer's favorite attitude of repose. The seats, made of plaited oak splints or strips of deer-hide, last almost as long as the hardy frames.

In another cove you will find the man or woman who weaves the picturesque melon-shaped "hip" baskets by means of which the people "tote" their possessions from place to place, either walking or riding horseback, the horse quite as often as not being a lop-eared mule. These weavers are oftentimes quite skillful in their art, being able, so they claim, to weave any kind of basket you can show them.

Brooms are made by anybody and everybody. The tall picturesque broom-corn that ornaments the landscape, however, is raised to sell, the universal sweeping instrument of the mountains being made from the "broom-straw," or wild sedge that so beautifully takes possession of every "old field" not yet grown up to bushes. All you need to do is to gather a bundle of the ripe sedge and "wrop," that is, bind, it about the end of a stick with a piece of wire if you have it, otherwise with a piece of string. But for brushing the hearth it is better to have your broom made from a bundle of tree twigs similarly "wropped" around the end of a stick.

There is a fascination about a life where the people themselves make what they need. It returns us in imagination to an age of peace and plenty for everybody, to an era of happiness free from hurry, worry, and sordid ideals, and if the reality falls short of the poet's fancy, there yet clings a touch of romance about the home-made chairs, baskets, and pottery of the Southern mountains. When can one forget the long, sweet days of wandering about the country in search of the "jug-makers"!—"jugs" being the generic title of every form of home-made pottery. It was while in Traumfest that one was fired with ambition to discover the makers of the rude but picturesque jugs in such general use there. The people tell you they are made in Jugtown, down in South Carolina, but when you go out to find Jugtown, there is no such place. At Gowansville, below the mountains and some ten miles from Traumfest, one makes a serious effort to find—not Jugtown, that quest has long since been abandoned, but the nearest jugmaker. The people do not seem to know, but finally a black girl whom we stop on the road tells us that Rich Williams, "A cullud man who lives three quarters away, yon side the Tiger River," makes them.

On we go, and in the end find Rich—this side the Tiger. Yes, he makes jugs, and he is at it. You get out of him that a great many people in that region make jugs, and you conclude that "Jugtown" is a jocular expression for the whole region of pottery clay, but having found Rich Williams, you bear no resentment.

He is an old-time negro, as black as ebony, evidently very proud of your visit, and you are soon watching the bony, black hands knead the clay and pat it into a loaf, then on the wheel coax it into shape. The veins stand out like cords on Rich's sinewy arms, his long hands draw the flat clay loaf up, up, into the stately two-gallon jug with its narrow mouth, or into the wide-mouthed butter crock, or the pug-nosed pitcher, big or little. Rich loves his work. He says he can make anything he wants to out of clay. Looking at him, you seem to see before you the original potter. His wheel, which looks as though he had made it himself, is in a little log hut, lighted by one tiny window. His outfit consists of the wheel, a tall stool, his clay, and a stick or two. He digs the clay from the bank of the Tiger River that runs near—slate-colored, adhesive clay that Rich says is "powerful good" for jugmaking. He grinds it in a wooden box by the help of a slow-footed mule that walks in a circle at the end of a long curved beam which turns an upright shaft fitted with wooden teeth at its lower end. Rich has a jug of water at his elbow, one of his own make, and there he sits all day, and every day, busy with his clay.

You watch tall jugs rise as by magic under his hands, and when they are done he lifts them off the wheel, and on every jug are slight indentations caused by the pressure of his hands as he lifts them. There are queer hollows in them, sometimes, and lopsidednesses, for Rich is not always in the best mood, and, while on some days jugs fly easily from under his hands, there are other days when they are contrary. Rich tells you that his glaze is made from ashes and clay, that he washes the jugs inside and outside with it, and then sets them in the oven. His oven, out of doors near the shed in which he works, is a long, low vault of bricks and clay, with a fire-hole at one end and an opening at the other. He sets in his jugs, makes up a wood fire, and bakes them until they are done.

It seems as though one could learn to tell, from looking at a jug, what manner of man made it—and whether he was black or white. Black men's jugs are like them, some way, careless, generous, picturesque. Rich's jugs are homely, but one likes them, they are so honest. A jug made by a potter who dug the clay out of the bank with his own hands, and soaked it, and ground it, and shaped it, and glazed it, and baked it, must be a wholesome sort of jug to have in any house. We had formed the habit of setting groups of Rich's jugs in the fireplace, partly to heat the water, and partly for the picturesque effect, long before we knew of the ebony hands that moulded them out of the gray clay of the Tiger River.

The place of the jug would seem to be firmly established in the mountains. Yet in these later days its existence is threatened. The tin lard pail has risen above the horizon. Everybody buys lard, and the "buckets" become family treasures. Even into the remotest regions the insidious foe has crept, until one finds the unlovely lard pail occupying the place where, a few years ago, only the decorative brown earthenware jug would have stood.

Penelope and Nausicaä

The mountain woman has her duties and her privileges. She loves, honors, and obeys, innocent of any knowledge of the suffrage movement. She can work out of doors, wearing a long skirt. She does much of the work elsewhere relegated to man, but is always deferential to her husband, whom she respectfully refers to as "him," as though that were his baptismal name.

In the mountain cabin "housework" has no terrors, an hour a day is enough for everything. "Bric-à-brac" has not been discovered, and there are no "things" to accumulate. Yet the people are not without ideas of decoration, in some places stray newspapers being eagerly seized upon, not for the valuable information they contain—the people manage to get on very happily without that—but for the purpose of papering the walls. Particularly upon the side occupied by the chimney these publications are put to a use believed by many to be ornamental. In some parts of this land of leisure, to have one's walls papered by "illustrated editions" is as much a mark of distinction as in another part of the world it is to have them hung with masterpieces of painting. Besides, they keep the room warm, so the people say. At times this might be figuratively, if not literally, true! As soon, however, as harvest-time comes, the atrocious effect is softened by the multiple strings of beans, of sliced pumpkin, and sliced apples that festoon the walls about the fireplace and shrivel decoratively in front of it, mercifully concealing and staining and otherwise harmonizing the luridities of the daily press. Papering the walls in this way is an exasperating boon to the storm-bound stranger who, unaccustomed to long reverie in a public place, turns for pastime to the papered wall. You follow a thrilling narrative through several columns, interested in spite of yourself, then at the most exciting point it stops short. You have reached the end of a page that cannot be turned.

You will often see the mountain woman in her big sunbonnet in the fields hoeing, or helping "lay by the craps," occupations which, if not pursued too arduously, and they seldom are, do her no harm. On the contrary, such work is good for her, although it so often excites the indignation of strangers, to whom the sight of a woman working in a field always seems to bring visions of terrible oppression and cruelty. Most of the mountain women would prefer their light field work to the far more arduous duties of their well-dressed critics. The woman milks the cow—she does not like to trust so important and delicate a task to a mere man—and she sits in the doorway or near the fire and chums the butter in a tall, slender earthenware or wooden churn. And when she is done, she has plenty of time to rest.

When berries are ripe, she and the children have an ever-ready occupation. Particularly in huckleberry season you will see little "gangs" of sunbonneted women and children, with stained and happy faces, and stained hands and clothes, plodding along the dusty road carrying heavy pails of shining blue-black berries. And sometimes whole families go to the "huckleberry balds" on the mountains, where they stay several days, sleeping in their tented wagons. It is only in recent years that the people have taken to canning their berries, sugar being a luxury in the mountains. But lately there has come a substitute for sugar which is vaguely referred to as "powders," and what these mysterious powders are we discovered one day when into a country store in the mountains, where we had gone in search of something to eat, came a little troop of women each with her tin pail full of berries and each demanding "powders" according to her needs. The clerk cast a critical eye over each pail of berries, then ladled out from a bottle a quantity of white powder sufficient in his estimation to cover the case. When the women had gone we asked him what the powder was. He said he didn't know, and rather reluctantly handed us the bottle, on which was the label printed in black letters—Salicylic Acid. It does not take much of this to preserve a jar of berries, though one should think that as a substitute for sugar it might be a little disappointing. However, any berries are better than none when winter comes, and there is no other fruit, excepting apples and peaches, which are dried in strings before the fire or simply spread out on one end of the porch floor, and the appearance of which makes one's mind turn with lessened repugnance to the thought of berries preserved in powders.

But the most cherished occupation of the mountain woman for generations was, and to a very limited extent still is, weaving, an occupation exclusively her own and which in a peculiar way relates her to a by-gone world. Traveling along the road, you glance through an open doorway to see a woman "sitting in a loom," a large, clumsy, home-made loom in which she is weaving cloth. One always experiences a thrill of pleasure at sight of a loom here in the mountains. Some memory of Penelope and Evangeline seems to linger about it. But the weavers of today are neither great ladies nor fair young girls. The girls of the mountains prefer machine-made cloth to the home product and the labor of weaving it. "I can't learn her noway," the mother says of her daughter who takes no interest in the ancestral loom.

In the corner near the loom stands the spinning-wheel, not as a mere parlor ornament with a ribbon around its neck, but in readiness to spin a thread. Sometimes loom and spinning-wheel stand upon the porch, where they lend a peculiar air of domesticity to the landscape. As a rule, however, they are inside the house, for weaving is the woman's winter work, or one might say her recreation, for like the woman of antiquity she loves to spin and weave. And she is proud of the result. Even the coarse "jeans" for her men's clothing and the "linsey cloth" for her own are regarded by her with affectionate pride, for has she not created them out of nothing, you might say? To convert a long thread into a piece of stout cloth might well make any heart thrill with pride. Besides this, she weaves towels and blankets and, most prized of all, coverlets of elaborate design for the beds.

"We used to have great gangs of sheep," the people say, "but now we have to buy all our wool, and it don't pay to weave noway." "I'd rather card and spin and weave than anything in my life," the older women who did this work in their youth tell you. It was the stock laws that drove away the sheep, for they had to be inclosed and this made raising them unprofitable—so the people explain, but one suspects it is really the cheap machine-made cloth, to be had at every country store, that has conquered the loom.

There are not many looms within easy reach of the larger places, prosperity and contact with the outside world, be it ever so slight, soon retiring the loom. Yet there are a few looms even there, and in the remoter regions, far from railways and summer visitors, they are still in common use. With what pleasure one recalls certain high valleys where under the shadow of blue domes and green slopes one finds in every second house a great loom taking up half the room! And those quaint log cabins whose beds are spread with blue and white coverlets such as are cherished in old New England farmhouses!

One penetrating into a certain "cove" of the mountains finds Mrs. Hint Tomson, still a "powerful weaver." Near her lives old Mrs. Robbins, who used to do "a heap of mighty good weaving work," too, but she is now blind in one eye, though she can still "design" sunlight with it, and she is ninety years old, so she says, and "plumb broke down." If she is right about her age, one can well believe the rest of the statement. There are other weavers living in the same neighborhood, some of whom yet "weave a power," and all of them will bring out from chests or shelves and display with pride the old coverlets made by dead and gone grandmothers or great-grandmothers, as well as by less industrious present-day weavers.

With what pride they display their favorite patterns! They know nothing about the latest novel or the opera or scandal in high life, perhaps they could not even tell you who is President of the United States at the present moment, but they are ready to give their opinion upon the relative merits of the "rattlesnake trail,"

Penelope

"the wheels of time," "the rising and setting sun," "Bonaparte's March," "the snail's trail," and other old and prized designs.

And as they show their treasures and talk, they tell you many a homely secret connected with the art of weaving.

"If you want to make a man jeans that he can't hardly wear out," one woman confides to your sympathetic ear, although you have no great expectation of needing the advice, "you dye the chain light tan with black walnut, then take the first shearing of lambs and weave it in white, then dye the cloth with walnut. The lamb's wool fulls up, it shrinks more than any other and makes a cloth he can't hardly wear out. You've got him harnessed up then to stay."

The "chain"or "harness," that is to say, the warp of these coverlets is made of cotton thread, usually white, and the "filling" of woolen yarn, generally blue, though it is sometimes red or green, or pink or black. Mrs. Levi Ward's "wheels of time" are black and white.

Besides the coverlets themselves, Penelope takes pride in showing her "drafts," the patterns from which the designs are made, and which have been handed down from generation to generation dating back to those days when the women vied with one another in inventing original designs, designs which were handed down with the loom—a true "heirloom" as one perceives. To this day each pattern keeps its name, and that of one, the "Missouri trouble," brings one suddenly close to a page of history, when the women were patiently weaving through the formative periods of a nation, tingling with the charged condition of the atmosphere, and through their looms giving expression to the emotions thus powerfully aroused. Those days are gone now. Lethargy has stolen over the souls of the people and no new designs are being made, only some of the old ones are copied, and that with lessening frequency. The coverlets made today are not so beautiful as those made before the use of chemical dyes. Then the people raised their own indigo and went out into the woods for walnut bark and certain herbs whose dyes defied both time and the washtub, only getting a little mellower as they grew older. Some of the prettiest of these old coverlets have a dark green pattern woven into a black warp, and one occasionally sees an old-rose counterpane, which is prettiest of all.

Even in the remoter districts it is only the older women who weave, and in another generation hand-weaving will have become a lost art, so far as the people at large are concerned. Schools to encourage weaving have been established here and there in the mountains, it is true, but philanthropic efforts of that kind cannot save a people from the onward march of progress. The work done in these schools is not sold to the people themselves—they cannot afford to buy it—but to summer visitors or it is sent to distant cities as a luxury to the rich. It serves a good purpose in providing remunerative work to a small number of the mountain women, but as to reviving to any extent the good old customs among the people themselves—the hand cannot be put back on the dial. Besides the immediate help they afford, these schools have doubtless another mission: by gathering up and recording the old patterns, and with them more or less of the old customs of the people, they are preserving valuable material for future historians and story-tellers.

In addition to the art of weaving, the mountain women have another picturesque occupation which is in no immediate danger of passing, and which, were it not for Homer, one might hesitate to enlarge upon. But after the glamour cast over Nausicaä beating out the family wash in the crystal waters of the Phœacian River, one ventures to present a woman of the Southern mountains standing under a laurel tree, her well-used wooden tubs ranged on a bench before her. On the ground at her side bright flames leap up about the large black pot, hung to a pole above or standing in the ashes. A cloud of white steam from the pot, a little curl of faint blue smoke from the fire, the deep-blue sky showing through the leaves of the forest, the murmur of running water from the stream close at hand—these are the rest of the apology, if any is needed, for presenting the subject in detail.

Whereas Nausicaä trod out the stains from her clothes with snow-white feet, the woman of the mountains lifts her clothes from the boiling pot on the end of a long stick, lays them on a stump leveled for the purpose, and soundly beats them with a paddle. There are no shining sands on which to spread them, so she spreads them on the shining bushes, and when they are dry loads them, not into a chariot drawn by firm-hoofed mules, but into a basket made of oak splints which she sometimes carries home on her head.

The washing-place down by the branch is always picturesque, and so is the woman at her labors surrounded by the beauty of nature that, as it were, embraces her. Even more picturesque than the white woman at her task is perhaps the black woman whom one often sees in the lower mountains standing under a great laurel bush or a shady tree, dipping the clothes from her steaming black pot, then valiantly paddling them on a tree stump. There is something so leisurely and yet so hearty about these black people—and they satisfy your love for the picturesque without exciting any feeling of pity. When you look into their great shining eyes you know that when all is said they love to wash. And they have never any feeling of shame about it. Though for that matter neither have the mountain women of the white race when you get far enough from the villages, where the ferment of civilization has crept in, the ferment whose first action is always to make people ashamed to be seen working.

In accordance with the customs of the country, the women do their washing as they do everything else, in the manner most convenient for the moment. They have no roof to shelter them in winter, but the year round wash "down at the branch" in the open air. Often the tub stands on the ground, the woman leaning over it in a way to make one's back ache in sympathy. But as usual your sympathy is wasted.

"Why doesn't your husband make you a bench?" you cry in indignation, and she, rising up smiling from the suds, replies—"I

Over the Tubs

like it better this way, a body don't have to lift up the water, nor lift down the tub to empty it."

Washboards of course are as unknown as darning-needles. Why waste money on a washboard when all your ancestors paddled their clothes on the end of a stump? But sometimes the woman has no tub, and that really is serious. Once, over towards the lovely Nantahala Mountains, we came upon a woman washing in a wooden box. She was young and a baby sat on the ground at her side. The blue mountains were a heavenly vision behind her, a clump of brilliant wild flowers rose above her head. But her eyelids were swollen, she had evidently been weeping, and the tiny cabin higher up the hill was very bare inside. Was there a "still" down in the ravine? Had her young husband been carried away by the "revenuers"? Or had he fallen a victim to the seductions of his own industry? Our hearts were troubled, but we could do nothing. She turned her head aside and would not look at us; so, respecting her sorrow, we passed in silence, flooding her with warm good will and heartfelt hopes that life would soon grow brighter.

A Vanishing Romance

To the outside world the most interesting character in the mountains is the moonshiner, who appears to the imagination as the Robin Hood of the Southern greenwood, sallying forth from his illicit "still," hidden in some cavern in the mountains, to pursue the relentless vendetta and contribute "spirits" to a grateful community.

Who is this romantic figure? When and how did he come upon the scene? Unfortunately for romance, he is not a survival of some ancient age and custom, but on the contrary, a product of conditions resulting from the Civil War. "Before the war" the mountaineer converted his grain into whiskey just as the New Englander converted his apples into cider. The act of distilling in itself was not a crime, and became so only because it was an evasion of the revenue laws. In these late years the wave of prohibition passing over the South has further complicated the act and made it reprehensible in the eyes of most people. But we have only to contemplate the immense quantity of distilling in Kentucky, Illinois, and other great places of production to see that it is not a question of morals but simply of money. In the mountains, where it is stigmatized not as illegal but as "illicit," a nice distinction, it is not a question of morals but of rights.

Formerly, when no odium was attached to it, the distillation of whiskey was universal and respectable, according to the customs of the time, and, in spite of the supply of whiskey kept in every house, the people were not intemperate. Even today, the word "whiskey" has no such sinister meaning in the mountains as it has acquired in the outer world, where its use has been so long abused in the cities, although its distillation, because of its secrecy, its hidden ways, its "illicit" character, has made it the most destructive to character of any one pursuit.

At the beginning of the Civil War for the sake of revenue a very heavy tax was placed upon all distilled alcoholic liquors. After the war was over, the tax was not removed, and this is the grievance of the mountaineer, who says the tax should have been removed, that it is unjust and oppressive, and he has a right to do as he pleases with his own corn, and to evade a law that interferes with his personal freedom. We read in the stories of English life much about the right of smuggling, the practice of smuggling being not only right but heroic, and it was doubtless in accordance with this sentiment, which may have been strengthened by his desire to taste the forbidden fruit, that the mountaineer continued as of old to make his own whiskey, omitting the costly formula of obtaining a government license and thereafter subjecting himself to government supervision. At first, because of his remoteness, he was not much hampered by the enforcement of the, to him, obnoxious law. As the country became more thickly settled, the struggle for existence harder, and the officers of the law more vigilant, whiskey-making became a special rather than a general occupation, and was carried on by the boldest and most executive spirits of the region, who called their illicit product "blockade," thus attaching to themselves something of the respectability and even the heroism of a man running a blockade against an enemy in a just cause. Hence some of the most valuable men in the mountains have been moonshiners, as well, of course, as some of the least valuable. Today the moonshiner is losing caste even among his own people, and the younger generation of mountaineers finds its way out into the world when in need of employment for its energies.

The people tell us that, in days gone by, the whiskey made in the mountains was pure, but since the more complete enforcement of the revenue laws, and the yet more limiting consequences of recently enacted prohibition laws, the path of the moonshiner has been so beset that he has resorted to various ways of increasing the value of his product, adding tobacco and other deleterious drugs to give it "bead" and make "seconds" look like proof whiskey. In short, he now makes "mean whiskey" that sometimes causes a curious form of madness in the drinker.

The old time mountaineer, so far as moonshining was concerned, had often to choose between two evils. His possession consisted perhaps of a large family and a small cornfield, the latter often on a mountain slope so steep that its staying there seemed little short of miraculous. His corn being his wealth, it had to buy the clothes of the family if they had any. He could with great labor "tote" it down the mountain many miles to the nearest market, get next to nothing for it, go home to his needy family, an "honest man" in the eyes of the law, but despised by his neighbors as being "no account" in the warfare of life. Or he could betake himself to some lonely gorge not far from home, "still up" his grain, easily transport the product and yet more easily dispose of it. There is always a market for corn in this form, and the price it brings is several hundred fold that of the raw material, and the man who "stilled," though a reprobate in the eye of the law, until very recently was not so in the estimation of his neighbors. His family was fed and clothed, he waxed rich, and the stranger who came to the mountains admired his picturesque home and praised him for his industry, unaware of the true nature of his labors. It must have been a nice matter for any judge, taking into consideration all the circumstances, to decide whether the moonshiner of yesterday, when no avenues to livelihood were open, was a "good" man or a "bad" one. The unsuccessful moonshiner, of course, was bad.

Within the past few years the moonshiner, along with many time-honored customs, has been rapidly vanishing. But before that one often met him in the woods, patrolling some lonely path, gun on shoulder. If you asked him what he was doing he looked at you with kind and guileless eyes and told you he was "lookin' for squirrels," and as soon as you had passed he discharged his rifle, not into your quivering body, but into the air to inform his confederates that somebody was coming. He wore no mark of Cain upon his brow, often he was a handsome fellow, clever and fearless. You might know him for months, even buy eggs or mustard greens of him or his offspring, without suspecting the truth.

The moonshiner required gifts of a high order to succeed in his precarious calling. If caught distilling, there was a heavy fine and a term in prison, and whoever pleased could get ready money for betraying his hiding-place, a severe strain on the loyalty of impecunious or unfriendly neighbors. He owned a piece of land and raised corn on it, but not corn enough. He was always buying meal or carrying corn to the mill to be ground. Sometimes he took a little to several mills, but that deceived no one. Everybody knew he got a bag of meal at Scrugg's mill on Monday, another at the Pumpkin Patch mill on Tuesday, and a third at the Bear Wallow on Thursday, and everybody knew what he did with it, though if you asked him you would be gravely informed that he "fed hawgs."

He was honest, always leaving full measure in the bottle he found behind a stump. The method of exchange was simple: You put your bottle in company with money behind a stump in the woods; then you told the first mountain man you met what you had done. Even though he might have no interest in the business, by some system of communication the news was conveyed to the right place, and when you went next day you found your bottle full. Of course you kept away from the bottle's hiding-place meantime. The system did not work under observation.

It is not impossible, even in these days, to get samples of exhilarating "corn juice," a colorless liquid with a peculiar, flower-like aroma that deceives the stranger. It seems, for the first second after it is taken into the mouth, as inoffensive as the water it looks like, with a delicate flavor of wild flowers. But wait another second, and you will think you have performed the juggler's feat of eating fire, but without knowing how. In time it might ripen, but it never has time. It is the only thing in the South that cannot wait. It is enough to strangle a crocodile, and yet the trained native finds it too mild to suit his palate and sometimes adds the juice of the buckeye to give it zest. If you have ever tasted buckeye juice, you will understand that it is able to impart zest.

A Moonshine Still

When his still was discovered, the moonshiner sometimes argued the case quickly and to the point with his gun, but generally he hid away. It was only from the "revenuers" or "raiders" that he hid, however. In the case of a "spy," as he termed those overzealous neighbors of his who for the sake of the reward paid for such services informed the revenue officers where to find his still, he seldom spared the bullet, and it was as apt to come from behind as anywhere else, such "varmint" not being considered worth a fair fight. The life of an informer, if he was discovered, was worth considerably less than the sum he got for informing. Sooner or later he came to grief. Of course the law made an effort to apprehend the transgressor in such cases, but the forest is vast, and the quest was about as hopeless as hunting for a very small needle in a very large haystack. The woods tell no tales, nor do good people very much regret the untimely end of the "informer," for usually his kind is more detrimental to a community than is an honest outlaw.

The moonshiner defended his still as other men do their hearths. When two moonshiners fell out, they got their deepest revenge by betraying each other's still. This was generally followed by the shooting of one by the other, when vengeance was sure to descend upon the slayer, the avenger in his turn being shot by a member of the first victim's family. Thus was sometimes started a blood feud that lasted for generations, or until the death of the last male on one side. These deeds sound wild, but they were not of common occurrence, and all shooting was strictly confined to quarrels among themselves. A stranger might go into the home of a man red-handed with the blood of his foe and be received so cordially that he would never suspect his frank host of being "wanted" in the criminal court. Such lawless deeds, although they sometimes occurred, were not frequent in the North Carolina mountains, nor were they gilded by romance outside the story-books and newspapers. Those frightful blood feuds that have given such notoriety to certain districts in Kentucky and Virginia, and which were sometimes though not always connected with moonshining, are unknown here.

That the day of the moonshiner is passing is well illustrated by the fact that when the road was surveyed up Tryon Mountain a few years ago, not less than half a dozen moonshine stills were routed on the little streams adorning that dignified eminence, while today there is probably not a single still on the mountain. Only the remains of the stills were found, of course, for by the time the surveyors got there the watchful owners had taken away the copper retorts and whatever else was valuable.

Six little stills gone off Tryon Mountain at that time undoubtedly meant six little stills set up elsewhere in the mountains near, for not unless the retort was found and destroyed, and he too poor to buy another, did the owner of a still abandon his occupation. To the young and active mountaineer there was for long an irresistible fascination about moonshining. In it he found combined, as it were, the excitements of war with the reward of industry. It was his Wall Street with a spice of personal danger thrown in. When he was caught and put in jail he was terribly ashamed, not of being in jail, but of getting caught. It was something of a shock when one first came to the mountains to have a woman tell you her husband was in jail as frankly and with as little consciousness of disgrace as she might tell you that he had gone to visit his relatives. To go to jail for moonshining was almost as good as being a martyr. When a man came out, his friends laughed and shook hands with him, and he went back to "stilling" with a grim determination not to get caught again. What happened to the stills on Tryon Mountain is fast happening everywhere; as roads and settlements come in, the "moonshine still" goes out.

Although the moonshiner existed everywhere in the mountains, his most noted retreat was in the Dark Corners, on the eastern slope of the Blue Ridge. Where is this mysterious and dangerous region? Nobody seems to know exactly, though in a general way it is over towards Hogback, across the South Carolina state line. In course of time one discovers the name to be generic. There are "Dark Corners" on the maps in various states of the South, but they are not related to each other, nor to us excepting through a common reputation for lawlessness. If nature had planned our Dark Corners on purpose for the successful distillation of iniquitous "corn-juice," she could not have planned better, made up as it is of valleys guarded by mountain walls, furnished with rushing streams, and with numerous obscure exits in different directions. Best of all, perhaps, it lies directly on the State line, for when the skein of the moonshiner's life becomes tangled by spies and revenuers, he needs another state handy to step into for rest and reflection, and whence he can in safety give spirituous consolation to his brethren.

The principal water-course of our Dark Corners is Vaughn's Creek, whose source is supposed to be in that lovely gap between Hogback and Rocky Spur, into which, as seen from Traumfest, the sun drops and disappears at the winter solstice, and whose upper waters were once believed to be bristling with stills. Of course no outsider was supposed to go into the Dark Corners, but any one might follow that road winding along high up on Melrose Mountain to a certain point, where looking down he could see directly into the forbidden region. With what breathless curiosity you peer down there the first time! And what do you see? Did you not know it to be in the Dark Corners, you might suppose it to be a corner in some paradise. In the distance, on a mound and surrounded by tall trees, stands a large, old-fashioned house. Below it are cultivated fields covering the bottom of a little valley through which winds a stream, one of the numerous tributaries of Vaughn's Creek. Almost beneath you is a cabin with a tall tree shading it, the green fields beyond it merging into those others. The term "dark," it is evident, cannot refer to nature, for sunshine floods the place, its woods we are sure are fragrant, and its streams murmur with sweet voices, and there is not the slightest sign of wickedness anywhere—which is a little disappointing. This of course is only one very small portion of the Dark Corners, the rest being hidden behind wooded ridges. And this valley, with its sparkling waters and high surrounding mountains, is so tempting in its possibilities that one longs for the means, including the ability of the landscape artist, to convert it into the dream of beauty it could so easily become.

But though we may look so safely down into one end of the Dark Corners, hold our breath up there on Melrose Mountain, and see nothing to hold it for, access to that charmed region is even today as difficult to the stranger as it has always been believed to be undesirable. There is a road in, but it appears to have been designed to keep people out. By far the easiest way to get there is to walk. And this we did many a time in by-gone days, having first made friends with the principal offenders against the excise law. It was the people of the Dark Corners who muddled our hitherto clear convictions about right and wrong. The young girls who came out of there to bring us flowers smiled as sweetly as any child of fortune. And one has seen the face of a moonshiner glow with an expression that assured one that, whatever the verdict of the world, he would not be counted bad in that final court where human prejudices are ruled out.

That the Dark Corners got its name from the flourishing but questionable industry carried on there is disputed by some, who say that the name was given, not because of moral obliquity, but because once a stump orator, trying to rouse the people at some political crisis, told them they were steeped in ignorance, that they lived in dark corners, and never came out into the light. "Dark Corners!" The name struck the fancy of deriding neighbors and stuck. However that may be, Dark Corners here came to be synonymous with the haunt of the moonshiner, whose boldest deeds were executed there in days gone by. Many tales are told of raids into the Dark Corners, of tragedies enacted there, and finally of the clever manner in which the "master moonshiner" conducted to a happy issue his perilous vocation, rendered ever more perilous by the encroachments of civilization. This kindly outlaw did not shoot the invaders; he invited them to dinner, cared for their horses, entertained them with his best, no doubt including an accidental bottle, then followed them to his still, looked on while they destroyed his expensive outfit, assisted them in loading the barrels of confiscated "stuff," even politely lending them his own wagon and horses to convey it away. It was difficult to get "stuff" hauled out of the Dark Corners, because nobody would do it. No negro driver could be induced to go in there at any price, so it was a real kindness to be helped out by the moonshiner himself.

Such conduct as this could not fail of its reward. The "raider," so it is said, did his duty to the extent of satisfying the demands of his office, and if he suspected that the stuff confiscated was but a part, and a small part, of what remained "hid out" in the ravines, he did not overwork his conscience nor risk his popularity trying to find it. Neither did he accuse the man, who had treated him so handsomely, of owning the still found so near his house. This was a coincidence which did not concern him. Neither did he come too often nor too secretly. It was whispered that it was not to the interest of the revenuer to destroy so good an excuse for his own office.

Of course a good deal depended upon the quality of the "revenuer" assigned to a district, but even that could be arranged, it not being unheard of for the brother or other near relative of a notorious moonshiner to be elected to that discreet office. There are a good many ways to evade an unpopular law in a country where the majority is "agin the government." Even the licensed stills have been known to be operated most successfully by clever moonshiners who knew how to satisfy the demands of the inspector and at the same time manipulate the machinery in a way to make licensed distilling pay as well as that not licensed.

It would be hasty to affirm that "blockade" is no longer made in the mountains, but it is not now made in the free-and-easy manner and on the comparatively large scale of former years, although as a matter of fact the amount of whiskey manufactured in the little mountain stills has never been worth the cost of trying to restrain it.

In these days those rows of demijohn-shaped jugs in which Traumfest used to transport her "vinegar" are no more seen standing on the platform of the railway station. It is astonishing the amount of vinegar that used to go out of Traumfest, in jugs. It had a powerful alcoholic smell, this vinegar, but those who handled it turned the olfactory equivalent of a deaf ear to this peculiarity, and having received it as vinegar, unquestioningly passed it on as such. It went to other stations, where it was received by those in waiting, and by them distributed to such as needed this sort of vinegar to their salad. Sometimes it was "molasses" jugs that had this peculiar smell, which was no odor of sanctity, nor yet of honest sorghum.

To visit a moonshine still was the natural desire of all good people, and this could easily be done after the confidence of the owner had been gained, for he then trusted you completely. It is psychologically an interesting experience. The forest seems full of eyes as you follow your guide through the lonely paths. You have a feeling that somebody is looking at you and reading the truth in your guilty heart. For the moment you, too, are an outlaw, and the mingled feelings that assail you are not wholly disagreeable. One's feelings undergo a curious change, however, upon finding the still, not in a cave on a wild mountain-side, nor in some all but inaccessible glen, but in a little ravine near the moonshiner's home, where live his wife and little children, those beautiful little children so common in this country. One notices the delicate framework of both parents, the small hands and feet characteristic of the people of the South, the well-formed features, the unfulfilled promise of a nature designed for a life of refinement.

The man leads you to his still as naturally as he would take you to see his corn-mill. You are astonished to find how near the still is to the house, until you reflect how far away the house itself is. The object of your quest is perhaps so hidden in the ravine that you do not suspect its presence until you are standing directly over it, and then would not know but for a faint line of smoke coming up through the tree-tops. The path to it is very obscure: you might have thought it a rabbit-path; and yet the still has been here undisturbed for ten years. To maintain a still without a path is part of the business. Following the steep trail to the bottom of the ravine, you soon find yourself at the still, which consists of a low roof covering a little furnace made of stones. In one end of the furnace is cemented the copper retort, a picturesque object suggesting wizards and alchemists. The pipe connects the retort with the "worm" that lies coiled in a keg of running water, and from which through a tube is escaping in a slender stream the precious liquor that resembles water in looks but not in taste. A vat or two of "beer," or fermenting meal, giving forth a sour, yeasty smell, a few jugs and kegs waiting to be filled—such is the moonshiner's still. The fire is made of rails or poles, one end burning in the furnace. To feed the fire, it is only necessary to push up the fuel as the ends burn off. It is better not to chop wood in the neighborhood of a still, lest chips betray the workman.

A visit to the moonshine still, no matter how often one may go, never ceases to be exciting. It may be the spice of danger attached to it that makes the fire glow with so red and sinister an eye in the rude furnace, and light up so dramatically the human figures in the wild glen closely curtained with laurel and rhododendron leaves. Sometimes the inside of the still is almost as dark as night, because of no windows and the close-pressing foliage, when one's feelings are heightened in proportion.

Notwithstanding the abundance of "moonshine" one seldom sees drunkenness in the mountains, though one would do well, so it is said, to avoid certain regions of a Saturday night, for then the lovers of strong waters betake themselves to secret places in the woods, where bottles change hands and young men on the way home sing out of tune.

It is not long since, walking along the roads of a Saturday afternoon one would see a fresh-cut laurel bush lying in the path or in the middle of the road. If you followed the direction in which it pointed, you would find another one at the first intersecting path, either pointing up the path or away from it. You might not notice these bushes, but there were those who would.

Every mountaineer, seeing a fresh-cut laurel bush in the road of a Saturday "evening"—it is evening here after midday—knew it to be what the gypsies call a *patteran*, and that to follow the direction in which it pointed would lead him finally to some well-hidden spot where a man with a jug was waiting for customers. The *patteran* would guide any one to the appointed place, but unless you were a regular customer or known to be going with honest intentions you would not find any one when you got there. You might notice, however, a man sauntering along the path ahead of you, loudly whistling.

Yes, the moonshiner seems almost to have vanished from many parts of the North Carolina mountains, with whatever of romance the story-books have attached to him. The people who still demand strong waters may know how to get them, but one no longer sees the *patteran* of Saturday evenings, nor those rows of odd-smelling molasses jugs on the platform of the railway station, fearlessly awaiting the coming of the train.

Church and School

When you see little groups of people assembled at the houses or moving from place to place, the men newly shaven, the women and children dressed in their best, you may know it is Sunday. When there is no church, everybody goes visiting, and one should think from the numbers collected in the dooryards of some of the houses that these visitations must strain the capacity of the bean-pot considerably. For whoever comes must be invited to dinner.

If it is "preaching-day" the people are found all moving towards one point, the settlement church, which, like the school-house, generally stands "at a point equally inconvenient for everybody." In the villages and larger settlements, the minister is resident, and the churches are like other country churches, but outside the villages, services are conducted in the barnlike little "church-houses" by an itinerant preacher, the frequency of whose visits depends upon the size of his parish and the distances he has to travel. Hence it happens that upon the death of a person in a remote district, although the actual "burying" takes place at once, one may be invited weeks or months or even a year or more afterward to attend the "funeral," a very important ceremony which is frequently deferred until the presence of some favorite preacher is obtainable, and to which come friends and relatives from far and near.

The itinerant preacher is nearly always a native who has very little more "book-larnin'" than the rest of the people, and who may be seen in the field on week days ploughing with his "ole mule" exactly like his neighbors. He chooses his calling because of his natural gifts, his reward oftentimes being the opportunity to exercise his talents. Once, asking the wife of a hard-working farmer preacher how much he got for his arduous Sunday services, sometimes requiring him to start the day before, the astonishing reply was, "Oh, he don't get nothing. He says it takes them as long to come and hear him as it takes him to preach, and the least he can do, if they take the trouble to come, is to preach to them." A novel and refreshing view of pastoral duty in these days.

The people as a rule are Baptists, though there are a few Methodist, Presbyterian, and Episcopalian centers which are rapidly enlarging, but the religion of the mountains may be said to take naturally the Baptist form, and when you see a crowd down on the river-bank some Sunday, you may be sure there is a "baptizing" going on.

The people are devout and good church-goers, but the old-time native preacher knows how to preach nothing but doctrine, he produces emotional effect by intonation and the frequent introduction of a long-drawn and hysterical "ah"—thus, "Oh, Lord—ah—be—ah—merciful—ah—to these thy—ah—children—ah," and so it goes, with increasing intensity for an hour or more. The effect of this must be heard to be appreciated. To preach less than an hour, no matter how much or what may be said, is a sign of incompetency.

On "preaching-Sunday" the people conscientiously go to church, however distant it may be, but the prayer-meetings introduced by newcomers have slight attendance. "I reckon they're clar plumb dilatory," the Baptist minister's wife, who washed clothes for summer visitors, explained of her neighbors who could not be induced to attend a mid-week meeting.

Besides the orthodox Baptists, there are various offshoots, such as the "Washfoot Babdists," and very popular just now, the "Wholly Sanctified," the mystic meaning of whose doctrine, being literally interpreted by some erring brethren, is a cause of much trouble both to the defenders of the faith and the community at large. Under the Smoky Mountain we heard of a sect of "Barkers," who, the people said, in their religious frenzy run and bark up a tree in the belief that Christ is there.

The mountain school, like the mountain church, varies with the locality, out in the country resembling the barnlike church-house, only being smaller and, until very recently, built of logs. It sometimes stands in the lonely forest so far from any one that finding the school-house seems to be the child's first step to an education, the second step being to acquire learning in spite of the opportunities offered. The log school-house was picturesque in the extreme, but as an educational institution it lacked many things. Sometimes it lacked windows, relying upon the cracks between the logs and the open door for light and ventilation. Its furnishing consisted of benches, and a chair for the teacher, while the books were few and as antiquated as the furniture. The condition of the school-house in the remoter regions, oftentimes did not greatly interest the people. Once upon protesting against a school-house with no windows, the father of several of the children in attendance replied that the children's eyes were strong and it did them no harm to learn their lessons in the dark.

"Book-larnin'" evidently is not the thing that most absorbs the remote mountaineer's waking hours. He takes his children's schooling as he takes their measles, not very seriously. A few parents are anxious to have their children educated, the rest are indifferent, not quite comprehending what good can come to the children from something they themselves have had so little use for. Nor can one blame those parents who prefer to keep the children at home rather than send them miles, it may be, through the forest and over rushing streams, to the schoolhouse where school "takes up" for only a few weeks in the year, and where the teacher, like the rest of the people, knows little more than how to be kind. The advantages of such schooling are apparent, and one wonders whether that father were more a philosopher or a humorist who, being condoled with because the school was so far away, "reckoned" it was just as well because the children were therefore better contented to stay at home. Another parent, philosophizing upon the questionable advantages of "book-larnin'" for his children, ended with the optimistic assertion, "Well, I reckon it don't hurt 'em noway— they so soon fergit it all." And the woman who said contentedly, "I can't neither read nor write, but I don't need to, for God has given me a pretty wit," summed up the ancient philosophy, of a large part of the mountains.

Passing a roadside school-house at "recess" time, one is astonished at the number of children crowding about the building. The forest may seem like an uninhabited wilderness, yet there are children enough to supply a small village. And even at the school-house far from the road, and hidden so well that it is cause for wonder that the children ever find it, one has seen them come darting out of the forest like rabbits, barefooted and sunbonneted, carrying such books as they had, and swinging their "dinner buckets"—lard pails most of them. If you expect to find these young backwoodsmen as shy as quails and overcome at the unprecedented appearance of strangers in their midst, you will be mistaken. They are not shy, and they are not bold, these children of the forest of Arden. They are glad to see you, and show it in smiles as broad as nature has made provision for. You feel that if you stayed a little longer they would all invite you to go home with them.

There is no truant officer in the mountains, and no need of one. The children love to go to school and go so long as there is a school day left, unless circumstances in the form of younger brothers and sisters and the stern hand of parental control forbid. Perhaps their devotion is partly accounted for in the length of the school year, which lasts from six weeks, to three or four months. You do not have time to get tired of going to a school that lasts only six weeks with forty-six weeks of vacation to look forward to.

The log school-house is fast vanishing from the North Carolina mountains where so many changes have been made within a few years. And while the schools hidden in the heart of the wilderness are undoubtedly still primitive enough to compete with any of the noted log schools that nurtured genius in former days, genius is not nurtured in them here, for it can quickly find its way to the better schools of the villages that are becoming more and more accessible. Indeed, educational opportunities are increasing on all sides at the same quick pace that characterizes the other "improvements" that are now transforming the wilderness into something else, though it must not be supposed that there is yet no room for improvement.

There are schools for higher education, colleges and industrial schools, in the mountains themselves, as well as in the country just below the mountains, and now a law has been passed which retires the unlettered mountain girl as a teacher in favor of the one who can show a normal school certificate, there being three normal schools in the mountains, as well as normal departments in other mountain institutions. The school-houses are being rebuilt, and even now the last log school-house may have closed its doors forever on the youth of the North Carolina mountains.

Ten years ago statistics of illiteracy in these mountains were almost startling. It was calculated that there was a school attendance of only about one third of the children of school age, while the condition of the buildings, the quality of the teaching, and the length of the school year in the country districts were such as to leave those who attended school little better instructed than those who did not. Since that time much has been done to wake up the people to the value of education, as well as in providing means to such an end, but necessarily there yet remains a large army of mountain people who can neither read nor write.

The older educational institutions are of course in or near Asheville, and these have steadily bettered their equipment with the passing of time. Now all through the mountains one finds the established village schools increasing in efficiency and new schools being started. Among the educational institutions none give better promise than the industrial schools that have sprung up here and there within recent years. The churches are now as a rule putting forth their most earnest efforts in this direction, wisely seeking to do that which the regular educational institutions leave undone, and many earnest souls are devoting their powers to teaching the people how to live as well as how to think and believe.

Perhaps no better illustration of the struggles and conquests of these workers can be given than that of Brevard Institute, near Brevard, in the French Broad Valley. This school, started in 1895, through the self-sacrificing efforts of one man has struggled on, kept alive mainly by that internal heat which alone gives any institution real growth-power. Today it enrolls nearly two hundred pupils, most of them girls, as the department for young men is not yet fully developed. Here come young people from all parts of the mountains and for a price within their means receive home, education, and training in the practical things of life. That the spirit in which the school was founded yet persists is felt the moment one enters its doors, when one becomes aware of such an atmosphere of love and helpfulness, from the principal down to the youngest pupil, that it is a pleasure to go there and bask in the warmth of it. Not that, even today, the equipment is anything like adequate to the needs, but the results prove that the poorest tools in loving hands can accomplish much.

Besides the ordinary academic subjects and special religious training, the pupils are here taught "a dread of debt, promptness in attending to business obligations of every sort, a love for thoroughness and accuracy in doing work of every sort, self-control in the expenditure of money, and a knowledge of simple business transactions." There is a business course, a department of music, one of domestic art where is taught dressmaking, millinery, and lacemaking, and a department of domestic science where the subjects taught are housework, cookery, laundry, and mending. In the normal department, "it is the intention to show young teachers how manual training, sand tables, dramatization, phonics, and so forth, can be introduced and profitably used even where there is no equipment." Thus young people are prepared to go home to the little mountain schools and there spread abroad the information and the ideals they have themselves received, as well as to go, if they are so inclined, into the world of action now opening below and in the mountains, and whose demands for helpers in all departments is in excess of a competent supply.

Brevard Institute is but one among a number of industrial schools that are doing their part, against all sorts of difficulties, to help on the transformation that is so rapidly taking place in the Southern mountains.

Another form of practical education is well illustrated in the Allenstand Cottage Industries, which is settlement work carried on in remote, and what one might call side-tracked, districts. This work began, with a day school as a nucleus, in a cove in the mountains in the northwestern part of Buncombe County, long before the present wave of prosperity had drawn near to the mountains. Here the difficult question of how to bring to the people material help without spiritually hurting them was finally answered, we are told, by the gift from a well-to-do "neighbor woman" of a home-woven coverlet forty years old, slightly faded but still beautiful in its golden brown and cream hues.

This worn old coverlet became as it were a palimpsest whereon love deciphered the history of the past for the enlightenment of the present. Looms had almost disappeared, chemical dyes had replaced the old-time vegetable dyes in coloring the "linsey cloth," still sometimes made, and the yarn spun for stockings. But the spinning-wheels were there and gave a clue by which the settlement workers ingeniously found their way out of the labyrinth. Wool from a neighboring valley was obtained and given out to be carded and spun by hand, then, in the words of one of the workers:—

"The coloring was the next business, and it was a matter of time to learn from the older women the secrets of the indigo pot and of the coloring with barks and leaves. We learned that for the best results the indigo dye should be used before the wool was spun. Whence the old phrase 'dyed in the wool.' The formula for a blue-pot demanded, besides the indigo, bran, madder, and lye, the ingredient of patience, till the pot, set beside the hearth to keep it at the right temperature, saw fit to 'come.' Then the dipping of the wool began. For a deep blue this dipping must be repeated five or six times, and the pot 'renewed up' between times, as the strength of the color was exhausted. The coloring with madder was less of a circumstance. Gradually we learned of many other dyes, of leaves and barks and flowers, giving us a variety of soft hues—browns, yellows, greens, orange, and also an excellent black. The true green is obtained by dyeing first with a yellow dye and then dipping in the blue-pot, but a good olive green is given by using hickory bark with something to 'set the dye.' Every year we gather the 'bay leaves' for the bright yellow, and harvest for winter use the 'yellow dyeflower' growing on the high ridges.

"But to return to the beginnings. When yarn enough for three coverlets had been prepared, the next step was to find a weaver of the double draft—that is, of the coverlet material with shotover designs. This requires four sets of harness in the loom, instead of two as for plain cloth, and four treadles as well. The warp is 'drawn in' and the weaving 'tramped' according to a paper pattern which is pinned up on the front of the loom. A number of women in the cove knew well how to weave plain linsey and jeans, but no one could weave the coverlets. Sixteen miles away, and farther from the railroad, we found a family where mother and daughters had great store of spreads, old and new, to which they were continually adding. As they showed these treasures to us, the variety of design was bewildering. At last we chose two patterns, and the women undertook to weave our yarn for us. It was an exciting moment when, two weeks later, our messenger returned carrying across his horse's back the long roll of weaving. Now came the question whether there was a market for such work. This was soon ascertained. Our first coverlets were sold in a few weeks, and the demand for more was enough to justify at least a small start in business. So an enterprising young woman near us volunteered to learn the double draft. A loom was found for sale in the 'Ivy Country,' and hauled to us, more wool bought and more spinners set to work."

Thus started what has grown to be an important industry to that part of the mountains. From this cove one of the settlement workers pressed yet deeper into the wilderness, to the "Laurel Country," as all that region drained by tributaries of Big Laurel Creek is called. Here, away up on Little Laurel Creek, near the Tennessee line, almost due north from Hot Springs, and close under the wild Bald Mountains, at a place called Allenstand, the work was begun again. Once Allenstand was a stopping place on one of those early roads over which passed the traffic in cattle, sheep, horses, and swine from Tennessee to the eastern lowlands, and from this it got its name, a "stand" being a place where drovers stopped overnight with their charges, this particular one being kept by a man named Allen. Allenstand may have been prosperous in those days, but the tide of traffic becoming diverted, the people living there were left to primitive conditions until the coming of the woman who was to open the doors to them, for it is to one woman that the "Laurel Country" owes its prosperity. It is always the individual who divines and conquers the difficulties in an undertaking of this sort, and so signal has been the success of this inspired worker that she is known to the outside world as the "Bishop of the Laurel Country," for about Allenstand as a center have sprung up a number of similar settlements at intervals of a few miles.

To the making of the more elaborate coverlets was added the simpler weaving of linsey which the country people themselves cannot afford to buy, it having become a luxury for dwellers in the outer world, to whom it offers itself, not only for outing wear, but also as suitable material for tailor-made gowns! Also floor rugs were made, as well as rag rugs for which the colors are chosen and blended with very pleasing results. Indeed, there is work done and experiments constantly being made in various kinds of weaving and embroidering, as well as in basket-work and simple wood-carving. And there is now a room at Asheville where the products of this settlement are on sale.

Younger than Allenstand, and more remarkable as an illustration of the possibilities of the mountaineer for a high type of development, is the industrial school at Biltmore. Here the rector of All Souls', the Biltmore church, recognizing the needs of the people, secured the services of two women gifted with the genius necessary to carry such a work to perfection, and who in ten years' time have developed to its present remarkable point what is known as the "Biltmore Industries," the history of which is as interesting as a story. The school was designed to meet the needs of the people connected with the Biltmore estate, and the enthusiastic founders started with four boys, the first one of whom had to be paid to come! Today some of those who first entered are carving chairs for the great establishment of Tiffany of New York, and more than one hundred of the pupils are earning a livelihood by their woodcarving craft. One young man, upon becoming engaged to be married, made for his future home a whole set of beautiful Chippendale furniture. The workers are paid from the moment they begin, and the older ones are not only self-supporting, but they are technically and artistically educated to the enjoyment of a kind of life which otherwise they could neither have attained nor appreciated.

Woodcarving is not the only work done at the Biltmore Industries, as witness the rolls of cloth lying on the table of the industrial rooms, cloth woven by the women in their own looms and colored by natural plant dyes. There is also embroidery, beautiful in color, design, and workmanship, and the girls, after some diplomatic manœuvres to overcome the opposition of the militant sex, now also carve. Thus in the embroidery, carving, and weaving the women, like the men, are getting far more than pay for their work. One of the pleasures of going to Biltmore is a visit to the rooms of the Industries where the work of the people is shown and explained.

The Cherokee Nation

The railroads that have triumphantly surmounted the Blue Ridge and taken the mountains, as it were, by storm, make it easy in these days to get within reach of the formerly almost inaccessible places. Besides those that have crossed the mountains, and the short line up the French Broad Valley to the "Sapphire Country," there is the "Murphy Branch" that connects Asheville with Atlanta, Georgia, by a circuitous route down the very center of the plateau around and over obstructing mountains.

At intervals along the Murphy Branch, villages have grown up, the largest of which, Waynesville, is beautifully placed close to the Balsam Mountains, and has long been a favorite summer resort. The next most important are Sylva and Dillsboro', lying between the Balsam and Cowee Mountains, and beyond these, Whittier and Bryson City, between the Great Smoky and Cowee Mountains.

From any of these villages one can start afoot or otherwise upon delightful trips through some of the finest scenery of the mountains, and from two of them, Whittier and Bryson City, roads lead into the Cherokee Indian Country that lies on the lower slopes of the Great Smoky Mountain. The Indian Country affords one a plunge into the wilderness in more senses than one, for not only does one find here wild scenery, but also the original inhabitants, or at least a very orderly remnant of that mysterious and picturesque race that before the coming of the white man roamed these solitudes.

The Indians of this region were Cherokees, and there seem to have been several tribes, not always on amicable terms with one another, judging from the number of arrow-heads found in certain fields near Asheville. The country about Asheville is believed to have been a common hunting-ground without permanent settlements, which would account for the arrow-strewn battle-fields as well as for the dearth of Indian names in that section.

The white man when he came did not enter upon the scene in a way to inspire confidence in the red man, who finally tried to hold back the hand of destiny by massacring the invaders. This resulted in an armed force entering the mountains in the summer of 1779, burning the villages, killing the Indians, and destroying their growing crops.

The treatment of the Cherokees by the white man affords no better reading than the treatment of the other Indian tribes by their civilized conquerors, and finally many of the more restless spirits among the Indians went West in search of new hunting grounds. Many, however, stayed at home and made the best of the new order of things, until the white conqueror finally decided to remove the whole Cherokee Nation to lands set aside in the Indian Territory.

Now, it is one thing to decide to move an Indian, and another thing to do it. You have first to catch your Indian, and when the hour struck for the Cherokees to go West—nothing was said about their growing up with the country—lo, the band had shrunk to half its size. This half was deported and men went out to hunt up the other half. Any one who thinks he can find an Indian hiding in the wilds of western North Carolina, has not seen the country. He might as well spend his time hunting for the lost ten tribes of Israel. In course of time the Indians returned to their homes and went on peacefully raising corn, grunting emphatic denials to any suggestion to go West. Finally, the large territory they now own, over one hundred thousand acres, was bought for them with their own money by one who championed their rights, so that the Indians who would not go West now occupy some of the most picturesque and beautiful as well as fertile land in the North Carolina mountains. They are known as the "Eastern band of the Cherokees," and are not "reservation Indians" in the ordinary meaning of the words, since they own their land by right of purchase and are true citizens of the Republic with all the privileges of citizenship. These Indians are as law-abiding as their white neighbors, more so, since they have never distilled unlawful "moonshine," but have only drunk it, when they could get it, until the chief of the tribe, becoming aware of the devastation being wrought among his people by the use of whiskey, did that which might have done honor to any civilized leader. Calling a council, he told the people that the only way to save their nation was to abandon the use of whiskey which he himself would do from that day, whereupon almost the whole tribe joined him, and although some fell from grace under temptation, there was a marked change for the better from that time.

The easiest way to get into the Indian Country is from Whittier over the road that goes up the Oconolufty River to Cherokee, the principal Indian settlement, and where is a government school. Another and more picturesque though longer way, a distance, if one remembers rightly, of twenty-five miles, is to go from Waynesville through the Jonathan Creek Valley and over Soco Mountain by one of the most nearly impassable roads in the mountains. But by going this way one enters the Indian country from the primeval forest, which has a certain appropriateness. Jonathan Creek Valley, deep, and so narrow that the neighbors say the cobblers there have to sew their shoes lengthwise, lies close under the north end of the high Balsam Mountain, and is one of those quaint survivals of other days that makes one feel, upon entering it, as though a door had been shut on the modern world. The road follows up through the peaceful valley, past the picturesque houses with the cornfields showing above the roofs, and the gardens full of flowers, past the high-wheeled mills, and across the charming fords banked in laurel where Jonathan Creek crosses and recrosses the road. You go on and up the mountain-side where the forest is stately, still, and ancient, and where underneath the trees, on all sides as far as one can see, a bed of dewy ferns covers the earth, the green fronds nested in shadows.

The road ascends through the ferns and you notice that Jonathan Creek has become a little rippling brook, a new-born child of the forest and the clouds. When you get to the gap of the mountains you find in the "old field" there, a large cold spring, the cradle out of which Jonathan Creek leaps to go dancing down the mountain-side, and away to the turbid plains below.

At the gap you see Soco Fall and hear it thunder down the lonely cliff. It is the wild beginning of Soco Creek that dashes down the other side of the mountain, and the road following down the gorge soon presents such an appearance that you adopt the Indian mode of progression, leaving the driver to survive or perish as fate ordains. To cross an Indian's conception of a footbridge over the torrent dashing uproariously against the boulders that strew its course is only one degree better than trying to cross the washed-out fords in a carriage. Yet nothing can dim your pleasure in the splendid freshness and mystery of the shadowy gorge where the water shouts in a thousand voices, for you are in the Indian Country where nature seems a little wilder and more secret. The writhing limbs and deep-green foliage of monster rhododendrons crowd the banks. Above them tower dark hemlocks. It is twilight in the gorge, although the sun shines brightly on the tree-tops.

Once in a while you get a glimpse of noiseless forms flitting through the forest. But you are not afraid, for the Indians long ago laid aside their tomahawks and arrows, along with their feathers and war-paint. They are watching us out of curiosity, and their presence adds the one needed touch to the romance of the road. As we get lower down, a lonely, neat-looking house occasionally stands near the rushing river, tightly closed and looking as though uninhabited, though your driver assures you that black eyes are peering at you through the holes between the logs. But when you meet Big Witch carrying his fish spear and clad all in shop-made clothes, and two Indian women dressed in calico, each carrying what should be a pappoose, but is only a little brown baby in a pink frock just like any other baby—when this happens, your romantic fancies take flight like a flock of startled birds. At the government school, well placed on a slope near the Oconolufty River, some two hundred young Indians are learning the white man's way of life, boys and girls in about equal numbers.

The Cherokee is not a noble red man in appearance, having the flat, broad type of face with wide-apart eyes, instead of the aquiline features of the wooden warrior that used to stand outside the tobacco-shops. The Indians cultivate the land, raise a few horses and cattle, make soapstone pipes to sell to tourists, and weave baskets. Their lack of progress is not due to want of natural gifts we were told at the school. They can, if they would, but they are utterly wanting in the first great incentive to work, a love of acquisition. The negro soon develops a desire to possess things, the Cherokee never. Perhaps he is the true philosopher, and seeing too far ahead asks, "What is the use?"

The Indian Country lies in a *cul-de-sac* between the Balsams and the Smokies, two of the grandest ranges in the Appalachians, and through it flows the Oconolufty River, swift, broad, and clear as crystal, its bed strewn with boulders, large trees guarding its banks, and rhododendrons dipping to the water. This romantic stream being too swift for a "bench" is spanned by air-line bridges, the thought of crossing which chills the blood. In its calmer reaches, one sees the long dugout canoes of the Indians tied to the trees along the bank, or perchance an Indian girl crossing the river standing securely at the bow of the craft and paddling against the current.

The Great Smoky Mountains

Is it the name, or the literary uses of the last few years, that has invested the Smoky Mountains with that feeling of mystery that seems always to hang about them? Those who have seen them rising in ghost-like beauty high against the western sky need, however, no explanation of their power over the mind. One approaches them with a peculiar feeling of anticipation, a feeling almost reverential, as though about to unveil some great mystery. One approaches them also with a little inner trepidation, they have always seemed so far away, so delicately blue and ethereal, or else as their name suggests they have been to the imagination pale emanations from a burning world—suppose that closer acquaintance with them should dispel a cherished illusion!

But have no fear. These mountains possess a double personality. The dreamlike slopes you have known and loved will remain, only there will be added to the domain of your memory another Smoky Mountain Range, the possession of which is also a rare pleasure. These new mountains, with their grand trees and wide spaces, their freshness and fragrance, their dangerous cliffs, steep slopes, and deep ravines, their rushing streams and their almost impenetrable wildness, become a refuge—glorious heights where you wander in imagination when weary of the dust of the world.

For the Smoky Mountains are at once the most ethereal and the most substantial of created things, ethereal when you see them exquisitely blue or pearly white phantoms in the containing heavens, tremendous realities when you are among their wild cliffs and inclosed by their primeval forests.

Unlike the Blue Ridge, the Smoky Mountains do not hold out inviting levels for man's occupation. They sweep in steep slopes up from both sides to a narrow summit, in places a mere knife-edge ridge, and their flanks are set with precipices, ravines, and deep moist coves out of which rise large forest trees. They are yet the home of the wild animals that have been driven from most other parts of the mountains, and their rhododendron and laurel labyrinths are so dense and so extensive that to get lost in them may mean destruction. Their feet lie in the pleasant valleys, their heads in the clouds. For a distance of over fifty miles the Tennessee and North Carolina state line runs along the crest of the Great Smoky Mountains without crossing a gap below five thousand feet high, while it surmounts Clingman Dome, Mount Guyot, and other summits at an elevation above six thousand feet. Below, these mountains are covered with the finest hardwood trees left in the United States; above, they are wrapped in spruce and balsam fir, a dark unbroken forest of which covers all but the very tops. For like the summits of all the highest mountains, these too are bare—no matter how small the opening may be, the mountain-top is free.

But while there are no large settlements and few signs of the devastation that follows the coming of man, the long line of the Great Smoky Mountains is not uninhabited. The valleys that run up into the mountains hold little nests of houses, and here and there, far up on the mountain-side, in a cove or on a fertile "bench," one may find a clearing with its lonely cabin and its cornfield, to be reached only by a trail through the forest.

The Great Smokies yet remain, as a whole, the most inaccessible part of the mountain region. No road crosses them, few paths penetrate into their fastnesses. To go to any of the high peaks is an arduous climb requiring a guide. And yet it is not difficult to ascend into their forests far enough to get a sense of the glory of the heights.

Being at Cherokee, in the Indian country, instead of following the road down the Oconolufty River to the railroad, it is far wiser to go up it and thereby get into the very heart of the Smokies. As you ascend the narrowing valley, you have a feeling of exhilaration, an increasing sense of splendid freedom, with which the increasing altitude may have something to do. The many streams,

A Good Footbridge

that come hurrying down from their birth chambers in the clouds, cross the road to enter the river. Hence there are fords, beautiful shady places under the trees and the vine-draped bushes. And then the way becomes so narrow that there is not room for both road and river, and the two, for some distance, become one, the river by this time having grown shallow enough to make such a liberty possible. This often happens in the mountains, and a stranger, seeing you slowly vanishing up a river with no apparent exit, might conclude that you had lost, not only your way but your senses. And you do feel a little as though you had taken leave of the ordinary ways of life and entered into a sort of enchanted world as you splash along through a tunnel roofed by tree-tops and paved with flashing water, the leafy walls embroidered with the strong, dark lines and white flower clusters of the *Rhododendron maximum.*

These roadways in the rivers, these entrancing halls paved with silver, and walled with chrysoprase, topaz, and emerald, are among the most cherished memories of the mountains. There is such a road—let us see—in the "Plumtree Country," where, in the springtime, the silver-floored tunnel is roofed with the delicate colors of coming leaves, and out of which you pass into a world radiant with plum blossoms, and where the road, no longer paved with silver, is bright red and overhung with blossoming trees. Clouds of airy white flowers float above you and about you, pouring intoxicating fragrance into the air you breathe—and what is more inebriating than the breath of the wild plum! Later in the season bright red plums replace the flowers, giving forth a spicy and joyous odor that tempts you to taste again and again the sparkling juices. The road is fairly covered with the bounty of the tree. The path you travel is red with plums.

One remembers another union of road and river near the headwaters of the Linville, and alongside which a footpath has been cut in the laurel. There used to be a short one near Traumfest, where the overarching bushes were twined with the clematis that bears large pink, urn-shaped flowers, and—but enough, one could recall a bookful about the fords and riverbed roads of the mountains.

When you get to where the shining Oconolufty forks, you take the left-hand "prong" and go on until the next fork when you turn to the right, the stream becoming ever wilder and narrower and, if possible, more sparkling. The farther you go the more difficult the road becomes. There are few people living as far as this, for you have gone beyond the Indian boundary and are close to the uninhabited mountain. Yet here one's artist friend got one of her loveliest pictures composed of a long, gray old house, pale-blue cabbages, bright flowers, and mountains so divinely blue as to make the senses swim.

When you reach "Jim Mac's place," you stop, for this is the end of what has ceased to deserve the name of road. There is nothing beyond but the steeply rising mountain with its primeval forest, where the red deer and the brown bear yet roam, and the panther and the wildcat make their home. Big trout lie hid in the bright waters of Laurel Fork that comes leaping down icy cold from its embowering springs three thousand feet above your head. At Jim Mac's one hears thrilling tales of fisherman's luck and hunter's adventures, while one young man reluctantly admits that he never did bear-hunt, but has only squirrel-hunted.

And from Jim Mac's you go to the very top of the mountain, there where you step on the Tennessee line without knowing it. Not to one of those grand fir-clad summits that few people reach, but to a gap at an elevation of some fifty-five hundred feet lying on the ridge of the Smokies somewhere between Clingman's Dome and Mount Guyot, two of the great mountains of the range, Clingman having contended long and ardently with Mount Mitchell for the honor of being the highest mountain in the East.

We follow an obscure trail that our guide says in wartime was a sort of road across the mountains, and that it passed near an alum mine where during those troublous times the women got something to set the dyes of their homespun clothes. The horses we ride were born and bred in the mountains, the only kind of horse one ought to ride here, for he knows the ways of the woods and will go over a log or under it, climb, one is tempted to say, anything but a tree, take the situation philosophically if he falls down or you fall off, get up himself, or, if he cannot, wait patiently for help, and when it comes he will assist rather than hinder by his efforts. This horse that never gets nervous or frightened is intelligent and companionable to a high degree, the mountain horses often seeming to share the kindly nature of the people with whom they are intimately associated in all kinds of work, from ploughing a furrow or working a sorghum press to hauling logs over almost impassable roads or bearing their owners over almost impassable trails.

The way up the mountain is now enchanting in its perfection of wildness. Oaks tower above you as you go, and tall locusts shade you, a giant chestnut here, a lordly cherry there, a stately ash, a royal tulip-tree, mammoth hemlocks, standing where they please, all remind you that this is a primeval forest, planted by nature and by her husbanded through the millenniums. Here, too, along the cliffs and the streams, the rose-bay, splendid in the literal meaning of the word, adds to the shining of its polished leaves that of regal flower masses, for up here it is yet in bloom, although the time is August. These noble rhododendrons, that blossom with a freedom and a loveliness of color that belong with these vast sky-domed spaces, sometimes are not purple at all, but a clear bright rose-color seldom seen at lower levels.

In the forest where the rocks are hidden from view under a thick carpet of moss, your horse wades knee-deep in luscious ferns, or his hoofs sink out of sight in tender oxalis leaves whose crowding flowers embroider a rosy and white design over the green floor. You pass into a parklike grove of great beech trees, still and sweet. You see a large turkey on the topmost limb of a dead tree suddenly expand his wings and float away with incredible speed and lightness. A domestic turkey walking on the ground gives no hint of the almost ethereal lightness with which the wild bird projects himself into and through the air.

As your body rises your spirits also mount. All the turmoil of mistaken humanity is down below those billowing forests that sweep into bottomless blue abysses of which you catch glimpses from some cliffside. The clean, cool air is filled with tree odors, about you the wild denizens of these untroubled heights are roaming and, it may be, unseen, are watching you and wondering. A crackle of twigs—a light crashing noise in the laurel—what is it?

The shadows among the trees are intensely blue, overhead white clouds sail in the boundless heavens, down the mossy cliffs streams leap like naiads newly escaped from some cavern of eternity. Where the view opens, fir-clad summits roll away like high green seas, to be transformed in the distance into that spirit-like semblance of mountains that seem to belong, not on earth, but to the realm of the sky.

In a high-lying primeval forest one is often stirred by what might be called primeval feelings. Out of the solitudes come revelations. You look at a tree, grand, alone, touching as it were both earth and heaven, and it awakens in you strong emotion. What is this tree that thus can move you? As you stand questioning, a light flashes through your consciousness. The forest has answered.

From this gap one gets no extensive outlook; we cannot see Clingman Dome, that lacks only about fifty feet of being as high as Mount Mitchell, nor Mount Guyot, nor any other of the high peaks of the Smokies; nevertheless we feel that we know the mountains, lacking only the supreme pleasure of traversing those balsam groves that cover the peaks. A new Smoky Mountain, strong and glorious, projects itself into the imagination alongside the wraith-like shapes of those other Smoky Mountains one has so long known and loved. And over these splendid slopes, one sees in imagination the protecting arm of the new national park reach out, as it soon will, to save them forever from the power of the destroyer.

HIGHLANDS

There is joy also in the valleys. From them you look up to the mountains transfigured by a light that crowns them in beauty. In the valleys are the homes of the people, the leafy inclosing hills, and the winding roads, following which a new picture unfolds each moment as you pass along.

Leaving Whittier and facing towards the Blue Ridge, one may follow the valleys across the plateau from one bordering range to the other. When you come to the beautiful Cullowhee Valley, you ought to be going the other way, however, for the Balsam Mountains, lying so splendidly against the sky, are behind you, and you are constantly looking back as the valley opens and shuts and those noble heights come and go.

And what does one now see beyond the Balsams?—those spirit-like forms high in the sky? It is the line of the Smoky Mountains, rehabilitated since we left them, and restored to their wonted place in the heavens. As the road winds on and up, you turn to see again and yet again the deep-toned Balsams and that line of dream mountains that grows higher as you ascend.

"It's been heavy draughting all the evening." These words from your driver bring your thoughts down to the road which, from recent rains and the passing of tanbark wagons, is, indeed, as he puts it, "terribly gouted out." But you are now up the mountain and crossing the gap where, at the turn in the road, that long white waterfall comes gliding down the slanting cliff, and beyond it in the distance the Balsam Mountains rise, purple, indigo blue, and deep green against a cloudy sky.

Just beyond here you get some one to guide you a mile or two along a wild ravine where the jack-vine grows, to the upper falls of the Tuckasegee, one of the grandest falls in the mountains, the thunder of which is heard for a long distance. Although not so

WHITESIDE MOUNTAIN

high as the other cascade seen from the road, it is far more impressive, for the much wider sheet of water leaps over a vertical cliff bordered on either side with stern walls of granite. Striking a projecting ledge it separates into two parts to leap again, a mass of foam, to the bottom of the ravine.

It is cool and sweet in the spray of the thundering waters and you reluctantly turn back and climb out of the shadowy gorge where the tall trees are draped in vines, among them the great jack-vine whose cables sagging heavily from the tree-tops produce a weird effect in the semi-twilight of the gorge. Nothing in the forest is more suggestive of tropical growths than these enormous vines with their large leaves, the bark peeling in tatters from the stem that when dead separates for its whole length into flat ribbons, black and strange-looking.

Out of the dark gorge, up to the bright sunlight of the road you climb, and continuing on your way, the cliffs that distinguish the country about Highlands soon begin to appear above the trees. Up you mount, now through a forest fragrant with hemlock and white azalea, now over cool, hurrying streams, now close to damp cliffs with little plants in the crevices, the way darkened by the hemlock trees that grow so freely here, on and up, finally to attain the very summit of the Blue Ridge—and find yourself at Highlands.

Highlands, nearly four thousand feet high, lies on one of those tablelands of the Blue Ridge that seem to have been designed for the occupation of man. But it differs from all other parts of the Blue Ridge plateau, and indeed of the whole Appalachian uplift, in the tremendous precipices that all but surround it, seeming to lift it up and hold it aloft. For about Highlands are the grandest cliffs this side the Rocky Mountains.

When at Highlands, one is always conscious of being in a high place, of inhabiting, as it were, the "Land of the Sky." From the village itself, which lies in about the center of the tableland, there is no extensive view, only that ever-present sense of being up high and out in the sky. But just out of the village one discovers the truth; there is no grander scenery in this part of the world than that immediately surrounding Highlands. And here, as in so many places in these mountains, one has that inner vision of beauty that man alone can add to a landscape. One sees in imagination the charms of nature enhanced by those human touches that send us sightseeing to foreign lands. Even in Italy, away from the seacoast there is nothing in the way of natural scenery more beautiful than our own Southern mountains, we lacking only that instinctive feeling for the beautiful that makes every son of that fair land build his house with pleasing lines and place it sympathetically in the landscape, the row of columns, the arcade, the terrace, the stone wall, the statue, put, as by inspiration, each in its perfect place.

Nowhere in the mountains does one find more beautiful natural growths than at Highlands, where the laurel and rhododendron grow to trees and flaming azaleas set whole mountain-sides ablaze, and here one remembers finding wild lilies-of-the-valley. But that which characterizes the scenery of this region, separating it distinctly from the rest of the mountains, is the presence of the many bare precipices that on all sides drop into unseen abysses, the most terrible of all being the long wall of Whiteside Mountain, that makes a sheer descent of fifteen hundred feet and has the distinction of being the grandest precipice this side the Rockies. Yet even these cliffs cannot give a cruel aspect to the country, because over all their savage tops hang delicate vines and dainty shrubs. Smiling flowers of the rose-bay look fearlessly over the edge and the white lace of the fringe-bush sheds its perfume down the stern front of the rock.

The nearest point of view at Highlands is perhaps Black Rock, that drops in a sheer wall nearly a thousand feet into Horse Cove, and from whose rim one looks into a wide abyss floored with tree-tops, and beyond this to mountains billowing away as far as one can see. At a point on the brow of the precipice, far in from the road and surrounded by flowers that have escaped from its gardens, stands a house as though on guard, the first house of importance in this region, although many pleasant homes have since appeared. It was built by Captain S. P. Ravenel, of Charleston, who came about a generation ago when life was yet so primitive that lumber had to be carted a distance of more than thirty miles up the mountains. The dining-room floor, made of alternate strips of black walnut and oak, reminds us that walnut trees were not uncommon in this region at the time the house was built. In the charming wilderness the Ravenel family not only made a beautiful summer home for themselves, but, through their interest in the people about them, they stamped a lasting impress upon the community. For besides building roads and making other civic improvements, they built a church, and by their contact with the native people brought inspiration and hope to many a longing heart, as well as a knowledge of those refinements of life which are man's latest and best inheritance.

A favorite walk from Highlands is to the top of charming, flower-graced Satulah that rises something less than a thousand feet above Highlands, and where one gets an open view in all directions. The granite walls of Whiteside, sheer and terrible, or else veiled in a misty blue atmosphere, sharp Chimney Top to the right of it and the bold form of Shortoff to the left, rise conspicuously above the countless mountains that reach away to the far Balsam and Pisgah Ranges, while against the western sky is seen the ever-beautiful form of the Nantahala Range. Turning now towards the south, away from the tumultuous sea of the high mountains, one looks off over the receding levels of Georgia, out of which rises the calm and beautiful form of the Rabun Bald, lending a great sense of peace to the landscape.

The road from Highlands to Whiteside Mountain winds along through a thin forest and gives no hint of what is coming until you reach the "bench" of the mountain, where all of a sudden the land drops in a vertical wall to the valley below. From this bench the mountain-top rises precipitously above your head, the path up through the trees and bushes being very steep, like a flight of steps in places; but it is also very sweet, and you stop every few moments to gather a flower, inhale the fragrance of some blossoming bush, and look off at the mountains lying far away.

The top of the mountain, although somewhat less than five thousand feet in elevation, gives one a feeling of being very high above the earth. For the air is singularly stimulating, and the rocks are covered with the growths of high places, among them "heather," as the people call the delightful little evergreen *Dendrium buxifolium*, and the hardwood trees through which the path leads are dwarfed and twisted, like trees that have had to battle with the elements for life.

To go to the edge and look directly down requires a steady head and should be done with caution, for the rock is bare and polished, and but for a ledge where bushes grow, a ledge scarcely noticeable a short distance away, it resembles, as some one has said, a stupendous petrified waterfall. In some lights this appalling front gleams white as snow, which has given the mountain its name. The characteristic feature of the scenery from

The Devil's Court House

Whiteside is the upspringing cliffs of the nearer mountains, impressive walls that would be more terrible if those close to you were not wreathed in verdure, and the more distant ones softened by the tender lights and the cloud mists that so often lie about them, although there are clear, hard days when the cliffs look savage enough.

And there are times when Whiteside Mountain becomes the theatre of a scene so terrific that to witness it is a landmark in one's life. It was on a cloudless summer day that one walked along the top of Whiteside far enough to see the cliffs of the Devil's Court House, as the turret-like northern end of the mountain is called. One remembers admiring the little cloud that suddenly appeared in the intense blue of the sky, and the merry massing of white clouds that came rolling sweetly up over the edge of the horizon. You started to descend because of them, but finally decided that they were going around. You did not know that no cloud ever goes around Whiteside. A great bird dropped suddenly out of the sky with half-closed wings and disappeared in a cleft of the rocks. There was something about the arrow-like descent of that bird into the mountain that made you feel uneasy and you hurried down, but before you got to the bench, the storm was muttering and clouds were boiling over the whole sky.

It seemed better now to wait until the storm was over than to risk driving through the woods. What happened next is difficult to describe. When the storm struck, you found yourself holding your large black horse by the halter, the mountain woman who had brought you there clinging to the other horse. At each crash of thunder the frightened animals plunged and reared, but when the one you held came down, it laid its quivering nostrils against your cheek, as though begging forgiveness and imploring you to save it. The lightning seemed pouring out of the clouds as from some devil's caldron. At each deafening explosion it was seen darting in all directions over the stony floor. Electrical fire fell about us like rain. The metal parts of the carriage were struck, strange electrical thrills coursed through our nerves. Rain fell in torrents icy cold, while an icy wind drove it against us in lines almost parallel to the earth, and threatened to sweep us over the cliff. It would have been dark almost as night but for the constant play of the pallid lightning. The face of the woman who, a little way off was clinging to her horse, was ghastly green in color— "Are we dying?" she sobbed—it seemed we were, but you put on as hopeful a front as possible to help her. And then—the whole earth seemed shattered to pieces, the woman and her horse fell as though shot, and lights played about them on the rock.

Heaven knows how long it lasted. It seemed hours. It vanished almost as suddenly as it came, and when the sun burst out we discovered we were yet alive, drenched to the skin, and our teeth chattering with cold and fright. The woman and her horse had struggled to their feet, she with legs so numb that she could scarcely stand and the horse quivering in every muscle. We managed to attach the trembling animals to the carriage, which, though repeatedly struck, had not been destroyed, and get back to Highlands. It was weeks before one fully recovered from the effects of the adventure, and one wonders if the poor woman and the horse she held ever fully recovered.

It was the worst electrical storm known for years, and why we chose that particular day to go to Whiteside with its Devil's Court House who can say? For from the bench of Whiteside the native people, those who live in that region, flee in terror at the slightest sign of an approaching storm. It is a noted battle-ground. To stand in the midst of a conflict of the gods where lightning bolts are the weapons is an experience one would not dare to court, but having survived it, it becomes one of those great headlands in life the existence of which is worth whatever may have been the cost of discovering them.

It is the hardness of the massive granite in this region which has preserved the great upright cliffs through the ages, and because of the hard and precipitous nature of the rocks, this part of the country is gemmed with waterfalls, of which there are half a hundred within a few miles of Highlands, each one worth a visit.

Characteristic of Highlands are the many roads that go from it as a center, or, perhaps one should say, go towards it, for here all roads lead to Highlands, that is, all upward roads. Our favorite in bygone days was perhaps the "Old Franklin Road," where the Nantahala lay so sweetly in the sky before us as we went. It was hard to get over the Old Franklin Road even then, and now it is probably all gone, the new road having taken its place.

But whether one goes to Franklin by the old road or the new, there is to be seen that lovely line of the Nantahala towards which one's course is directed. In the picturesque Cullasagee Valley—"Sugar Fork" the people call it, rudely translating the soft Indian name—you leave the main road and go through the woods to the fall whose thunder prepares you for the headlong leap of the stream down nearly a hundred feet of vertical cliff. It is one of the noblest falls in the region, and when one went there, the way to it was made memorable as well by the ginseng seen blossoming in the woods. This mysterious little plant, "sang" the people call it, whose roots are so potent to cure the Chinaman of all his ills, has been nearly exterminated because of the eager search the country people have made for it. They sold it at the stores, where one large root was worth a week's wages. This inconspicuous little plant, with its power of healing Oriental ills, belongs to that mysterious brotherhood of the two continents, appearing only in the eastern United States and eastern Asia.

Returning from the fall and following down the clear Cullasagee, Franklin in time comes to view where it lies so prettily on the blood-red waters of the Little Tennessee, with the Nantahala rising, an exquisite background, behind it. And seeing it thus in the mystical light of the summer day one has again that vision of what the earth might be, and will be, when future generations are moved by the power of beauty that is finally to conquer the world.

Seven or eight miles before reaching Franklin, one passes the noted Corundum Hill, at Cullasagee, the site of the mine where, besides other less attractive minerals, men are in eager search of the gems that lie hidden in the heart of the ancient rocks.

Near Highlands

Franklin, although it is the county seat, seemed at the ends of the earth to us travelers from the wild interior, and now one hears with dismay that the railroad has come to it up from Tallulah Falls in Georgia, which makes one tremble for the next news from Highlands. The railroad does very well in some places, but imagine a locomotive smoking and puffing and screaming up that romantic valley of the Cullasagee where log houses and spinning-wheels consoled the eye in former days! And imagine it bringing up at a smart station among the flaming azaleas of Highlands!

From Franklin you can go out to climb the steep sides of the Nantahala, where the road winds up among gigantic trees—which, alas, may be all gone now—and on over the gap and down to the lower but very picturesque country beyond, where Standing Indian, the last and one of the highest summits of the Blue Ridge, looks calmly over the head of Chunky Gal Mountain crouching at his feet.

Although the Nantahalas abound in beautiful flowers, they also have a reputation for the production of "ramps," as the people call the wild onions that are abundant enough in some regions to be a nuisance to the farmer. Cattle sometimes eat ramps and are poisoned, though it is said that, if they eat them in the spring before other greens sprout, they get used to them and can consume them without injury. Ramps are pretty notwithstanding their malodorous and other bad qualities, and "ramp coves," with the thousand other plants that fill them, are not as bad as the name implies.

The Nantahala Range rises steeply to a narrow edge whose summits are five thousand feet or more high, and one discovers that it is this steepness, together with the absence of near, high mountains, that gives the range its strong individual line against the sky.

Another favorite road winds down through the forest from Highlands to Whiteside Cove, where one ought to stay awhile and become acquainted with the appearance of grand old Whiteside from below, for from the many intersecting ridges and coves the great mountain with its Devil's Court House appears to advantage. The country about Whiteside Cove is extremely wild, for it is on the eastern slope of the Blue Ridge and streams rush through it from all directions. And yet how can you call it wild with apple trees in bloom and that soft, Southern caress in the air!

Beyond Whiteside Cove the road leads down to Cashier Valley and on to the "Sapphire Country," whose natural beauty man has enriched by the introduction of lakes into the landscape. Cashier Valley, with its open spaces, its cultivated farms, and its views of the surrounding mountains, has long been a favorite place of residence, and it was here that General Wade Hampton had his summer home.

The Sapphire Country

The romantic name of this region is said to have been given to it because of the prevailing color of the sky and the waters. There are moments here, as in all these mountains, when the celestial hues of the heavens seem to have diffused themselves through the tissues of air and earth, and we have about us a world which "Sapphire Country" well expresses.

There are three large artificial lakes in the Sapphire Country, Lake Fairfield, the upper one, occupying a beautiful little "cove" in the mountains at an elevation of about three thousand feet; Lake Sapphire, a short distance below it, longer, narrower, and more winding, lying in the enlarged bed of the Horse Pasture River; and Lake Toxaway, lying some ten or twelve miles to the east of the others, and some two hundred and fifty feet lower. Lake Toxaway is larger than either or perhaps both of the other lakes, having a shore-line of sixteen miles.

These charming lakes, with their steep wooded banks here, their green and level shores there, the outreaching points of land, the mountains, clouds, and trees reflected in the water, the splendid rhododendron and laurel that in places crowd to the water's edge, give to the scenery something that to many seems essential to its perfection. The lakes have been finished long enough to have settled into the landscape like works of nature, so that to visit these sheets of water, that lie like jewels in their beautiful setting of trees and flowering shrubs, leads one to the reflection that man can make as fine a lake, on a small scale, as can the cosmic glacier, he following nature's method of clearing out the bottom—but with quick-working shovels of steel instead of the slow push of ice—and of damming up the exit with a symmetrical stone wall instead of an irregular haphazard moraine.

The outlet of Lake Toxaway is Toxaway River, that, rising west of the Blue Ridge, breaks through that barrier—the only river, unless it may be the Linville, that does this—and joins the Horse Pasture part-way down the mountain. For the Horse Pasture, although so close to Toxaway River, rises on the western slopes of the Blue Ridge that makes several sudden curves in this region, the Sapphire and Fairfield lakes lying on its eastern slope, and Lake Toxaway west of it. To the east of Lake Toxaway the streams run to the French Broad Valley that begins just below here, and along which a road leads from Toxaway down to Brevard, lying so pleasantly on its slopes just above the level river bottom.

This upper part of the French Broad, although less impressive than where the river breaks through the mountains beyond Asheville, has a gracious beauty of its own, possessing that indefinable charm of level spaces below uprising hills. The French Broad, it is interesting to know, in the early history of the country lay on the boundary line between the English and the French possessions, the French acquiring by treaty all the territory in this region drained by waters running to the Mississippi. Since there were several "Broad" rivers in the mountains, this one became the "French Broad," a name that it retains to this day. Up the French Broad Valley as far as Toxaway comes that branch of the railroad, from Hendersonville. So it will be seen that Highlands now lies between the terminals of two railroads, the joining of which one fears is only a matter of time.

The largest and finest of the group of hotels that has sprung up at these lakes is at Toxaway, where the visitor will find all the amenities of modern hotel life. And now an electric car line is being projected from Toxaway to Fairfield, the first thread in that web of steel which the eye of prophecy sees woven over the mountains in the near future.

The whole Sapphire Country is remarkable for its scenic beauty. The points of view to go to, the mountains to climb, the streams to fish, the waterfalls to visit, the forests to explore, afford inexhaustible entertainment to the nature-lover, to which has been added tennis, golf, boating and hunting for those who enjoy such sports; for the property of the hotel company, which includes some twenty-eight thousand acres, is mostly wild land where the forests, kept as game preserves, are full of deer and birds and the streams and lakes are well stocked with fish.

Waterfalls are a characteristic of this country that lies so near the steep walls of the Blue Ridge. In whatever direction one may walk, ride, or drive, there are the waters leaping down, sometimes in deafening volume, sometimes in exquisite veils, or white, winding threads, or ethereal fabrics woven of air, water, and light, sparkling and gay. Whatever form of waterfall one likes best can here be found, for these jewels of the landscape are everywhere strung on the silver streams that embroider the green robe of the Sapphire Country—and along the watercourses and bordering the cascades the smaller rhododendrons, those the color of a blush rose, hang their exquisite flowers over the rocks.

Among the roads that run in every direction is one up Toxaway Mountain, or Great Hogback, as it is called on the maps, on whose summit it is worth while to spend the night and see the sun rise over one of the finest panoramic views in this part of the world, there being no near heights to obstruct the outlook. But sometimes, instead of rising over a world of mountains, the sun shines across a level expanse of white cloud out of which as time goes on mountain-tops appear one after the other, phantasmal islands in an unearthly sea. As the sun mounts, the ineffable abyss of mists, lights, and shadows changes and acquires substance, finally resolving into far-reaching mountains, green, blue, opaline—some of them free of clouds. Others with cloud banners floating over them, or soft cloud lakes cradled in their hollows. But sometimes the clouds lie higher and you wake up shivering to discover that these mists are beautiful only when wrapping up your friends below.

One remembers with pleasure the sweet things that grow on Toxaway Mountain, fragrant white azaleas, tall, orange-red lilies, saxifrages, columbines, laurel, everything in its season, the flame-colored azaleas converting it into a blazing garden in their blooming time, while sweet-fern, suddenly discovered growing at your feet, sends your thought in a flash back to those New England pastures forever fragrant in memory with the sweet-fern that clothes them.

You will not be in the Sapphire Country long, nor anywhere in the higher mountains for that matter, without hearing the magic word "corundum." Upon investigation corundum proves to be, on the surface, a useful but prosaic mineral which, because of its extreme hardness—it is next to the diamond in that—is made into emery wheels, sandpaper, and other abrasive instruments. But this is only one side of corundum. When you penetrate into its history you find it the product of very old rocks, the oldest rocks on earth—which is interesting, but not vital to anybody but the geologist. But, and here corundum becomes not only of absorbing interest but positively dazzling, mysteriously connected with it, born from it like fancies from a poet's brain, are the most beautiful and precious gems in the world, gems surpassed in value by the diamond alone.

When corundum crystalizes in an ecstasy of red, we have rubies—true, or, as we say, Oriental rubies—gems next to the diamond in value, or in their best form equal to it. When the crystals form in other moods, they shine forever as purple amethyst, or Oriental sapphire, or pink or white sapphire, or they glow with the deep and thrilling green of the emerald, rarest of gems and equal in value to the ruby, or they emit the yellow light of the topaz. Corundum crystals take all the colors of the rainbow, each gem named from its color, and all of them, no matter of what color, are known under the general name of sapphire crystals, or sapphires. Sapphire crystals of all colors are found in the North Carolina mountains, some predominating in one section, some in another.

Corundum, the mother rock of the most precious gems, is found throughout the North Carolina mountains excepting in the extreme northern part, and there are several mines in the

Sapphire Country, which is a famous corundum region, and these mines, although not worked primarily for gems, yield many fine ones, particularly blue sapphires, to which circumstance some attribute the name of the region. It is a fortunate place that has more than one reason for deserving such a name.

It is interesting to know that corundum mining which has grown to so important an industry here, began its history in a gem mine. This was at Corundum Hill, near Franklin, and the mine, which was opened in 1871, among other treasures yielded what is said to be the finest specimen of emerald green crystallized corundum in the world. It must not be supposed, however, that this remarkable crystal, measuring four and a half, by two, by one and a half inches, and which is now in the Morgan-Bement Collection in New York, is what we should call an "emerald." If that were so, we should have the most precious gem on the face of the earth. For a gem must be transparent, and while there are in this crystal transparent places from which gems could be cut, the crystal as a whole has not realized absolute transparency throughout, even a crystal reaching perfection only at rare intervals, which is why the great gems are so noted, so few, and so costly. When we buy a gem stone we are buying the highest expression of inorganic life, the poetry of the rocks.

The Cullasagee corundum mine began as a gem mine, but since the finest gems of the rocks, like the most inspired fancies of the poet, are few and far between, the mine in time became worked principally for corundum, which, having been unable to crystallize into gems, was set to sharpening and polishing. Not that gems are no longer found in this mine: many a fine one appears, like an occasional inspiration, from the rocks which are now valued principally for their lower service of utility.

But there are other gem mines in the mountains today, one of the most remarkable lying in the valley of Cowee Creek, whose waters enter the Little Tennessee only a few miles north of Franklin. Here are found true rubies, concerning which a government report on this region says: "In color and brilliancy they are equal to the Burmah ruby, and if the percentage of the unflawed, transparent material increases but little, this new field for the ruby would be a well-matched rival to the Burmah fields."

This is very pleasant, the only thing lacking to make perfect the fascination of these flower-graced mountains being the discovery that the rocks beneath are graced with Burmah rubies. Burmah it is true, has not yet yielded up her sceptre to the proud corundum rocks of the New World, for years of unfulfilled hopes have passed since that report was made. But one is comforted by the reflection of how short a time it is since any efforts have been made systematically to explore these rocks.

Although the field of sapphire gems is so extensive, it must not be supposed that in the course of millenniums the crystal flowers of these mountains have blossomed in corundum alone. If the ruby has remained but a dazzling hope, another source of gem stones has yielded a treasure which is not only very beautiful, but is abundant enough and occurs in large enough stones to make mining for it profitable. It is also peculiar to this region, an original product of the North Carolina mountains, which from some points of view is better even than duplicating a Burmah ruby. This new gem is found also in Cowee Creek and near the ruby deposits. It is a peculiar form of garnet and its name is rhodolite. It is remarkable for its transparency and great brilliancy, the color shining out with peculiar brightness in artificial light. If you ask how it differs from the true ruby, the answer is that the finest sapphire gems have an intensity of color never equaled by any other stones, and the ruby is valued for this and its wonderful lustre, although other gems may surpass it in brilliancy. Rhodolite, like rhododendron, gets its beautiful name from the Greek word meaning rose, for it is the color of roses and rhododendrons.

In the valley of the Cowee Creek these two lovely gems, the ruby and the rhodolite, have blossomed side by side in the rocks, each extracting from them what it needed to bring to expression the spirit of inorganic life, just as in the crumbling soil above them the roses and rhododendrons have blossomed each in its own rare colors to express the inner spirit of the plant. And who shall say that the same necessity, impelling the crystals through cycles of cosmic pressure to emerge in permanent forms of beauty, does not impel the flowers of the upper air to clothe themselves in transitory loveliness?

Other members of the garnet group besides rhodolite have been found in the North Carolina Mountains, but perhaps none other of important gem value, although immediately below the mountains Bohemian gem garnets, or Cape rubies, as they are also called, are found in abundance. But the garnet of the mountains exists as a rule in massive form, in places pure enough to be cut into wheels—"emery wheels" made of garnet!

In addition to the corundum or sapphire gems, and the one precious garnet stone, there is, in the mountains, a remarkable series of gem crystals found in the mica veins. For while mica may not itself create gems, there is in company with it, born as it were from the same mother, the group of beautiful crystals belonging to the beryl type and which are among the most valuable of the precious stones. Large sea-blue aquamarines, that for beauty of color have never been surpassed, and beryls, both sea-green and yellow, than which none richer have ever been found, as well as clear green and blue stones, occur in different parts of the mountains in sufficient quantities to make mining for them profitable, although none have been found in the Sapphire Country where the beryl-bearing rocks are less prominent.

The most important of the beryl mines thus far opened are in the Black Mountain Country, particularly near Spruce Pine, where mining operations have brought to light many lovely gems, notable among which are blue stones of large size and equal, we are told, to any from Brazil, with lesser numbers of fine aquamarine and honey-yellow gems. And the beryl-bearing rocks of North Carolina have, like the corundum rocks, given a new gem to the world, although it has not been found in the mountains. It is the beautiful new emerald known as hiddenite, which is being profitably mined at a place called Stony Point, in the foothills just below the mountains, and where some very valuable stones have been found.

Mica, which occurs plentifully and of very fine quality in the North Carolina mountains, was mined there even in prehistoric times, as has recently been discovered, and it is from these mica mines that beryls were first obtained, the discovery of the sapphire gems coming later. No one can be in the mica mining regions of the mountains without noticing the glitter of the dry roads as well as the sparkling appearance of man and beast when these have traversed the highways, thereby becoming covered with "diamond dust."

As well as the sapphire and beryl gems, the rocks of these fortunate mountains yield beautiful crystals of the cyanite group, closely related to topaz and named from a Greek word meaning blue, because of their prevailing color, the finest of these blue stones resembling Oriental sapphires. As to tourmalines, they seem to be awaiting their discoverer, only black ones of gem quality being generally found, although what one might call the haunts of the tourmaline are frequent enough.

Very beautiful quartz crystals are abundant in different parts of the mountains, the finest gem of which is the purple amethyst, not the Oriental or sapphire amethyst, but still an exceedingly beautiful stone. A valuable mine of these gems was once brought to light in an unusual and romantic manner. This happened on Tessentee Creek that enters the Little Tennessee a few miles south of Franklin. Here a landslide exposed a large vein of crystalline quartz to a depth of twenty feet, and in the decomposed rocks of this vein amethysts were found in large quantities, there being many beautiful ones from half an inch to three inches long, both light and dark in color, the dark spots often of the deepest purple. These gems, thus offered open-handed by nature, were equal, it is said on authority, to those found in any country of the globe.

Beautiful smoky and citron green quartz crystals abound in the Black Mountain region, and the choicest form of quartz, rock crystal, also occurs abundantly there, masses of several hundred pounds' weight having been found. From these have been cut many beautiful objects by the Tiffany lapidaries of New York, among them a crystal ball five inches in diameter. One mass of rock crystal was found encrusted with a green substance so that when polished it looked like moss under clear water.

Aside from those gems, whose very names have so long exercised a spell over the human heart, there are found here many lovely crystals bearing unfamiliar scientific names, but from which beautiful jewels can be cut; and while few of us will be fortunate enough to find priceless stones in the crystal streams that sparkle under the laurel, or stumble upon a newly disclosed amethyst mine, any one with a fondness for crystals and a little knowledge of how to proceed can gather many a lovely, unfading flower of the rocks to recall the days of happy wandering over the oldest and most gracious mountains in the world.

Besides the crystals there are many rare and beautiful minerals not only valuable to the collector, but available for purposes of art, among which quartz yields a lovely fawn and salmon-pink chalcedony, as well as agates, green chrysoprase, and red and yellow jasper. And there are choice building stones to be found almost everywhere, among them serpentine and beautiful marbles, in some places the marble being white and fine enough for the sculptor's chisel. So that one who should, like Kubla Khan, a stately pleasure dome decree, could find choice materials for its construction close at hand, with beautiful and rare stones to ornament the interior and even encrust it with jewels—all from the rocks that otherwise adorn the earth with their covering of beautiful plant growths.

And beyond the minerals that are beautiful, there are many that are curious or useful, among them asbestos, that seems so little like stone and which is here found of the finest quality; and there is pure talc from which our best toilet powders are made, and soapstone, a form of talc, and graphite, and the queer flexible sandstone, a bar of which bends when you lift it; and kaolin is mined for the making of fine white china. Indeed, almost everything one can ask from the rocks—even to the newly valued "rare earths"—here await man's pleasure.

Crystals and the other rare minerals from the North Carolina mountains are treasured in the greatest collections of the world, in this country very fine ones being on exhibition in the Metropolitan Museum of Art and the American Museum of Natural History, both in New York, in the United States National Museum at Washington, in the Field Columbian Museum at Chicago, as well as in many smaller museums and private collections, and they have been shown in the great expositions of the world, where we are told their absence would leave a vacancy that could not be filled.

Hunting in these later days has been transferred almost entirely from the destruction of animals to the finer sport of finding and treasuring precious stones and rare or beautiful plants. The animals that once abounded here are practically gone. The crystals, hidden away in the recesses of the earth and affording more difficult hunting, are only beginning to be objects of general interest. But the plants have long attracted attention, and the beautiful Sapphire Country, with its sparkling waters, its crystal flowers of the rocks, and its glorious plant flowers, is the home of a beautiful little blossom which has the most romantic history of any flower in the mountains, it having been the quest for nearly half a century of every botanist who came hunting to this paradise for botanists. It is the *Shortia galacifolia,* with a leaf closely resembling the galax, to whose botanical family it belongs, but which, instead of blossoming in a spike of small white flowers, bears a single large and beautiful white or pink blossom on a slender stem. The flowers, with their delicate wavy petals standing close together above the clustered leaves, are extremely beautiful, although it was not this beauty that at first excited interest in the plant that became an object of eager quest long before any one had so much as seen its flowers!

It was more than a hundred years ago that the French botanist Michaux came to these mountains to explore the plant world, taking back to France many living specimens as well as a large herbarium. After him came other botanists, among them our own Asa Gray. In fact all botanists of note had first or last to come here, but it was a long time before all the wild flowers had been captured and named, if they are yet. Meantime, Dr. Gray being in Paris one day discovered in the collection of Michaux a little unnamed plant marked as having come from the high mountains of Carolina. The specimen was imperfect, consisting of only the leaves and one fruit—the leaves but not the fruit of the galax. This little nameless plant with its interesting peculiarities became an object of vain search to Dr. Gray, but he finally ventured to describe it, and named it in honor of Professor Short of Kentucky, whereupon *Shortia* became an object of general quest. Meantime Dr. Gray found a specimen almost identical with *Shortia* in a collection of Japanese plants, which of course greatly increased his desire to find it. But it was not until nearly a century after the specimen of Michaux had been gathered, and nearly half a century since the search for it began, that *Shortia* was really captured, not by Dr. Gray, but by Professor Sargent who was exploring the Sapphire Country so rich in beautiful growths.

The strangest part of the story is that having been traced to its home at last, *Shortia* was found, on the Horse Pasture River a few miles south of where Lake Toxaway now lies, literally coloring acres of the earth with its charming flowers, and there any one so inclined will probably find it today, although it has been carried away by the wagon-load, not, however, becoming thereby exterminated, as happens to so many of our wild flowers when the thoughtless visitor tears them rudely from the soil. For it was not the thoughtless visitor who removed *Shortia,* but skillful gardeners, who took it and cultivated it with the greatest care and sent it out to beautify the gardens of the people all over the world.

THE FORKS OF THE PIGEON RIVER

"You ought to go to the Forks of the Pigeon, the coves are so thick up there, there is scarcely room for the mountains." Thus the people advise, and to the Forks of the Pigeon, if you are wise, you will go, not for the reason given so much as that up there you will find a new and very interesting country to explore. Besides the coves there are Cold Mountain, Shining Rock, the redoubtable Sam Knob, and Pisgah itself, which is accessible from the East Fork.

For you must know that the Big Pigeon River starts in the most remarkable *cul-de-sac* in the mountains, a *cul-de-sac* formed partly by Pisgah Range, which, sweeping down in a southwesterly direction, meets a line of high balds coming down from the northwest. These two mountains ranges form, as it were, the prongs of a mammoth pitchfork, whose handle is the Tennessee Ridge reaching down nearly to Toxaway Mountain. At the point where the handle joins the prongs, forming, as it were, a strong connective, is the beautiful Tennessee Bald, its summit covered with blue-grass and white-clover.

The cup-shaped space between the prongs of the pitchfork is occupied by the nearly circular Cold Mountain uplift, that, at Sam Knob, its highest point, rises to an elevation a little over six thousand feet. The two Forks of the Pigeon almost surround Cold Mountain, receiving the waters that rush down its steep sides as well as those from the western slopes of Pisgah and the eastern slope of the line of balds. The two Forks come together at the north end of Cold Mountain just above the settlement of Garden Creek, forming the Big Pigeon, one of the wildest streams of the mountains, and that speeds along in a general northwesterly direction, finally to break through a gorge of the Great Smoky Mountains some miles south of where the French Broad makes its exit in gentler fashion, the Pigeon entering the French Broad when both rivers are well out of the mountains.

Garden Creek, with its restful levels, its grainfields and apple-orchards, and its fine outlooks to the western mountains, is a good place from which to explore the interesting country of the Forks. It is reached by driving up the valley of the Pigeon from Canton on the Murphy Branch. If Mr. Osborne is still at Garden Creek, he will tell you of the Indian mounds he helped to open, as well as of many interesting things of the surrounding country. There is one mound at Garden Creek with an apple tree growing out of the top, but the greater number have been found, and opened, in the present Cherokee boundary, and in those larger valleys like that of the Valley River, where the more important Indian villages stood.

The contents of these mounds, principally bones, pottery, and stone implements, which do not differ essentially from the contents of other Indian mounds, have been placed in various museums of the country, principally in that of the Valentine Museum at Richmond, Virginia.

Henson Cove, under Sugar Top Mountain, is not one of the wild Fork coves, but being at Garden Creek you will often go there for the sake of the pleasant walk through the woods and past the little farms, where the catbird and the thrush sing to you along the way, and for the sake of the friendly people who live there. As you go along in the fresh morning, the air perfumed by the wild grapevine draping the tree above your head, the wild roses blossoming along the slopes, white azaleas on the edge of the woods, ripe strawberries hiding somewhere near in the grass, as you go along, the warm summer sun drawing the fragrance out of all sweet things, you decide that there is no better walk than that to Henson Cove.

One of the joys of the road is the complete recovery of one's senses. In the city you have no use for anything but eyes and ears, and not for the finer offices of those. But in the open—how many delicate sounds attest the unsuspected register of the ear! Day by day you hear new cadences in the treetops, in the shrubs and the grasses. Voices, silent at first, grow audible, sometimes you almost hear the flowers sing. And the eye, recovering from the dust and glare of the streets, sees finer tones of color, detects delicate movements in the leaves and in the clouds, your spirit is stunned by depths of black thunder abysses and exalted by the softly shining tints of the morning sky.

And in the open you acquire a new sense. You learn to smell. The most sensitive and poetical of all our senses, in the cities becomes deadened from disuse. But one day, in the sweet, clean air of the mountains, one makes the charming discovery that one can smell! Perhaps, going along a lonely road, there comes a sudden waft of delicious fragrance—ah, strawberries!—where are they? There is no one to tell, but the fragrance is wafted to you again, a little more certainly, and so you go in the direction indicated; again it comes, but fainter; you turn and try again, and soon you are sure and go straight to the knoll beyond the fence where the ground is red with the ripe fruit. Sitting down and tasting a berry here and there, you detect a flavor that exists only for him who has smelled his way to the feast. With the tuning-up of the senses come pleasures unguessed in the grosser uses of these divine faculties. One sometimes hears music in the fall of water over a cliff, in the sweep of the wind through forest trees, in the mingling crashes of a thunderstorm, or smells harmonies in the flowers, or tastes rhythmic cadences in a wild berry.

And then at the spring of icy water you quench your thirst with something of the same elation you felt in the flavor of the strawberries, for did you not trace your way to this spring by reasoning out where it ought to be, and then finding the path that led straight to it? To what better use could one put the attribute of reason?

With what pleasure one remembers those walks to Henson Cove, with its friendly people and its picturesque houses, in which still linger interesting old customs, old counterpanes, and old looms. Is Melissa Meese still weaving in Henson Cove? Can one still see charming coverlets in the home of Mrs. Nancy Blaylock? Who was it told us that "when a few funerals are made in this country the old weavers are all gone"? Is that picturesque cabin yet standing under Pizen Cove Top? And do they still have to guard against the "milk-sick" over there in Pizen Cove?

It was in this region that one first saw a "milk-sick pen," and heard of the curious sickness which, attacking cattle that eat grass or leaves in certain well-defined spots, through the milk poisons the people, sometimes fatally. What causes this strange illness no one seems to know, the vegetation in these places being the same as elsewhere; but what the people do know is just where these poisonous spots are, so that when you see a little space fenced off anywhere in the mountains for no apparent reason, you will generally be right in concluding it to be a "milk-sick" spot.

Dutch Cove, also under Sugar Top, but separated from Henson Cove by a pathless ridge, is considerably farther from Garden Creek, from which it is reached by a trail over the mountains. Larger and more thickly settled than Henson Cove, it has a road leading out towards the railroad, that is to say, it is connected with the world. Its name betrays its origin, and you hear of old Dutch Bibles in the Cove, although you do not succeed in finding any. The people of the more secluded Henson Cove consider Dutch Cove altogether too thickly settled, one of them assuring you, as proof of the degeneracy of the rival settlement, that you could stand in her cousin's door in Dutch Cove of a morning and hear nine coffee-mills going at once.

You can walk to Henson and Dutch Coves, but when you go up either of the Forks of the Pigeon you will get up "soon" in the morning, and you will not go afoot, for the fords of the forks are not to be trifled with. There are not even foot-logs to cause the timid to tremble, for the Forks of the Pigeon are master-hands at "getting up" and tearing to pieces everything they can reach. If one remembers rightly there are about twenty-six fords within six or seven miles up the East Fork—which is as far as the road goes—and heaven knows how many up the West Fork.

To explore the West Fork you cross the main river just below the Forks, that is to say, you cross it if the river is down. If it is up, you stay at home. Having crossed—how innocent the stream seems!—you are surprised to find the valley of the West Fork very much like that of Garden Creek. Fertile acres lie about you, elderberries bloom in the fence corners, blossoming chinkapins hang over the roadside, the smell of warm, ripe strawberries lurking somewhere near in the grass makes your sympathetic mouth water, while the roadside is gay with the pale leaflets and large bright-yellow, pea-shaped flowers of the Alleghany thermopsis. Green meadows where the cattle graze, orchards, thrifty-looking farmhouses, blue mountains showing in the distance—the West Fork does not seem so very wild.

Then you enter a ravine under shady trees. The road crosses and recrosses the stream over fords that are deep and full of rocks. The horse at times seems about to disappear permanently. The water runs over the sides of the wagon-box as the wheels sink in a hole on one side or mount a rock on the other. That you will be precipitated into the laughing waters of the West Fork seems inevitable. But then the kalmia clusters thickly at the water's edge, and a bird is singing in a tree-top.

At the narrowest places you meet loaded tanbark wagons, or a long line of oxen moving slowly forward with a load of lumber that looks absurdly small until you think of the state of the road, when the wonder is that they can move it at all. Where the river forks, one branch of it—there are no "prongs" to the streams here—goes to the right, the other to the left of Fork Mountain, a spur of Cold Mountain that lies between the two nearly parallel arms of the stream. The left-hand or Little East Fork lies at the bottom of a long narrow "cove" so tightly squeezed in between the sides of Cold Mountain and the wild Fork Mountain that road and river continually become one. And here on either side are the promised "coves" running up into the mountains, close together, one after the other, choked full of laurel and rhododendron, grown with forest trees, and each contributing a wild little stream to swell the waters of the Little East Fork. No wonder people stay at home in this part of the country when the waters are up!

At the end of the road you come, not to a lumber camp, but to a house with a clearing where the occupants apparently have lived for generations. The people here are glad to see you. A visitor up the Little East Fork is no everyday occurrence, and presently they are telling you all about themselves, their neighbors, and the surrounding mountains.

Shining Rock, the southern end of Cold Mountain, and over six thousand feet high, is just above your head, with a trail only four miles long up to it over the Scape Cat Ridge. Scape Cat has no name on the maps, being one of those countless ridges which are waiting for some one to come and, discovering how beautiful it can be made, occupy it and name it according to his fancy. In this way, let us hope, will be preserved some of the beautiful Indian names, the liquid sounds of which harmonize so well with the character of the landscape. For no matter how wild this mountain country, how inaccessible and rough, it is at the same time exquisite in the soft lights, with the all-pervading fragrances and the enchanting growths. Even the Little East Fork, now one sees it, is found to be lovable. Scape Cat owes its present name to the fact that "old man Campbell" went up there with a boy hunting for stock, and while they were off, some one stole their rations. Next day Campbell hid them and said to his boy, "Well, Andy, we'll 'scape them cats tonight." Old Sally Reese took the rations, everybody knew, and the ridge from that day was named, in her honor, "Scape Cat."

In all this region turkeys, domestic as well as wild, are common, and a "gang of turkeys" is about as ordinary a sight as a gang of chickens, but we were not prepared way up here on the Little East Fork of the Pigeon River to behold a gang of peacocks. When we admired them with a sort of anticipatory pleasure in the time to come, when peacocks will sun themselves on the walls in the charming gardens that charming people will make here, we were brought violently to earth by learning that the real value of the peacock is in its superiority to chicken meat. Peacocks, you learn, provide the finest dish you ever ate—and their tongues are not even mentioned.

If you want to climb to Shining Rock, you will find a trail going up from here, and at the top one of those balds so common to these mountains, and always so delightful. The top of Shining Rock Mountain is so level that we were told that men and women had been seen running footraces all over it. There are small firs here and there, and splendid groups of *Rhododendron Catawbiense* whose royal red flowers must transform Shining Rock into a garden of delight at their blooming season. Also huckleberries grow up here in the greatest profusion, your new friend of the Little East Fork informing you that she would not mind climbing up to Shining Rock and picking and bringing home half a bushel of huckleberries any day.

Shining Rock is named from the remarkable mass of white quartz, more than an eighth of a mile long and from thirty to sixty feet thick, that lies along the crest of the mountain and which is a conspicuous landmark for miles around. From Shining Rock one looks across to the Richland Balsam, Lickstone Bald, and a dozen other high bald mountains, while on the opposite side rise the summits of Pisgah Ridge. Indeed, the short Cold Mountain Ridge stands separated by deep valleys from a circle of high mountains that completely surround it. Its southernmost and highest point, Sam Knob, almost separated from the main ridge and rising without spurs in wild precipices to an altitude of over six thousand feet, is such a labyrinth of cliffs, gorges, and impenetrable laurel and rhododendron thickets that the mountain cannot be approached from any side. It is considered inaccessible even by the hardy mountaineer, so that when a hunted bear reaches Sam Knob he is not pursued. The hunters consider him at home. There are not many bears left in the mountains, though each year records a number of captures in different parts of the wilderness. That Bruin was once common, however, is shown by the frequency with which his name occurs in the Bear Wallows, Bear Creeks, Bear Pens, and Bear Ridges throughout the mountains. All this region was noted for big game until very recent years. But now the lumbermen, before whose advancc all life perishes, have found their way even into the coves of the Forks of the Pigeon.

The road up the East Fork, closely following, constantly crossing and recrossing the river, is, like the way up the West Fork, delightful on a summer day. Each ford is a picture, no matter how the crossing of it may affect your feelings. From Cruso, near the end of the road, the trail to the top of Cold Mountain is a trail up into the sky, where tall forest trees gradually lower their heads and finally disappear to be replaced by small firs and great gardens of the red-flowering *Rhododendron Catawbiense,* the glorious shrub that so loves to blossom high up under the dome of the sky. The trail leads at first up Cold Creek, under the chestnuts, oaks, locusts, and tulip-trees; then under rocky ledges and along such narrow crests that you look down on either hand into deep-lying coves filled with trees and wonderful in their intensity of lights and shades. The sun smites hot as it strikes you on one side, while a cold north wind strikes you on the other side.

The walk up this trail was made forever memorable by the fear your guide entertained of snakes. He was accompanied by his little son whom he constantly cautioned to be careful. Neither himself nor any of his friends or neighbors had been "snake-bit," yet every step of the way through the laurel was beset with unseen dangers, and from every ledge, close under which we had to pass, a snake was expected to precipitate itself upon us, and every time we had to grasp the rock to help ourselves over a difficult place we were in danger of grasping also a snake, while from him walking on ahead floated back a monologue in a minor key whose subject was ever the same, and of which we caught such fragments as this, "Be mighty careful now, look where you step! I'd rather give a thousand dollars than get you snake-bit up here." And so we continued our fearful way up the shining slopes and over the rocky ridges of Cold Mountain on a bright summer day.

That there are snakes, the names of the many Rattlesnake Ridges, Dens, Knobs, and Mountains, stand as evidence, and that there are certain dry, rocky places frequented by these reptiles, there is no doubt, certain parts of Cold Mountain, we were told, being infested with them; yet few people have been bitten, as the rattlesnake never acts on the offensive, but tries to escape unless cornered or frightened, and it does not strike without giving warning.

Having wandered over these mountains at short intervals for more than a dozen years, and never having seen a living rattlesnake and but very few dead ones, one seldom thinks of them. The only precaution necessary is to be careful about going into huckleberry bushes or other thickets where the growth is so close that you cannot see the ground. No one can blame a snake for striking if it is stepped on, also when pursuing Rattlesnake Knobs, or Branches, or Ridges, or Dens, one may as well look first and give plenty of notice of his approach. But as a rule one does not go to such places. The people know where they are and carefully avoid them, one man who had killed many rattlesnakes summing up the sentiment of the mountains when he said, "I am not afeard of a knife, or a gun, or a varmint, but I am afeard of a snake."

The top of Cold Mountain, to which cattle and sheep are driven for the summer, is an extensive pasture of blue-grass and white-clover, where a large spring of water, cold and delicious, wells forth. To spend a summer day roaming about one of these high balds is a pleasure one cannot repeat too often. In the splendid exhilaration of the air, which is not thin enough to be oppressive, and through the cold tissues of which the sun sends a delicious flood of warmth, the body seems taken up and rejuvenated. And where else is the sky so luminous, the clouds so purely white? From one point and another you look out over a world of mountains many of which are well-loved and familiar friends. The most beautiful wild flowers have arranged themselves in gardens to please you, and out of the rocks leap sparkling waters still more to refresh you. From the Forks of the Pigeon how many of these charming balds can be ascended by trails known only to the kindly natives, who will go with you if necessary or tell you the way where it is possible for you to go alone!

Pisgah and the Balsams

Pisgah, lying between Toxaway and Asheville, is the most noticeable and the favorite mountain seen from Asheville. Everybody knows it. Rising, as it does, above the other heights, its beautiful form outlined against the sky, it inspires a feeling of affection in those who see it day after day. It is the highest point in the Pisgah and Tennessee ridges, that long mountain barrier winding in a southwesterly direction from Beaverdam Creek, a few miles from Asheville, to Toxaway Mountain, a distance of some twenty-five or thirty miles. There is said to be a trail along the whole length of this crest, a sky walk to be envied the mortal who can take it.

It does not detract from the interest one feels in Pisgah to know that it has retained its height above other mountains of the region because its rocks are crystalline—that, in short, Pisgah is high and strong because it is largely composed of garnets, of garnets and cyanite, the latter one will remember being very closely related to topaz.

At Garden Creek, Pisgah often comes to view in your walks, and from Cruso, near where the trail goes up Cold Mountain, there is a road up Pisgah, that portion of the mountain now being included in the forest attached to the Biltmore estate. There is also an automobile road from Biltmore to Pisgah, a forecast, no doubt, of what will be true of many a high place in the near future.

There is no sweeter road anywhere than that up Pisgah. In the coves and clearings at the foot of the mountain the people live in the homes of their forefathers and give you a welcome that is more than cordial if you choose to rest awhile on their porch, or drink from their spring, and they will urge you to stay to dinner so heartily, that only the thought of finding some wind-swept, sun-bathed slope, where you can sit in the open air and look off over the distant mountains while you eat the luncheon provided at your last stopping-place, prevents you from accepting. Lying on the ground to rest and maybe sleep a little in the deep stillness of nature, you think with sympathy of the woman living far back in a certain cove from which she never emerged, and who in reply to a question, answered, "No, I don't want to go away. I ain't a lonely-natured person noway. I like a quiet life."

The road follows up Pisgah Creek, which, after the fashion of streams here, winds back and forth, so that for more than two dozen times you have to cross the swift water on those marvelous footways the people find sufficient for their own use, but whose vagaries present difficulties to the stranger.

What you get from a mountain road depends upon how you go. If alone, you hear and see and feel things that you never hear or see or feel with even the most considerate and sympathetic comrade. Your comrade you need for the halt at the end of the day. But you should also often walk alone. And whether alone or companioned, you must never walk right on. You must linger along and listen attentively, and sniff the air for news, and you must look, not only at the clouds and the blue of the sky, at the distant landscape and the colors on the near slopes, but you must look at the ground. For there also you will get things to remember when the doors are shut on the wander-life. You will be able to recall, for instance, that brown slope where in the early summer you suddenly became aware of a round bright eye shining out near the ground close to a log. As you continue to look, a striped and speckled form becomes outlined among the fallen leaves, the sticks and the stones. Ah, yes!—a ruffed grouse, but why so still? Why did it not escape at your approach? You look attentively at the ground close about you—nothing—yes—there so close to your foot that another step would have crushed out its little life is a round brown puffball with a stripe down its back, and close to it another, and another and another, until you have detached five new birdlings from the protective coloring of the ground. There are more, you know, but do your best you cannot find them. So you pick up the two nearest you, one after the other, and lay them in the palm of your hand. They show no sign of life excepting the shining wide-open eyes. They are just hatched, yet here they are, the accomplished young frauds, exercising the most practiced deceit, no doubt secure in their faith that you cannot see them, although you have them in your hand. You hold them thus only a moment, your pleasure in the contact clouded by thought of the suffering of that motionless little mother under the log. Yielding to a whimsical impulse, you place a light kiss on the top of each little head, then lay them on the ground side by side, and retreat backwards at some distance, and watch to see them go. But they do not go. You stand with your eyes on that one spot until they ache, and then in a moment of forgetfulness you look off to the blue mountains beyond. But only for a moment, a little sound like a quick sigh brings you quickly back to business. You focus your eyes on the spot—it is vacant! You know it is the spot, for you carefully marked it in your mind; the stone is there—but they are not. Neither is that bright eye any longer visible under the log. They fooled you, after all. Not the slightest sound, the least motion that could attract attention, and they have vanished very much like a dream. They have fooled you? They think so, but it is really the other way, for see, those two you held in your hand did not really escape—you have them yet, and they have never been able to grow up or change since that day. Two little downy birds, like happy dreams, must run about the pleasant aisles of Pisgah forest to all eternity with a kiss hovering like a butterfly above each little head.

The ruffed grouse, "pheasant," the people call it, is native to these woods and an encounter with one is always a surprise, and nearly always pleasant, though you once got a shock from a grouse that must pretty nearly have balanced the bird's own distress of mind. It happened on a long, steep mountain path one spring day. Going along thinking of anything but danger, you suddenly stop as you hear the sharp hiss of a snake. You stand perfectly still and search the ground with your eyes. You see nothing, and all is silent until you move, when again comes that terrible danger signal. You begin to feel shaky at thought of the near invisible reptile, no doubt coiled ready to strike, when something moves from over a fallen log and your startled eyes behold a long thin thing stretching towards you. But to your infinite relief and amusement the snake's head resolves into that of a ruffed grouse, and presently there fairly boils up over the log such a mass of irate feathers all on end, and outspread wings and tail, so crazy looking an object, with open mouth and hissing tongue, that you take the sufficiently obvious hint that your presence is not desired, and pretending all the fear the bunch of feathers thinks it is inspiring, you beat a hasty retreat, it after you, swelling, hissing, and triumphant. But you escape, and it no doubt goes back to its nest all self-complacency and with a fine tale to tell those children, as soon as they shall be hatched, of how it saved their lives one day and drove away a terrible human monster. Yet you wish it could someway know how that monster loved it and only ran away to please it.

Thinking of the many pleasant encounters you have had in bygone days with the woodland folk, and keeping eyes and ears alert for more, you follow up the winding way until you reach the bench of the mountain where Buck Spring, one of the famous springs of the mountains, gushes forth large, free-flowing, and icy cold. Near it now stands Mr. Vanderbilt's Buckspring Lodge on the edge of the bluff that looks off across the French Broad Valley to the Blue Ridge at the east and towards Asheville and its background of mountains at the north. The waters from Pisgah flow into the Pigeon River on one side, but into the French Broad on the other, and directly under the steep cliffs upon the top of which the lodge stands is that charming, far-famed level of the Blue Ridge plateau known as the "Pink Beds," because of the gorgeous garden of flowers it becomes in the springtime.

There is every variety of surface on Pisgah, from dense forest growths to open treeless slopes, bushy benches, and rocky cliffs—

and everywhere a bewildering variety of flowers. On each mountain you find characteristic flowers, as though each kept its own garden somewhat distinct from its neighbors. Not that you will not find these flowers elsewhere, but perhaps nowhere else the same species in equal abundance. And each mountain you remember because of some great floral outburst in process at the time of your visit, so that when you think of Pisgah, for instance, it is covered with the later summer flowers—gardens of pink and white turtlehead, asters, goldenrod, dozens of well-loved flower forms in luxuriance abound, as well as some you do not know—instead of with a cloak of flaming azaleas, or wearing a crown of rose-bay, as would have been the case had your first visit been earlier in the season.

From the top of Pisgah you get a wide view, and a very beautiful one, though perhaps the best is that plunge of the senses down among the rhododendrons, kalmias, and tree-tops that cover all the near slopes with a lovely surface of green, in which deep shadows lurk, and over which the light plays so beautifully.

To the west from Pisgah, across the *cul-de-sac* in which lie the Forks of the Pigeon and the high form of Cold Mountain, rise the Balsam Mountains, and from Garden Creek, that lies about halfway between Pisgah and the Balsams, a road leads through Davis Gap and on to Waynesville at the very foot of the Balsam Mountains. As one follows this winding road, beautiful views of Pisgah come and go, as also of Cold Mountain, Sam Knob, Lickstone Bald, and other familiar forms.

Then, upon crossing the Davis Gap, the glorious high Balsams rise up to view. The road passes a picturesque old mill with its tall wheel, where one stops to drink from the cold spring, and soon after reaches Waynesville, which has long been a noted summer resort because of its elevation of over twenty-six hundred feet, its beautiful outlooks, and the fact that it lies on the railroad.

Waynesville is not on the Pigeon River, but in the fertile and charming valley of Richland Creek which enters the Pigeon a little to the north of here. The village lies, as it were, in a nest of the Balsam Mountains, which rise so close about it that one cannot see them to advantage, but from various points in the village one can look out towards the Newfound Mountains where the fine large mass of the Crabtree Bald immediately attracts the eye. Crabtree Mountain!—and below it and running half around it Crabtree Creek—what a picture rises before the imagination at those two names! For the wild crab is one of the most precious gems of the forest. In the spring it blossoms, the first you know of this being the exquisite fragrance that pervades the woods. If, then, you go abroad you will find the wild orchards loaded with flowers like apple-blossoms, excepting that they are old-rose in color, delicately shaded with clear pink and white. No tree is more wonderful in appearance, and none is so wonderful in fragrance. The perfume, powerful yet delicate and very refreshing, rises in a vast cloud of incense from the fire of the flowers until the whole forest seems steeped in it. And if you choose to press a few of these ardent blossoms between the leaves of a book, or drop them among your papers or your clothes, you will have reason to remember the ecstatic blooming of the crab tree for a very long time.

The wild crab is not the only apple found in this fortunate land, for the orchards of Waynesville and the country roundabout yield apples that would not discredit the proud apple states of the North. Indeed, when we of Traumfest get a particularly good apple the question some of us ask is, "Did it come from Waynesville or New York?"

There is a white sulphur spring near Waynesville, but that which most powerfully attracts the visitor is its nearness to the Balsams, into whose recesses one can penetrate by paths and trails to the very haunts of the bear, only that poor Bruin has been so driven from pillar to post that he has very few haunts left. The Balsams are among the highest remaining of these once towering mountains, and they, like Pisgah, owe their preservation to the cyanite and garnet in their rocks.

The Balsams, as well as the Blacks, are named from the mantle of balsam firs that covers all their higher parts, so dark-green as to look black at times, although in the distance the magic light causes them to assume that wonderful blue color which is the prerogative of all these delectable heights. Balsam trees as a rule cover the higher slopes of all the mountains that rise above fifty-five hundred feet, sometimes on the highest ones running down the ravines much lower than that. These wide black mantles laid over the shoulders of the high mountains give strength to the landscape. As seen from below, they seem completely to envelop the mountains, but at a higher elevation, or upon approaching the summits, one discovers that the mountain-top is always treeless. This is true of the higher mountains, whether they are fir-clad or not, the "bald" varying in size from a few yards across on some mountains to rolling meadows hundreds of acres in extent on others. The large balds, such as that of the Roan, the Big Yellow, and other well-known forms, also give character and added beauty to the landscape, in which they appear like peaceful islands in the billowing sea of tree-clad mountains.

There is a road leading out of Waynesville and up to what is known as the Eagle's Nest, on one of the Junaluska spurs of the Balsam Mountains. This road, which is brown in color instead of red, winds up through a forest of hardwood trees, and towards the top there opens out a wide, gently concave meadow of mingled blue-grass and white-clover, one of those beautiful natural meadows that occur so frequently on the slopes of the higher mountains, and where the fragrance of white-clover mingling suddenly with the manifold sweet odors of the forest gives one a sensation of waking into the past interpenetrated with the events of the present.

There is a hotel at the top near a large spring of cold water that wells forth close to a fine outlook, as though nature had planned it that way on purpose. There, before your eyes, Pisgah, Cold Mountain, Shining Rock, Lickstone, and the other balds we know so well, stand amidst the lesser mountains; and that far blue line to the southwest between nearer heights they tell us is Cullowhee Mountain. But that which most strongly affects one here is the colors of the balsams that are close enough for you to look into the deep, soft hollows that lie on the wonderful green of the slopes like lakes of midnight blackness.

Not far from the Eagle's Nest is another outlook, to the north this time, whence you get a glimpse of the Smokies, and can look off to Craggy and Mount Mitchell, while down at your feet lies the picturesque little valley of Jonathan's Creek; but here, too, the eye turns ever to the massive form of one of the near Balsam Mountains, big Cataluchee, with its wonderful deep colors.

Walking over a beautiful natural meadow to get a full view of Plott's Balsams, you encounter such diversions as red columbine, gardens of pink turtlehead, fragrant and charming evening primroses, fire-pinks, phlox, lilies, and—sourwood, with its incomparable fragrance. The Plott Balsams that run southwest from here in a short and massive range are named from a family early inhabiting this region and among whom were several noted hunters. The grandfather of the present generation, some of whom still live up the wild and picturesque Plott Creek, killed a panther where the hotel now stands; but a hunter's fame here rested on the number of bearskins he could show, to hunt these dangerous animals with the primitive weapons of early days being well considered the true test of a man's courage. But though dangerous when brought to bay, the brown bears of the mountains are quite harmless if let alone. "There hasn't a bear in this country hurt a man in my memory, or my father's or my grandfather's," an elderly man assures you; and a hunter then present adds, "A bear ain't goin' to hurt a man noway unless he's hemmed, then he'll kill you." There are many bear stories yet told, though the most famous of the old hunters are no longer here to tell them. The railway train, thundering under the very walls of the Balsams and climbing across them through the high Balsam Gap, bespeaks a new era when people come in throngs to the mountains for other purposes than bear-hunting.

Mount Mitchell

From the top of Tryon Mountain on a fair spring day, a snow-white cloud was seen lying above the northern horizon. It was so beautiful in the pure blue of the sky that the eye involuntarily turned to it again and again; and then, some trick of the light revealed an opalescent world below, and all at once one realized that the cloud was the snow-covered crest of the Black Mountains, which can be seen from Tryon Peak on a clear day.

After this one saw the Black Mountains in the distance, like the Smokies ethereally blue or again pearly white. But unlike the impression created by the Smokies, this of the Blacks vanished upon near acquaintance, perhaps in part because the name stamped another vision on the mind. It is hard to escape the influence of a name, and the Black Mountains live in your memory as a group of night-black domes topping a long black mountain crest that lightens to varied shades of green as it descends towards the valleys, or else loses itself below in depths of blue shadows, which is the way it appears when one is near it.

Nowhere is the rounded contour of the Southern mountains so striking as in the high balsam-covered summits. Mitchell's High Peak, as it is now called, used to be the Black Dome, a name poetical and profoundly descriptive. When near enough, perhaps on some neighboring slope or summit, the balsam-covered mountains are impressive to solemnity. The dark, unbroken mantle of fir trees covering all heights and hollows throws back the light with singular depth and softness, the color varying from deepest green to inky black, in which lie intense indigo shadows.

The range of the Black Mountains, which is only fifteen miles in length, has, it will be remembered, thirteen summits above six thousand feet high. This short, high range, standing on a base less than five miles wide, its slopes sweeping up from either side to the crests more than three thousand feet above the surrounding valley bottoms, is, wherever visible, the most notable feature in the landscape.

It runs north and south, its southern extremity merging into the Blue Ridge, which here, in its very irregular windings, comes so close to the Black Mountains as to leave only a narrow and deep valley, that of the South Toe River, between. Two of the highest points of the Blue Ridge, Graybeard and the Pinnacle, noted landmarks, lie close to the Blacks.

To the southwest of the Black Mountains, practically a continuation of them, lies the short high chain of the Great Craggy Mountains in which Craggy Dome and Bullhead Mountain rise, in the one case a little above six thousand feet, in the other, a little below. To the west of the Black Mountain Range, tightly inclosing the narrow Cane River Valley, is a jumble of wild mountains, among which Yeates Knob reaches an elevation of six thousand feet, while to the north of the range lies the valley of Little Crabtree Creek between the Blacks and the rugged mountains beyond. Hence the valleys that nearly surround the Black Mountains are deep and narrow, and the streams rushing through them are very swift, clear, and, from the rapidity with which they rise during a storm, dangerous, the Estatoe, or Toe River, as it is commonly called, and its branches being among the most dangerous of the mountain streams.

There is the same glorious wildness in the Black Mountain country that one feels in the regions of the Smokies and the Balsams; and whoever ascends the Black Mountains, excepting perhaps over the trail to Mount Mitchell, unless he is a mountaineer of experience, must take a guide or run the risk of getting lost in the rhododendrons that heavily clothe the slopes of the mountain. To get lost in the rhododendron on one of these big mountains, where the foliage is too dense for one to see the sky, and where the strong, twisted limbs form a labyrinth in places utterly impassable, is an experience none would court, for, besides the trap woven by the rhododendron limbs, wild streams rush down, ledges and chasms obstruct the way, and fogs, the real danger in the mountains, are frequent.

But on a pleasant summer day what is more delightful than a climb to the top of Mount Mitchell! One can easily get to the Black Mountain country by way of the railroad that now crosses the Blue Ridge a few miles to the north of there; or one can follow the old route from the Black Mountain Station in the Swannanoa Valley, taking a long ride to the summit of Mount Mitchell and spending the night in a cave; or there is that two days' drive from Asheville to the foot of the mountain, over roads which, speaking after the fashion of the Italians, are carriageable—though barely so. The road, good enough for some miles out of Asheville, runs northward to the Ivy River up which it follows through the "Ivy Country," so named because of the luxuriance with which the mountain laurel or "ivy" densely covered this region.

At the forks of the river the road goes up the North Ivy, where the Craggy Mountains loom into view at the gaps, and where the valley, squeezed tightly in between the steep sides of the mountains, is as wild as a valley can be that contains picturesque little houses and has its slopes all tawny with chestnut bloom. It is a wild valley where sourwood loads the air with dainty perfume, morning-glories twine smilingly about the bushes, and deep-red or lavender bee-balm makes flower-gardens of the damp places.

The road, zigzagging endlessly about, finally gets up out of this valley, crosses a wide gap, and descends into the Cane River Valley near the house of Big Tom Wilson, the most famous bear-hunter of this region. Continuing up Cane River for a few miles you cross a picturesque ford and soon reach the house of Adolphus Wilson, Big Tom's son, at the foot of Mount Mitchell. It is very wild here, the glorious wildness of this country where everything is softened and sweetened by the beautiful growths and the touch of the sun in the sparkling air. Near the house the woods are fine, the path through them takes you past basins of clear green water and past damp places full of flowers and down to a stream that hastens along, broad, swift, and clear, and famous for its trout.

The Black Mountain country seems to you different from the country south of Asheville. Indeed, all this northern region has a quality of its own. It seems so free, so superbly wild, so very remote from the world, and for ages it has been remote, there having been no railroad within easy reach until very lately.

One advantage of settling down for a while in the Black Mountain country is that you will be more certain to visit Mount Mitchell in good weather; you can start when the right morning dawns. For this is a rainy country; the clouds hug close about the tops of the mountains sometimes weeks in succession; so that it is better to go to this region immediately after a general storm and there await the one perfect day. Not that this whole region is constantly deluged; on the contrary, the valleys are often clear when the mountain-tops are smothered in clouds.

One can easily walk to the top of Mount Mitchell, but it will be well, if you mean to stay, to have your blankets and provisions for the night taken up on horseback. The best way is to let the guide go ahead, and then loiter on as you please, the hoof-marks affording a sure protection against getting lost. With a long staff you can cross the rushing trout stream dry shod on the projecting rocks, after which you begin a most joyous ascent into the clouds.

The lower part of the mountain is covered with hardwood trees, the path leading past a tulip-tree that twenty years ago measured over thirty-three feet in circumference—no one seems to have had the "ambition" to measure it since. This majestic column had a narrow escape from destruction a few years ago when a mountaineer was with difficulty dissuaded from chopping into it to get an imaginary bee's nest. The fine natural forest is composed of many kinds of trees, among which the path winds, now in the woods, now across a stream, now through an open glade. The air, heavy with the honey-like odor of linden trees in full bloom above your head, murmurs with the myriads of bees that hover about the flowers. The uneven floor of the forest is covered with moss and large violet leaves. The white flower clusters of treelike rhododendrons gleam on the slopes. Laurel presents dense tangles on all sides. Hemlocks darken the way, ferns and moss everywhere carpeting the earth beneath them.

About three miles up, you pass through what is known as the beech nursery, a level bench grown with small beeches where grass and flowers cover the floor, a friendly vestibule to the dark forest that lies above. For a little beyond here you enter the balsams, and it is like entering another world, for in the balsam groves no other trees grow, and the young trees and the bushes that so lighten other forests are entirely lacking here. The tall, dark columns of the trees stand so close together that looking ahead there seems scarcely room to pass. The overarching roof shuts out the light. The pillared aisles are dark and sombre. A deep-green, fernlike moss covers the ground with an unbroken surface. This wonderful moss, sometimes a foot thick, curiously intensifies the loneliness of the forest. Over humps and hollows the flawless mantle lies, deep, soft, interminable, here and there patterned with lighter green oxalis leaves, always moist, always sucking in and holding fast the clouds that enter, the rains that fall. Continually saturated with the mists of heaven this exquisite monster with its insatiable pure desire becomes the constantly renewing mother of the rivulets that trickle through the mossy carpet, uniting to descend in crystal streams to the earth below.

This still, dark forest, its sombre aisles unlighted by flowers, unwarmed by the sun, covering immense spaces of the upper world, seems to exist for itself alone, to resent, as it were, the intrusion of human life into its mysteries. But it does not exist for itself. It is lonely because absorbed with the gigantic task of endlessly and without rest transforming the clouds into the life-giving streams of the plains. For man to slaughter the trees and tear that marvelous veil of moss would be to strip fertility from the cotton- and the cornfields that lie thirsting from the mountains to the sea.

Ascending through the balsam forests one seems under the spell of the Black Dome. The Black Mountains have received their baptism. No matter how delicately blue and ethereal distance may paint them, to think of them or to see them must ever after recall these sombre depths beneath the dark boughs. The path is wet and muddy in places, and also steep, but at last you pass up out of the dark balsams into a sunny meadow where blue eyebrights look up from the grass, and from which a stony trail bordered with rose-bay leads through stunted firs to the open top, where a monument standing alone on the very summit of the mountain gives a feeling of solemnity to the place. It was erected here in 1888 to the memory, as the legend on the side reads, of the "Rev. Elisha Mitchell, D.D., who, after being for thirty-nine years a professor in the University of North Carolina, lost his life in the scientific exploration of this mountain, in the sixty-fourth year of his age, June 27th, 1857."

Dr. Mitchell, being greatly attached to the mountain, then called Black Dome, and convinced that it was the highest in the Appalachians, had often been to the top to make his observations and prove his theory. One day he went up alone, and did not return at the appointed time. As soon as this became known, search was made, men and even women collecting from far and near, for Dr. Mitchell was greatly loved. The search, led by several old bear hunters, was finally given up when Dr. Mitchell's son, according to Big Tom, said to the men, "I give you a thousand thanks, but please hunt again tomorrow." Upon which Big Tom volunteered to take the lead and it is said he went searching for the missing man crying all the way.

The first trace was found eleven days after the disappearance, when Big Tom, sure of signs that no one less experienced in woodcraft could have seen, the mark of heel-tacks on a root, a stone displaced, weeds bent, a mark on a rotten log, went from point to point until he saw the missing man's hat on a log by a streamside. Above was a deep pool at the foot of a waterfall—the hat had floated down from there. Big Tom at this point tells the story thus. "I yelled and they answered me. They came on. 'I've found his hat.' They all huddled up. And I walked on a log and saw him. 'Come around, boys, poor old feller, here he is.' 'Have you found him?' 'I have—'" and old Tom's voice breaks and the tears are streaming down his face. Dr. Mitchell, although so well acquainted with the mountain, was believed to have become lost in a fog and to have fallen over the precipice above the cataract whose icy water kept the body in perfect condition until it was found. It was finally buried on the summit of the mountain so dear to him, and whose name was changed in his honor.

Big Tom was the most famous bear hunter in this region, but when we saw him years ago his hunting days were over, and his tall form was bent with age, but he loved to tell of the by-gone days and his bear hunts, and to show you the heavy, old-fashioned rifle he prized above all modern inventions. But best of all the old man loved to tell of how they went in search of Dr. Mitchell and found him looking as natural as life in the pure water of the mountain pool. So strong an impression has this brave and gentle old hunter made upon his community that the spot where his little house stands in the Cane River Valley is marked on the government map—"Big Tom Wilson's."

The extreme top of Mount Mitchell is bare of trees excepting a few stunted firs; but yellow St. Johnswort blooms in cheerful profusion over the rocks that are daintily fringed with saxifrage and sedum, a few twisted rose-bays show traces of earlier bloom, and prickly gooseberry bushes are maturing fruit for the birds, while sounds in the leaves and a flutter of wings betray the presence of a flock of juncos. On all sides the dark fir-clad slopes descend into the shadows below, where streams rush through ravines choked full of rhododendrons, and mossy slopes are impenetrable with laurel. Below the firs glorious hardwood trees cover the mountain-sides, the ravines, and the valleys, their intermingling hues of green blended and lost in tremendous depths of blue or purple spaces.

The view from the summit, off over the ocean of land that rolls in stormy waves to the far horizon, is stupendous. Beyond the impressive and dark masses of the near heights, the great mountains of the region, from the Grandfather to the Smokies, crowd the scene, melting as they recede into blue and misty shapes. Past the strong headlands of Craggy and the Blue Ridge, the mountains towards the south subside to rise again in far blue domes and pinnacles. Cultivated valleys, beautiful balds, uprising slopes, long curving lines, overlapping summits—it is difficult to disengage individual forms from the wonderfully blended whole. And here as elsewhere that which most moves the senses is the sweep of the near majestic slopes down into the deep blue spaces.

The cave near the top of the mountain is formed by an overhanging ledge, and here it is customary, for those wishing to watch the sunrise from the summit, to spend the night. And it is worth the effort, even if one only sees the mountains emerge from the clouds for a moment to be again swallowed up by them, for it is seldom that the visitor gets more than a glimpse of the whole world at one time, from Mitchell's cloud-capped peak. It was in this cave on top of Mount Mitchell that one once arrived in a pouring rain, after a perilous climb up the eastern slope, to find, as sole trace of former visitors, a little can partly full of condensed milk, which saved, not one's own life, but that of a young squirrel rescued on the way up, and who became the hero of many pleasant subsequent adventures.

The Black Mountain Country is very wild, and also very beautiful, the ascent of Mount Mitchell being but one of many reasons for going there. The streams are crystal clear, and everywhere picturesque houses are hidden away in the coves and valleys from which one gets superb views of the cloud-capped mountains that lie on all sides. There is no more romantically beautiful valley in the mountains than that of Cane River, which, in its upper part, is over three thousand feet high, and nowhere falls below twenty-five hundred feet. It runs along the whole western base of the Black Mountain Range, and from it one sees round-pointed mountains delightfully grouped in the landscape, and quaint houses placed in a superb setting of mountains and streams. Cane River is named from the heavy canebrakes that clothe its banks in places, supplying fishpoles, pipestems, and reeds for the loom, but the river valley is more noted for the products of its farms—grain, grass, and apples. No one can visit this region in the summertime without noticing the orchards loaded with handsome apples, fruit of so fine a quality that it took a prize at the Paris Exposition, the people tell you with pride. The land in the Cane River Valley is valuable, not only because it is fertile, but because the people love it so. One man we were told refused a hundred dollars an acre for his farm because "he was that foolish over it." And the inhabitants of the valley are fine and friendly, as you would expect of people who so love their homes.

Up Cattail Branch, and doubtless elsewhere, you can yet find men able to fell a tree and with the primitive whipsaw convert it into boards on the spot, and in the Black Mountain country one has seen a man sitting under a tree in front of his house shaving shingles by hand, those broad, strong shingles that add so much to the picturesqueness of a log house, and that last forever.

As you drive on down Cane River, now along the bank, now crossing a wide ford, you see a village ahead of you very beautifully placed in an opening between surrounding mountains. This is Burnsville, one of the most important and interesting mountain villages north of Asheville. Here are schools as well as hotels, and from points in and near the village are superb views of the high mountains. Within a short time Burnsville has come into easy communication with the outer world by way of the railroad that crosses the mountains a few miles to the north of here, and it is safe to predict that this gem of the mountains will not be overlooked by those who are on the way with money and love and knowledge to help transform the wilderness for the few into an earthly paradise for the many.

The Forks of the River Toe

The Estatoe should have kept its full name, but as the matter was not attended to in time, so that the river went down on the government maps as the "Toe," it will probably be long before the mistake is corrected.

The South Toe skirts the eastern base of the Black Mountains as Cane River skirts the western base. The North Toe, a long and winding stream, carries the waters from one side of the steep and high Yellow Mountain region, in places forcing its way through narrow gorges, and joins the South Toe a few miles east of Burnsville, the resulting river being known as the Toe. The Cane River finally enters the Toe, the two forming the Nolichucky River.

While the Cane River Valley is comparatively well peopled, the wild valley of the South Toe has as yet few inhabitants, but you will want to go there because the river, strong and wild and clear as crystal, has coming into it the merriest of trout brooks straight down from the sky, and because the valley itself is a most glorious wilderness, to be in which gives one a feeling of having escaped. Enormous trees grow on the slopes of the mountains—oaks, chestnuts, beeches, and magnolias mingling their foliage above your head as you wander along the woodland paths where brooks murmur among the ferns, and the rhododendrons are grown to trees. From Burnsville one can get to this fair, wild valley by following down the Little Crabtree Creek four or five miles to Micaville, a village that consists of a post-office and very little else.

The Toe River throughout its course is famous for its floods, which may be why the South Toe Valley, which is quite wide in places, is so sparsely settled. But it is the North Toe that holds the prize record in this matter. After the memorable floodyear when

Ford and Bridge of the South Toe River

Bakersville was so nearly washed away, one saw debris in the tree limbs some twenty-five or thirty feet above the level of the stream in the narrow cut near Spruce Pine. Everything had given way before the fury of the waters, including the iron bridge that had recently been built across the troublesome stream. To have an iron bridge meant much to the people, you may be sure, and no doubt the story told was true of how they gathered together on the riverbank and stood for hours watching the bridge as the water rose and covered it, and how when at last it gave way and went with a crash downstream some of the watchers wrung their hands and wept.

It is a memorable experience to cross the ford at Spruce Pine when the waters are up, as one discovered when, after waiting for days weatherbound at Marion, the chance came to ascend the mountains and attempt the ford. The road up the Blue Ridge crosses Armstrong Creek several times, a good preparation for the graver perils of the Toe, for Armstrong is one of those streams that come like a millrace down the mountain-side, dangerous not only in time of general flood, but because it rises without warning, becoming impassable almost in a moment after a sudden downpour somewhere up in the high mountains.

The entrance to the Toe ford, one found to be a newmade sandbank down which was a steep pitch into the rushing yellow-red water, while in the trees high above your head you saw the debris stranded there by the flood. The river was terrifying enough to look at, and once in, it seemed for a few moments as though the end had come. Although the driver headed well upstream so as not to be washed below the ford where was no exit through the rocky wall, it seemed as though we were being borne swiftly down to destruction. The water suddenly rose about your knees and the horses disappeared all but their heads: they were swimming. This lasted but a terrible few moments, however, while the driver sat still and pale, his eyes riveted on the horses, the reins held loosely in his fingers. It was discovered afterward that this foolhardy feat was the result of courage stored in a bottle in the driver's pocket. He had gone down the mountain before a long rainstorm came and raised the waters, and he had been detained so long that he was ready to take any chance to get home. Of course one did not know these things until afterwards, and the fording of the Toe in retrospect has something of the emotional value of the conflict with the powers of the air on Whiteside.

Doubtless there is a bridge over the river again, as this happened several years ago, pedestrians at that time being obliged to cross by way of a chain bridge. There is probably nothing worse than a chain bridge short of the bamboo bridges such as one sees in pictures of wild countries. The narrow footway is suspended high above the water, the floor being made of slats so far apart that you cannot help seeing the water rushing below, which gives you the feeling that you are going to step through. But worse than this is the motion of the bridge, that, the moment you step upon it, billows up and down as though trying to shake you off, the rope hand-rail on either side being but one degree better than nothing. These suspension bridges are used where the stream is too swift to allow of a "bench," and the people very truthfully say, "Strangers don't like them noway."

One coming up the mountain now will not be likely to drive, as the railroad disdainfully spans the torrents and has a station, if you please, at Spruce Pine itself. In the old days upon reaching Spruce Pine one always stopped at English's. To enter this part of the country meant to stop at the large, picturesque log house set back among the trees with its vines and flowers, and than which no place was better known the mountains over. It is also near Spruce Pine, it will be remembered, that one finds the most noted of the beryl mines, whence come shining crystals for ladies' necklaces and rings and brooches.

Wild as parts of the Southern mountains yet remain, it is seldom one can get any real sense of the perils of primitive life. The wolves are gone, the bears are almost gone, the larger rivers are being spanned by safe bridges, contests with lightning are only for those peculiarly favored of the gods, new methods of lumbering are retiring the old-time logging train; yet it is in the forest that we can get closest to the eternal conflict between nature and man carried on by the early settlers, in the forest where the great immobile trees resent, as it were, the power that lays them low. Even to be an onlooker at the conflict is exciting, as one discovered that day in the woods when one sat down to rest near the upper edge of a rough, newly made trough that extended down the mountain-side. As far as one could see, on all sides, stood large trees, oaks, tulips, and chestnuts. Shouts were heard in the distance and loud crashing sounds. Nearer came the noise, and then down the steep hollow of the trough a yoke of oxen moved slowly, very slowly into view. They were straining forward until they were almost on their knees. Foam hung from their mouths, their eyes bulged, the veins stood out like cords under their sides and on their legs. A long whiplash came suddenly, out of space apparently, and stung their panting flanks, a man's voice shouted commands, and the cattle strained yet harder down the slope.

Behind them came a second yoke of oxen, fastened to the same chain. They, too, were leaning forward on the yoke. They, too, dropped foam from their mouths and their flanks heaved. As these passed the opening in the trees, a third yoke followed, straining like the others, their noses almost touching the ground, their flanks ridged with whiplashes. The descent was steep and rough, men shouted frantic commands to the near cattle and far back in the woods. Following the third yoke came a fourth, leaning forward like the others, disfigured with welts like the others, foaming at the mouth and with bulging eyes. Behind them came a fifth pair of cattle, their weight on the yoke, their muscles standing out, toiling as though they were trying to move the mountain itself.

Suddenly there was a cry along the line, men came running, whiplashes stung the faces of the oxen, and they halted in their steep descent. The chain slackened and rattled, then suddenly tightened again, jerking some of the cattle out of their tracks. Wilder shouts came from the woods above, mingled with a rumbling and then a crashing sound. An instant's ominous silence and the commotion was renewed with tenfold vehemence in the rear. The men who had come forward ran back. The cattle stood panting in the trail.

Minutes passed while the sounds of a struggle of some sort came loudly through the forest. At last the command to advance was given, the long lashes of plaited hickory bark swung out and the ten huge forms bent strongly to the yoke. Behind them came the sixth yoke, foaming at the mouth, with protruding eyes and every muscle tense. Slowly, terribly, the long line of cattle pulled down the rough descent, now stumbling, now jerked from the narrow trail to be at once mercilessly whipped into line. The seventh yoke, with lowered heads and panting sides, was followed by the eighth, a lordly pair, for the creatures were larger as the line advanced. These great brutes were dark-red with white stars on their foreheads, their breathing was audible, they were almost groaning, their flanks rose and fell in quick, short jerks, foam dripped from their mouths, their tongues hung out as they strained forward against the yoke.

Suddenly the commotion in the rear was renewed, the taut chain jerked, the cattle veered, the chain suddenly slackened and one of the great red oxen lost his footing. He stumbled frightfully against a tree trunk, his foot sank into a hole, it seemed as though his legs must be broken and his great sides crushed as he fell forward against the tree on his neck, his head stretched out. Several whiplashes swung out and descended with sharp reports upon his quivering skin, a dozen men yelled, and he struggled to his feet with bloodshot eyes.

Again the long line started, again the living engines bent to their herculean task, and the ninth yoke came into view. The noise increased and the sound drew nearer as of a tremendous weight crashing down the mountain-side, waking the forest to horrid clamor. The tenth yoke passed, a pair of enormous brutes with bloodshot eyes and heaving flanks, like the others leaning their weight on the yoke, foam dripping from their open mouths. Behind them came the eleventh and last yoke bending to their task, suffering with dumb endurance the agony of their brutal labor.

The chain was longer behind these, and then there appeared at the opening and stopped, as the cry to halt rang down the line, the end of an enormous tulip-tree log. Not less than ten feet in diameter nor less than forty feet long, it lay in the trough that had been ploughed out by other logs. As it lay there it seemed malignant and conscious, as though resenting being torn from its place of pride in the forest where it had so long towered above the other trees.

The trail changed its direction at this point and the great log had to be turned. Shouts from the men, cracking of whips, creaking of yokes, rattling of chains—and finally the long line of cattle stood in the new line of advance. But the log lay as before: it had to be turned, not by the cattle, but by the army of men that had now come to view. Along the sides of the great column they ranged themselves, cant-hook in hand, and at the word of command tried to move it, pivoting it on the chain end and striving to swing the other end about until it should lie in the new line of direction. As the cattle had toiled, now toiled the men. The veins started on their temples, their eyes stood out, they were silent during the effort.

The log moved, it turned, and then—in spite of their almost superhuman efforts, it rolled. Over it rolled down the slope, twisting the chain, dragging four yokes of oxen into the bushes as though they had been so many straws. There were shrieks of command and of fear as the men on the lower side leaped out of the way, while others horribly whipped, goaded, and shrieked at the cattle that had fallen down the hillside. The log had come to rest perilously near the perpendicular wall of a low ledge of rock and the men had the dangerous task of returning it to its place. Some below steadied it and pushed with levers, while those above struck into it with their strong hooks and put all their strength to the task. For an hour the struggle between the log and the men continued, a struggle fraught with danger to the lives of both man and beast. But the more active power won, and the great log lay in the new path. All was ready again, the whips cracked, the men shouted, the cattle bent to the yokes, the log yielded, the long line moved on.

The way was very dangerous now, as a steep incline lay just ahead. The men with their iron hooks jumped now this side and now that to keep the log in its track. The trail grew steeper and the great bolt began to move too rapidly. The men with their hooks in its sides held back with all their strength, others shrieked at the cattle and goaded them brutally that they might keep clear; they made a sudden pitch forward and fell over each other, the last yoke but barely escaping a lunge from the dreadful object behind. The noise of the shouting was deafening.

Thus had the great log been coaxed and driven, held back and drawn forth, out of the roadless forest. At last it was pulled up a gentle slope and on a level space came to rest alongside a group of others like it—to have its bark removed and await its turn at the portable sawmill that stood a few rods away. The logs are never barked in the forest; the men say they would be killed getting them out unless the bark was on to keep the logs from slipping.

On the platform of the mill a log had just been rolled; it was placed against the saw, it seemed to the imagination to shiver, then a long, piercing shriek rent the air, and a slab dropped from its side, the first step in the process of converting a tree into a pile of boards. These boards are placed in what seems light loads on rude wagons, before each wagon a line of oxen is attached, and over the rough roads the load is drawn, sometimes many miles, to the nearest railway station. Thus does the forest inflict its penalty of pain, and thus has the world been supplied with wood from the stricken giants of the beautiful, devastated forests of the Southern mountains.

LEDGER AND THE ROAN

The name of Micaville explains itself. It lies in the most important mica region of the mountains, where the rocks sparkle, the roads glitter, and nearly everybody is engaged one way or another in working in mica. You see women and girls sitting under sheds cutting plates of mica into regular shapes, and piles of mica-waste glinting by the roadside or flashing near the mouths of the mines on the hillsides. Yet there is nothing here to suggest the hardships of a mining country, for the mines are for the most part near or at the surface, and the workers are the mountain people themselves. It is here that, walking on a dusty day, you come home sparkling like a Christmas-tree decoration, and here that the laurel bushes glitter with little points of light that do not come from their glossy leaves. Not only at Micaville, but all through this region the earth sparkles prodigiously.

If you follow the road northeast from Micaville, you will not only get some very fine views of the Black Mountains, but you will cross a charming ford of the wild North Toe that enters the South Toe a little below here, and best of all you will soon come to Ledger, which, though it may be little more than a name on the map, is much more than that to those who have enjoyed the hospitality of the friends once living there, and from whose home as a center this whole beautiful country lay open.

Ledger was as remote as any place in the mountains when one first went there, but now the new railroad, that has performed the feat of crossing the mountains by ascending the wild Toe Valley and descending the Blue Ridge, has a station on the river a few miles from Ledger.

Ledger will long be remembered as the home of Professor Charles Hallet Wing, who, after many years of notable service as professor of chemistry in the Boston Institute of Technology, came here before there had been any change in the customs of the country, to escape the turmoil of the outer world. Professor Wing vehemently disclaimed any share in changing—he would not call it "improving"—the life of the people, but he made his charming log house, his barn and outbuildings, also his fences with their help. In his carpenter and blacksmith shops the youth of the neighborhood learned the use of tools, and how to make many things. They also laid pipes to carry water to the house, and became familiar with the electric motor that lighted the place.

Professor Wing, with no thought of course of benefitting the people, built a school-house and library building, the schoolrooms seating one hundred and twenty-five pupils, provided two teachers, and himself conducted a manual training department which he fitted up in the basement. At the time of Professor Wing's first coming scarcely any one in that region could read or write, but that this was the fault of circumstances alone was shown by the fact that there were two hundred and fifty applicants the first year the school was opened, these ranging from six years old to forty, and this school was successfully conducted without the infliction of any sort of punishment.

The library was in time supplied with some fifteen thousand books which were sent to Professor Wing by friends who wanted to help from all over the country. The library was kept by a native youth who was trained for the purpose and taught to rebind books, a very necessary art, since some of the most-used books were those that had been discarded by the Boston Public Library. At the little Good-Will Library in the heart of the Carolina mountains, the old volumes were cleansed and repaired and books sent out all over the mountains, being loaned not only to those who came for them, but sent in the form of small, traveling libraries, each box containing seventy-five books, wherever a man would "tote" them in his wagon, be responsible for their distribution, and after three months bring them back again—and get another set if he so desired. The library was free, with rules but no fines, and it is illustrative of the quality of the people that the rules were not broken and that at the end of the first year not a book was missing, none had been kept out overtime, while less than six per cent of those taken out had been fiction! What a boon it was to come upon one of these cases of books when storm-bound in some otherwise bookless place! One remembers whiling away several stormy days reading Froude's "Essays" from one of these libraries, which among more popular reading always contained a lure for the more sober-minded.

In the home at Ledger the housework was done by mountain girls trained by the genial hostess, who loved her girl charges and taught them everything they might need to know in making a home for themselves. One remembers the pretty sewing-room in a cabin in the woods, with its sewing-machine and work-table where the girls went afternoons to chatter together and sew for themselves, with an occasional visit from the beloved lady who dropped in to advise or praise.

We accused the Professor and his wife of ruining the picturesqueness of the country for a radius of miles about their place, for paint and upright fences and buildings, tidy yards and farms, with everywhere signs of modern methods of life, had somehow followed their coming. But there were still left plenty of log houses to repay one's wanderings along the shady roads where the picturesque foliage of the buckeye mingled so prettily with the leaves of the other hardwood trees, and where wild plums offered you high-flavored fruits in the summer, and chinkapins showered bright brown nuts about you in the fall.

Is it Uncle Remus with his Brer Rabbit who has cast such a glamour over the chinkapin—that miniature chestnut tree whose little sweet nuts are scattered so plentifully about the roadsides in the fall? And what a pretty custom it is to speak of coins of small denomination as "chinkapin change." It quite takes the sordidness out of money. The buckeye, too, has over it a glamour of romance, and while its large glossy nuts are not to be eaten, it lights up the forest in an enchanting manner with its large clusters of red, pink, and yellow blossoms that cover the tree and open about the time the tulip-tree begins to bloom. Throughout the hardwood forests of the higher mountains it grows to perfection.

One never thinks of Ledger without recalling delightful walks in search of pictures, for there are no better fireplaces and looms, nor more picturesque little mills and bee-gums any where in the mountains than in the neighborhood of Ledger. Can one ever forget Bear Creek and the friendly people there!—how one would like to speak their names, for the names of the people recall cherished memories of the mountains, each region having its own names. It was up Bear Creek that we found an old lady of ninety spinning on her porch, and up Bear Creek we learned new patterns on old coverlets, and got many a picturesque washing scene and interior where the great fireplace was draped with strings of beans or of pumpkin, and where we saw big wild grapes strung like beads, and hung up to dry.

Wandering about the country, how many an open-air cane-mill we visited where the people were grinding out their winter supply of "long sweetening," and who never failed to offer you a cupful of the boiling syrup. And following the pleasant fragrance of wintergreen, we found the "birch still" hidden in the woods, though not for reasons of secrecy, as no penalty is attached to the distillation of the essential oils that are, at the country stores, exchanged for shoes and sugar.

One's youthful conception of birch bark, that it was something that grew out in the woods to be chewed, is here enlarged by discovering the birch still, wherever the sweet birch abounds, zealously extracting the fragrant oil that goes to flavor our candies and perfume our medicines under the name of "wintergreen." Another youthful belief, gathered from literature that oil floats, is also modified by the discovery that birch oil at least could never be cast upon the troubled waters, because it is red and heavy, and sinks to the bottom of the bottle of water into which it runs from the "worm" in the still. The only objection one has to the birch still is the pathetic bare trunks left standing in the forest where the bark has been completely cut from the trees.

This objection does not attach to the delightful pennyroyal still that one sometimes finds near the dry banks, where pennyroyal grows in intoxicating abundance, and the gathering of which seems to leave no scar nor in any way diminish the supply. Pennyroyal oil floats, as oil ought, on the surface of the water into which it drops, and the pennyroyal still has so thoroughly scented the halls of memory that one can never again smell the aromatic herb in any form whatever without seeing those open sunny banks hot with pennyroyal that lie on the side of Roan Mountain. And how many know the refreshing quality of a sprig of pennyroyal on a hot summer day. To chew this, or one of the pungent mints that also grow here in abundance, can sometimes add a mile or two to the day's walk. There are oil stills in the mountains south of Asheville, but it happened to be these of the more northern regions that one first and most often happened upon, and about which cling so many fragrant memories. Pennyroyal and ginseng are by no means the only herbs gathered in the mountains. Indeed, the higher Appalachians are a principal source of supply for a great variety of medicinal herbs, many tons of which are yearly shipped to all parts of the country and to Europe. In the season you are always meeting the herb collectors, either gathering herbs from the immense wild gardens where they grow or "toting" them down the mountains in great bags on their backs. One remembers gardens of balmony on the Grandfather Mountain, where after the collectors had gone you would not notice that any had been removed, so dense was the growth. The herbs are taken home and dried and exchanged at the country stores, that carry on a lively traffic in this industry which keeps many a mountain family in the necessities of life. You see the herbs, each in its season drying everywhere, spread out on the roofs, on the porch floors and—under the beds.

The curious names of some of the places in the mountains owe their origin to the sudden demand on the part of the Government for short, distinctive titles for post-offices. It takes either a great deal of time or a very quick wit properly to name a place, and so we have Spruce Pine not because spruce pines abound—there are only two there—but because somebody happened to think of it. For the same reason, no doubt, Ledger got its name, the true significance of which dawns upon you when discovering a few miles away a place called "Daybook!"

The pretty name of Lofus Lory, that so pleased and puzzled you until curiosity overcame discretion and led to inquiry, was not a sudden inspiration, though the reason for it is obscure, one being unable to discover that it in any way deserves its orthographic title. For "Lofus Lory" when spelled out becomes "Loafer's Glory." As it has no post-office, and has not yet been printed on any map, there is hope that phonetic spelling may be adopted in time to save it. The principal and perhaps the only family at Lofus Lory is distinguished for nothing worse than its efforts to raise melons in a sandy bottom near the Toe; but when you inquire about the melons, with interested motives, you learn that the river one day removed a part of the farm with the melons thereon, leaving the ambitious Lofus Lory like unto the rest of the world so far as melons are concerned.

The temptation to linger about Ledger is difficult to overcome, but there is the great Roan waiting but a little way north from here, to reach which one follows the road to Bakersville, preferably afoot, for it is only a few miles, and there are those charming views of the mountains, deep indigo in one direction, while in the other the Blacks appear, sombre, solid, and strong, or else seeming to hang suspended, half dissolved in gray rain-mists. To enjoy the way properly one should not only walk, but take time to sit on a rock and consider how the tall white spikes of the black snakeroot shine out of the dark woods, and ponder over the peculiar, penetrating odor of the sourwood that on a hot day pursues one like a dream, the fragrance seeming to lie in wait at the turns of the road to embrace one, the trees whence it comes standing somewhere unseen in the depths of the forest.

Bakersville lies in the valley of Cane Creek that runs down the middle of the village with houses on either side, the road and the creek identical in places. This confidence in pretty Cane Creek was ill-requited when, in the terrible floods that occurred a few years ago, it rose and roared and thundered through the valley and nearly wiped out of existence Bakersville, which is the largest village in this part of the mountains, and which like Burnsville, is an educational center. Now the railroad that has made its way up the wild Toe River passes close, making the fortunate village easily accessible to the outer world that stands knocking at the gates of the mountains.

But to the visitor who comes to explore, Bakersville's principal attraction is its proximity to the Roan and the Big Yellow, the most famous balds in the region, perhaps in all the mountains. The coves and valleys at the foot of the Roan are thickly settled, and a road crosses over the summit of the mountain connecting the hotel there not only with the new railroad to the south, but with another railroad to the north that originally came in from the west for the use of the iron company at Cranberry, and now crosses the Blue Ridge, so that the northern part of the mountains within a few years has become almost as accessible as the regions about Asheville.

The ascent of the Roan from either side is delightful. From Bakersville the road leads up the picturesque Rock Creek Valley that lies squeezed between the Pumpkin-Patch Mountain on the south and the slopes of the big Roan on the north. The Roan, standing boldly out in the landscape, is remarkable as being without trees excepting in the ravines and a narrow belt of firs towards the top. For this reason it is a mountain of pastures, as are Grassy Ridge Bald and the Big Yellow Mountain connecting with it towards the east. Near the top of Roan, which is over sixty-three hundred feet high, is Cloudland Hotel where one dines in North Carolina and sleeps in Tennessee, the hotel being cut in two by the state line.

Roan Mountain has long been famous for two things, the circular rainbow sometimes seen from the summit, and the variety of wild flowers that grow on its slopes, it being reported that

A Pasture on the Roan

more species are found here than in any other one place on the continent. One not a botanist going up in the summer will be delighted with the luxuriance and variety of colors assumed by the bee-balm, blood-red prevailing, although some of the springs and damp hollows are painted about with lavender, blush-rose, dark rose-red, pale honey-yellow or white bee-balm, and all of them, no matter what the color, are full of humming-birds. The botanies have no idea how many colors this charming plant assumes on the open slopes of the Roan. From these slopes one gets fine views of the surrounding mountains, views sometimes framed in rose-bay bushes, when your imagination paints a glowing picture of the scene when the rosebay is in bloom.

Near the summit you notice the little houstonia, with plumy saxifrage and pink oxalis everywhere in the mosslike growths that cover the rocks, and you will also notice, although you may not know how rare it is, the large buttercup-like flower with a geranium leaf, the *Geum grandiflorum.* If it is summer you will see the bright flowers of the lily named after Asa Gray, it having been first captured on the Roan, although it is abundant all through the mountains. And you will be sure to taste the little high-flavored strawberries hiding on the grassy ledges.

There are a few spruce and fir trees, mountain ashes and alders scattered about near the top, but otherwise the Roan presents wide reaches of pasture land where flocks and herds are grazing, and where, as you stand looking over the mountains beyond, a heifer, that has long been gazing stolidly at you, draws near and licks your hand, probably to find out what that motionless figure is really made of.

There is no mountain whose name you more often hear than that of the Roan. And the estimation in which the people hold this great bald was shown one day when a stranger, seeking to entertain a mountain woman, told her about Italy with its Vesuvius, its great churches, and its people with their strange customs. When the story was done, the woman looked intently at the narrator and then asked critically, "Have you-all been to

Roan Mountain?" Being answered in the negative, she added, somewhat condescendingly, "Well, if you want to travel and see something, you ought to go to Roan Mountain."

From the summit of the Roan you can continue on and down the north side to the Roan Mountain Station on the railroad, or you can follow the long trail over Grassy Ridge Bald, along the side of the Big Yellow and Hump Mountains down to Elk Park, where you can take the train by way of Cranberry and its famous iron mines to the Linville Country. On a fair day the long walk over the trail is the better choice, but you will have to take a guide, though one remembers sitting down on a mountain-top where two paths crossed, and studying out the situation on the government map while the mountain woman who had come to show the way looked on. Of course we were not lost, nobody ever is, the nearest to it ever known being by a mountain man who admitted that he had once spent three days plumb bewildered in the woods.

The Topographic Maps of the United States Geological Survey are the best guides one could have for general use; indeed, many of them are so detailed that one could follow the obscurest trails by their help. And they are always present, being printed in sections on sheets that can be folded small enough to be carried in the pocket, and they cost only five cents apiece. These maps are a splendid tribute to the work done by the Department that issues them. To get them it is only necessary to write to the Director at Washington D. C., who will send a plan of the maps, from which you can select those you need.

Linville Falls

One goes to Linville Falls to see the beautiful river at the point where it takes that leap into the gorge, forming the most noted cataract in the mountains. Linville, under the Grandfather Mountain, lies in a green bowl with tree-covered hills for its sides. Above the hotel, on the edge of the green bowl, look out cottages and summer houses, for Linville is a well-known resort. The river flows sparkling and dancing along one side of the bowl on its way to the falls ten or twelve miles south of here. The Linville is a delightful river, a clear trout stream from its birth-spring back of the Grandfather down to the falls and on through the ten-miles-long canyon below them, the canyon it has worn between Linville Mountain and wild Hawksbill and Tablerock.

The way to Linville from Ledger is by a pleasant and varied route up the North Toe River, then over ridges, up the Plumtree Creek, across the Blue Ridge, past Crossnore under the Snake Den Mountain, and on through Kawana, where you will stop to visit the Highlands Nursery that has done so much to make the beautiful growths of these mountains known to the outside world. It began twenty-five years ago with half an acre of land as an experiment. Now it covers one hundred acres, and every year sends out many carloads of the beautiful things that grow here and which find their way, not only to different parts of our own country, but all over Europe. This nursery owes its existence to Mr. S. T. Kelsey, of New York State, who came here from Kansas, and, with the energy and optimism of the North and the West combined, tried to transform the mountains. But he came too soon; the hour of awakening had not struck; so when he laid out a whole town on the Highlands plateau after the Western fashion, the people looked on in amazement and Highlands remained untransformed, as remained the rest of the mountains at that time, excepting for the roads he projected. For Mr. Kelsey had yet greater genius for making roads than towns, and laid out the finest of those first made in the mountains, among them the beautiful Yonahlossee Road that crosses the southern slopes of the Grandfather Mountain, scarcely changing its grade for a distance of nearly twenty miles. It was also Mr. Kelsey who planned Linville with its hotels and its lake. But the best thing he did was making the gardens and taming the most decorative and beautiful of the wild growths, not only the royal rhododendrons, laurel, and azaleas, and the noble forest trees, but the silver-bell, the sourwood, the leucothoë, the yellow-root, the wild lilies and orchids, and a hundred other charming wild flowers, including *Shortia* that gave the botanists such long search, inducing them to tolerate the limitations of a man-made garden, and also to bloom yet more freely, if possible, there than in the wilderness. Although no longer alone in its work, the Highland Nursery was the first native enterprise to distribute the decorative plants of this region from the North Carolina mountains, and from it the estate of Biltmore supplied its first needs.

It is an interesting fact that, long before the people of America had learned to appreciate the beautiful plants with which their country is so richly endowed, these were used and highly valued in European gardens, and English estates were beautified with our rhododendrons, laurels, and azaleas long before we had learned to value them as ornamental growths for cultivated grounds. It was Michaux, who, transported by the beauty of the wild flowers of the New World, took many of them home and introduced them to the people of Europe. It was he also who taught the mountain people the value of ginseng and how to prepare it for the Chinese market.

It is but a few pleasant miles from Kawana to Linville, along a road very much interfered with by little tributaries of the Linville River, among them the pretty Grandmother Creek. But if you want to go directly to the falls from Kawana, you turn towards the south instead of the north, and follow the road a few miles down the river to the Linville Falls settlement: this is about a mile from the falls to which a rough road leads, for the country about here is extremely wild: the woods are choked with dense growths of laurel and rhododendron, and the land is torn by ravines. For we are now on the outer side of the Blue Ridge adjoining the peculiarly wild foothill country, and whether the Linville River breaks through the wall of the Blue Ridge depends upon whether you consider the narrow Linville Mountain a part of the Blue Ridge or a part of the foothills, for it is over the upper edge of the deep gorge that separates Linville Mountain from a high ridge of the foothills that the river makes its escape. But however geology may decide the matter, in appearance the Linville Mountain belongs to the Blue Ridge, and one always thinks of it as ending the mountain plateau at that point.

Across the clearing, at the end of the rough road that leads to the falls, stands a house on the very brink of the precipice. As you approach it, the thunder of the water grows louder: you have a sense of nearing some catastrophe in nature. At the brink the mountain stops short without the slightest preparatory slope, without a buttressing spur. It drops in an upright wall, along the face of which a path descends through the rhododendrons that have grown along a narrow ledge. Down the path you take your way. At a certain point in it you can step out on the top of a large rock and see the river raging between cleft walls directly below you. As you continue the steep descent beyond here, rhododendrons offer you long, curved arms to hold by, and lend you their roots to step on. Finally, you jump down to a broad stone floor, and before you in its bed of solid rock lies the large pool of the upper falls into which the river enters in two wide, low cascades that are separated from each other by tree-covered rocks.

The shining Linville steps down from the forest, through which it has sparkled and sung all the way from its source at the back of the Grandfather, to rest as it were in the beautiful pool and make ready for that great leap down the wall of the mountain. High walls clad with living green encircle the pool on whose calm surface are mirrored the trees and the sky. To the eye it is a scene of peace, but in the ears is the tumultuous beating of the waters. The outlet of the pool is a deep and narrow crack. It is as though the broad river-bed had suddenly been set up on edge. The water plunges with a roar into this winding channel, rages about the impediments there, and finally escapes through a cleft in the rock to leap over the wall of the mountain.

Across a wide stone floor one walks to the scene of commotion in the narrow channel, but it is impossible to get a view of the final plunge without gaining a point of vantage by a jump too dangerous to think of. It fills one with a sense of impending danger to stand shut in by the high walls and hear the strife between the water and the rocks: and if it is terrible at this safe season of the year, imagine it in the spring floods! Standing on the wide, dry pavement, you look up to see a drift-log caught in the bushes on the cliff-side high above your head. It is hard to realize it, yet you know the water put it there. It was at a time of high water that the upper rim of the lower fall gave way, forming a step, and considerably lowering the final leap, thus taking away something from its impressiveness.

Climbing up again to where the path branches, if you want to go to the foot of the fall, where you can get a near view of it, you turn aside here—and take the consequences. A stream of water trickles down the slippery path, which is half rock, half rhododendron roots. The limbs of the rhododendrons twist about you like enormous snakes. You step down where you can, but where the distance is too great you have to jump, that is, you jump if you dare, but it is not likely you will dare, knowing what is below. The alternative is to sit down and slide over the rocks covered with black and sticky mud. It is a breathless scramble and your arms ache from holding to the rhododendron cables. Finally you reach the narrow ledge of rock that borders the deep pool into which the river drops. There it is, close to you, a high, white mass of foam and deafening you with its thunder. If the sun is shining you may see rainbows playing about it, and in any event you will get a wetting from the spray. A wall of rock rises above you and there is scarcely room to take a step, so close to your feet lies the deep water. There are big wise trout in this pool, the people say, but it takes a very wise angler to lure them out.

Getting back again is worse than getting down. Unfortunately gravity prevents sliding up, and a sudden descent into Avernus seems quite fearfully imminent as you slip and struggle and cling to the rhododendrons. But before starting up you can if you like follow along the edge of the cliff, as far as your nerve lasts, for the path is over rhododendron roots that have fastened themselves into the face of the rock. How they got footing here is a mystery; but here they are, and in behind their contorted limbs you creep along like an ant, hoping with every step that the roots will not give way.

This path, that grows less as it goes on, is followed by ardent fishermen, who either go back if it gets too lonesome for them, or else keep on. For if you keep on long enough you can get down to the bottom of the gorge—not so hastily as the description may seem to imply, though that too is possible—and when you get down, it must be almost worth the effort, for you will find yourself in the famous Linville Gorge that for the next ten miles is seldom traveled by a human being, although it is the finest trout stream in the mountains. The river runs between walls that rise many hundreds of feet high, and in some places the gorge is so narrow that there is room only for the river, and he who ventures in must wade as best he can through the swift water as it dashes about and over the rocks and boulders. Those who have been in the gorge speak enthusiastically of its grandeur and beauty.

Ordinary humanity, however, views the fall from a point down the ravine, on top instead of at the bottom of the mountain wall. To get to this point you follow a path partly through a scrubby undergrowth, partly through dark pine reaches that make soft walking, and where the edge of the abyss is hidden by impenetrable rhododendron jungles.

When you get to the open, rocky edge, you forget to look upstream to the fall, because of the wonderful blanket of trees that covers the opposite side of the narrow gorge. There is nothing like it: the walls seem made of foliage; the river far below runs through walls of living green, the crowns of superb forest trees that have managed to grow on what appears to be an upright cliff. You scarcely see the stems, only the green crowns of the hardwood trees blending their colors and their shapes with black interspersed shadows and interwoven with the dark-green of firs and the pale feathery effect of white pines, a marvelous tapestry wrought by the hand of nature.

The steepness of the walls makes this growth of large trees the more remarkable, and your heart aches to recall that this whole gorge, one of the wonders of the mountains, has been bought by a lumber company. But looking at that tapestried wall falling sheer into the mountain torrent below, your sympathy takes a humorous leap to the side of the lumber company. Any tree they can get out of there they will have earned! Float the logs downstream? "Not down *that* stream, unless you want to collect wood pulp somewhere beyond the foothills," a man who knows the gorge assures you.

As you stand on the brink of the precipice you hear the confused thunder of the fall, that at this distance is a mere white ribbon hung from the end of the gorge. Its voice alone asserts its importance. And how insistent, how unbroken, how hard and tiresome it is, a stupid unchanging roar, and blended with it is an echo as unresonant and monotonous as itself. You find yourself listening for a change that never comes, except a loudening when the wind blows towards you.

Irritated by the monotonous sounds you go on and around a curve out of sight of the vociferous ribbon. You seat yourself on a bed of dry, crackling moss that sends out waves of fragrance every time you move. Here the murmur of the far-down river blends with the dull roar of the cataract. This voice of the river is full of modulations, the harsh sound of conflict has given place to gentler tones and the subdued roar of the fall itself now makes an agreeable accompaniment.

To the song of the river is here also added voices from the forest, a sighing from the pine trees overhead, gentle rustlings from the crisp shrubs, a staccato chirp from the grass, a trill from some bird in the air, the clapping of a woodpecker on a dead tree, the drumming of some unknown creature, the ticking of a borer in a dead log. There are drowsy notes in this orchestra of the summer, with which the mighty perfume of the earth seems gradually to blend, and the warmth of the sun to mingle and hold all together in its tenuous threads—and—and—the sun conquers and you are sound asleep on the fragrant mosses, although it is mid-afternoon and you have planned a walk down that long ridge where the huckleberries grow. Thanks, oh, sun!—there is something altogether lovely in falling thus asleep against one's judgment.

There are "chimneys" over the edge of the precipice, whose tops have been conquered by brave little fir trees, and mossy things and a few flowers. And the precipice itself, do you realize that you are hanging your feet over the edge of the mountains—that the wall across the river belongs to the foothill formations?

What a sweet place is this edge of the high world! On a mountain-top all things unite to smell sweet, and on none more than on this. Crisp moss crackles whenever you move, hard-leaved, red-stemmed huckleberries crowd the crevices of the rocks, and *Dendrium buxophyllum,* whose thick carpet is seen to be made of tiny imitations of rhododendron bushes shares the crannies with other lovely growths. But everywhere, and by far the choicest thing here, is a species of dwarf rhododendron with a charming architectural structure, the curving brown stems crowned with upward-pointing, curled little leaves, green above, the under side dusted with a rich brown bloom, the red-tinged veins and red petioles giving a red flush to the whole plant. Seed pods on these charming shrubs tell of bloom earlier in the season, and who would not be here then! It would be hard to imagine a wilder, sweeter place than this edge, overlooking the gorge. To be here fills you with contentment. You imagine you would like to stay with the rabbits the rest of the summer.

The long and narrow Linville Mountain that borders the gorge on the west is not very well known to outsiders, but the people tell you of wonderful minerals there, among them large quantities of flexible sandstone. The Linville Country is very wild, but nowhere does the galax more riotously abound, this region being one of the favorite collecting grounds for this charming little plant.

Blowing Rock

The noble Grandfather towers head and shoulders above the sea of mountains that surrounds it. It is the giant of the Blue Ridge, and in a sense dominates the whole Appalachian uplift, not because of its superior height—we know how many higher mountains there are—but because it is so commanding. For Nature fashions mountains as she does men, here and there one so striking that it becomes a landmark for its era.

The Grandfather was believed to be the highest mountain in the eastern half of the United States until, not so very long ago, the surveyors came with their instruments and told the people there were forty mountains in North Carolina and Tennessee higher than the Grandfather. But of course nobody believed it: the people who had always lived under the shadow of the great mountain knew better than those men who flew in one day and out the next.

The surveyors were doubtless right in a way, but theirs was that mere scientific accuracy that proves nothing but the fact. Beyond that lies the real truth of the matter; forty mountains may measure higher, but to those who know the Grandfather, not one is really quite so high. In 1794, the French botanist, André Michaux, wrote of the Grandfather Mountain, "Aug. 30, climbed to the summit of the highest mountain of all North America with my guide, and sang the Marseillaise Hymn, and cried, 'Long live America and the French Republic! Long live liberty!'"

The mountain owes its supremacy not only to the comparative insignificance of its near neighbors, but to its position at the point where the Blue Ridge makes a sudden turn, swinging as it were about the Grandfather as about a pivot, the mountain rising in splendid sweep directly up from the abysmal depths of the foothills, with no intervening terraces. It has the effect of standing alone, its feet in the far-down valleys, its head in the clouds. It is also notable for its striking summit of bare rock as black as ink, a long, scalloped line as seen from Blowing Rock, a sharp tooth as seen coming towards it from Linville Falls. These bare, rocky summits are peculiar to the mountains of this region, as cliffy walls are of the Highlands country. None of these summits, however, can approach the Grandfather's black top in size and impressiveness, it being a landmark far and near.

The most impressive view of the Grandfather is from Blowing Rock that lies some twenty miles to the east of it on a brink of the Blue Ridge, which there makes a drop of a thousand feet or more into the foothills below. From Blowing Rock to Tryon Mountain the Blue Ridge draws a deep curve half encircling a jumble of very wild rocky peaks and cliffs that belong to the foothill formations. Hence Blowing Rock, lying on one arm of a horseshoe of which Tryon Mountain is the other arm, has the most dramatic outlook of any village in the mountains. Directly in front of it is an enormous bowl filled with a thousand tree-clad hills and ridges that become higher and wilder towards the encircling wall of the Blue Ridge, the conspicuous bare stone summits of Hawk's Bill and Table Rock Mountains rising sharp as dragon's teeth above the rest, while the sheer and shining face of the terrible Lost Cove cliffs, dropping into some unexplored ravine, come to view on a clear day. Far away, beyond this wild bowlful of mountains, one sometimes sees a faintly outlined dome, Tryon Mountain, under which on the other side one likes to remember lies Traumfest, Fortress of Dreams.

Off to the left from Blowing Rock, seen between near green knobs, the shoreless sea of the lowlands reaches away to lave the edge of the sky. And looking to the right, there lies the calm and noble form of the Grandfather Mountain, its rocky top drawn in a series of curves against the western sky. Long spurs sweep down like buttresses to hold it. Trees clothe it as with a garment to where the black rock surmounts them.

The view from Blowing Rock changes continually. The atmospheric sea that incloses mountain and valley melts the solid rocks into a thousand enchanting pictures. Those wild shapes in the great basin which at one time look so near, so hard, and so terrible, at another time recede and soften, their dark colors transmuted into the tender blue of the Blue Ridge, or again the basin is filled with dreamlike forms immersed in an exquisite sea of mystical light.

Sometimes the Grandfather Mountain stands solidly out, showing in detail the tapestry of green trees that hangs over its slopes; again it is blue and flat against the sky, or it seems made of mists and shadows. Sometimes the sunset glory penetrates, as it were, into the substance of the mountain, which looks translucent in the sea of light that contains it. As night draws on, it darkens into a noble silhouette against the splendor that often draws the curves of its summit in lines of fire.

Blowing Rock at times lies above the clouds, with all the world blotted out excepting the Grandfather's summit rising out of the white mists. Sometimes one looks out in the morning to see that great bowl filled to the brim with level cloud that reaches away from one's very feet in a floor so firm to the eye that one is tempted to step out on it. Presently this pure white, level floor begins to roll up into billowy masses, deep wells open, down which one looks to little landscapes lying in the bottom, a bit of the lovely John's River Valley, a house and trees, perhaps. The well closes; the higher peaks begin to appear, phantom islands in a phantom sea; the restless ocean of mists swells and rolls, now concealing, now revealing glimpses of the world under it. It breaks apart into fantastic forms that begin to glide up the peaks and mount above them like wraiths. The sun darts sheafs of golden arrows in through the openings, and these in time slay the pale dragons of the air, or drive them fleeing into the far blue caverns of the sky, and the world beneath is visible, only that where the John's River Valley ought to be there often remains a long lake of snowy drift. Sometimes the clouds blotting out the landscape break apart suddenly, the mountains come swiftly forth one after the other until one seems to be watching an act of creation where solid forms resolve themselves out of chaos. The peaceful John's River Valley, winding far below among the wild mountains, is like a glimpse into fairyland, and one has never ventured to go there for fear of dispelling the pleasing illusion.

Near the village of Blowing Rock, at the beginning of those green knobs between which one looks to the lowlands, is a high cliff, the real Blowing Rock, so named because the rocky walls at this point form a flume through which the northwest wind sweeps with such force that whatever is thrown over the rock is hurled back again. It is said that there are times when a man could not jump over, so tremendous is the force of the wind. It is also said that visitors, having heard the legend of the rock, have been seen to stand there in a dead calm and throw over their possessions and watch them more in anger than in mirth as they, obedient to the law of gravity instead of that of fancy, disappeared beneath the tree-tops far below.

Blowing Rock, four thousand feet above sea-level, is a wonderfully sweet place. The rose-bay and the great white *Rhododendron maximum* crowd against the houses and fill the open spaces, excepting where laurel and the flame-colored azaleas have planted their standards. And in their seasons the wild flowers blossom everywhere; also the rocks are covered with those crisp, sweet-smelling herbs that love high places, and sedums and saxifrages trim the crevices and the ledges.

Blowing Rock is also noted for the great variety of new mushrooms that have been captured there, though one suspects this renown is due to the fact that the mushroom hunters happened to pitch their tents here instead of somewhere else. For other parts of the mountains can make a showing in mushrooms, too.

It sometimes rains at Blowing Rock, but there are other times when one stands there on the brink in bright sunshine and sees, it may be, four showers descending on different parts of the country at once.

Blowing Rock has long been a favorite summer resort, and at present is most easily reached by way of a drive twenty miles long, up the ridges from Lenoir, where a short branch railroad connects with the main line at Hickory.

At Blowing Rock, the Blue Ridge, as so often happens along its course, presents a steep wall towards the foothills, but keeps its elevation at the top, extending back in a wide plateau; hence the country back of Blowing Rock and the Grandfather Mountain has a general elevation of from three thousand to four thousand feet; that is, the valley bottoms are thus high, which is what gives to this part of the country its peculiar charm. It is the walker's paradise, deliciously cool all summer, and totally free from any form of insect pest. South of the Grandfather the valley bottoms average about a thousand feet lower, although one there finds the highest mountains. But there are no finer views anywhere than from the Grandfather, the Beech, and other high summits of the Grandfather country. And here as elsewhere the people are so friendly and so good that one can if so inclined start out alone and with perfect safety spend weeks walking from place to place, stopping at the little villages for the night or where there are none, with whoever happens to be nearest when the sun goes down.

Leaving Blowing Rock one day in mid-June, you perhaps will walk away to Boone, some ten miles distant, three miles of the way a lane close-hedged on either side with gnarled and twisted old laurel trees heavy-laden with bloom so that the crisp flower cups shower about you as you pass and the air is full of their bitter, tonic fragrance. Large rhododendrons stand among the laurel, but their great flower clusters are as yet imprisoned beneath the strong bud-scales. When the laurel is done blooming, you will perceive that you must come this way again for the sake of the rhododendrons. Little streams of crystal clearness come out from under the blossoming laurel, flash across the road, and disappear under the laurel on the other side. How sweet the air where all the odors of the forest are interwoven with the bitter-sweet smell of the close-pressing flowers! How the pulse quickens as one steps along. Is that a bird? Or is it your own heart singing?

Before the first freshness of that laurel-hedged road has begun to dim from familiarity, you emerge into the open where the view is of wide, rolling slopes, green hills and valleys dotted with roofs, and beyond these the great blue distant mountains soaring up into the sky. That steep hill to your left is bright red with sorrel, a sorry crop for the farmer, but a lovely spot of color in the landscape. You climb up this sorrel-red hill to the top of Flat Top Mountain, up over the rough stones and the dark-red sorrel to where the view is wide and fine. But Flat Top Mountain offers you more than a view. It is noon when you get there, for you have not hurried, but have stopped every moment to smell or to see, or just to breathe and breathe as though you could thus fill your bodily tissues with freshness and fragrance to last into your remotest life. As you climb up Flat Top, you detect a fragrance that does not come from the flowers, a warm, delicious fragrance that makes you look eagerly at the ground. Seeing nothing, you go on half disappointed, half buoyant with the certainty of success—ah, it comes again, that delicious warm fragrance. You abandon yourself to primitive instincts and trusting your senses turn about and walk straight to where the ground is red with ripe strawberries. You sit down on the warm grass and taste the delectable fruit. A bird is singing from a bush as though sharing in your pleasure. When you have gathered the best within reach, you lie back and watch the clouds sailing like white swans across the sky. Then you take out the bread you have brought, the most delicious bread ever baked, for it has in some magical way acquired a flavor of blossoming laurel, and rippling brooks, and blue sky, and the joy of muscles in motion, of deep-drawn breath, of the lassitude of delicious exercise, with a lingering flavor of the spicy berries whose fragrance is in the air about you. Such bread as this is never eaten within the walls of a house. And then you rest on the warm hillside fanned by the cool breeze, for no matter how hot the summer sun, there is always a cool breeze in the high world at the back of the Grandfather. Before starting on, you must taste again of the exquisite feast spread for you and the birds, whose wings you hear as they come and go, fearless and ungrudging, for there is enough for all.

Farther along on the mountain stands an old weather-boarded house whence you see Boone in the distance lying so sweetly among its mountains. A path here leads you down to a deserted cabin in a lovely hollow. That well-worn path at the doorstep leads to the spring only a few steps away, such a spring as one is always looking for and always finding at the back of the Grandfather. Its water is icy cold and it is walled about with moss-covered, fern-grown stones. This cabin in the lovely hollow, with its ice-cold spring, the surrounding fruit trees, the signs of flowers once cultivated, gives you a strange impulse to stop here, like a bird that has found its nest, but you go on along a woodsy by-road whose banks are covered with pale-green ferns, and where the large spiræa in snowy bloom stands so close as almost to form a hedge. The velvety dark-green leaves of wild hydrangea crowd everywhere, its broad flat heads of showy buds just ready to open. Enormous wild gooseberries invite you to taste and impishly prick your tongue if you do. The blackberries make a great show, but are not yet ripe. The roadside now and then is bordered with ripe strawberries. This shady way brings you again into the "main leadin' road" you left some distance back when you climbed the sorrel-red hill to the top of Flat Top Mountain, and which now also has its wealth of flowers, among which the pure-white tapers of the galax shine out from the woods, while here and there a service-tree drops coral berries at your feet.

Soon now you cross the deep, wide ford of Mill River on a footbridge, substantial and with a handrail, and where you stop of course to look both up and down the stream overhung with foliage, and just beyond which is a pretty house with its front yard full of roses. It is only two miles from here to Boone, and you breathe a sigh of regret at being so near the end of the day's walk; yet when you find yourself in Mrs. Coffey's little inn with its bright flowers you are glad to sit down and think over the events of the day.

Boone, at the foot of Howard Knob, is a pretty snuggle of houses running along a single street. Boone says it is the highest county seat in the United States, and that Daniel Boone once stayed in a cabin near here, whence its name. However all that may be, the lower slopes of Howard Knob are pleasantly cultivated and valleys run up into the mountains in all directions, as though on purpose to make a charming setting for Boone the county seat.

That first visit to Boone!—what a sense of peace one had in remembering that the nearest railroad was thirty miles away; and then—what is that?—a telephone bell rings its insistent call and Boone is talking with Blowing Rock, or Lenoir, or New York City, or Heaven knows where! For though this part of the country was the last to get into railroad communication with the outer world, it was by no means the last to grasp the opportunities within reach.

With what delicious weariness one sinks to sleep after the day's walk over the hills! Your eyes seem scarcely to have closed when a loud noise wakens you with a start—what is it? Nothing excepting that the day's work has begun, broad daylight flooding in at the window. Breakfast is ready, coffee, cornbread, fish from some near sparkling stream, rice, hot biscuit, eggs, wild-plum sauce, honey and wild strawberries—you can take your choice or eat them all. And what a pleasant surprise to find every thing seasoned with the wonderful appetite of childhood, that reappears on such occasions as this!

Your body seems borne on wings, so light it feels as you leave the inn and again take to the road. Back to Blowing Rock? No, indeed; not even though you could return, part way at least, by another road. The *Wanderlust* is on you—the need of walking along the high valleys among the enchanted mountains. That seems the thing in life worth doing. As you leave Boone you notice a meadow white with ox-eye daisies, and among them big red clover-heads, and, if you please, clumps of black-eyed Susans—for all the world like a summer meadow in the New England hills. Ripe strawberries hang over the edge of the road.

From Boone to Valle Crucis you must go the longest way, for so you get the best views, the people tell you. And so you go a day's walk to Valle Crucis, where the Episcopal settlement lies in the fine green little valley.

From Valle Crucis to Banner Elk, under the Beech Mountain, is another day's walk, when again you take the longest way, up Dutch Creek to see the pretty waterfall there, and where the clematis is a white veil over the bushes, and up the steep road by Hanging Rock where the gold tree grows. This is an oak, known far and near because its top is always golden yellow. The leaves come out yellow in the spring, remain so all summer, and in the fall would doubtless turn yellow if they were not already that color. The people say there is a pot of gold buried at the roots, but this pleasant fancy has not taken a serious enough hold to menace the life of the tree.

Stopping at a picturesque, old-time log house to rest, a little girl invites you to go to the top of Hanging Rock, which invitation you gladly accept, thereby getting one of the most enjoyable walks of the summer, your little guide telling you all the way about the flowers and the birds, and stopping under an overhanging cliff with great secrecy to show you a round little bird's nest with eggs in it cleverly hidden in the moss. One suspects it was the chance to show this treasure that led the child to propose the long climb to the top of the mountain. The gooseberries of Hanging Rock are without prickles, perhaps because the wild currants growing there have stolen them. Imagine prickly currants! There is plenty of galax on Hanging Rock, and mosses and sedums and all the other growths that make mountain-tops so agreeable. The top of Hanging Rock is a slanting ledge, from which the mountain gets its name. At Banner Elk you will want to stay awhile, it is so pretty, and you will also want to climb the beautiful Beech Mountain with its grassy spaces and its charming beech groves.

From Banner Elk you take the short walk over to "Calloways," close under the shadow of thc Grandfather, and from here the long and beautiful walk down the Watauga River at the base of the Grandfather, then along the ridges back to Blowing Rock, watching as you go details of the mountain beneath whose northern front you are passing. The open benches, the rocky bluffs, and abrupt, tree-clad walls, of this side of the mountain, which we call the back of the Grandfather, are not impressive like those long southern slopes sweeping from a summit of a little less than six thousand feet down into the foothills. For the mountain on this side is stopped by the high plateau from which it rises. Yet it is good to be at the back of the Grandfather. From the Watauga road we see the profile from which the mountain is said to have received its name, although one gets a better and far more impressive view of it from a certain point on the mountain itself.

And so you return to Blowing Rock after days of wandering, only to rest awhile and start again, gaining endurance with every trip until the ten miles' walk that cost you a little weariness becomes the twenty miles' walk that costs you none. You cannot tire of the road, for every mile brings new sights, new sounds, new fragrances, new friends, new flowers, one charm of walking here being the endless variety. No two days are alike, each has its own pleasant adventures.

The Grandfather Mountain

Down in the plains and in all the cities it is August. Up here it is some celestial month not mentioned in any calendar. For we are camping at the back of the Grandfather Mountain; our tents are pitched on a slope that is separated from the base of the mountain by a narrow, wedge-like little valley down which ripples the silvery beginning of the Watauga River. To be at the beginning of a river is guaranty of many pleasant things. Opposite us the mountain rises, steep, rough, and covered with beautiful growths. It is so near we can see the shades of green and even make out the forms of the tree-tops. On its side the clouds form, welling up as from a caldron of the storm gods. We are shut in by tree-clad slopes, excepting towards the east, where the view opens down the valley upon distant blue hills.

Ripe blackberries hang over the roadside, and the bushes growing about the rocks in an abandoned field near us are loaded with extra good fruit. There is a certain pleasure in gathering one's food from the bushes; one is apt to gather so much more than bodily sustenance. You think of things in a berry patch, for instance, that never come to you anywhere else; you solve the problems of the universe differently. In a brier patch you think in cycles and flavor your food with dashes of cosmic philosophy. And there is profit as well as pleasure in gathering your food from the bushes. At the back of the Grandfather, berries are important in our daily fare. We eat them as they grow, and also prepared in many ways. We make discoveries in culinary æsthetics as well as in cosmic philosophy, dealing with blackberries. You have never really tasted a blackberry pudding, for instance, until you have stood on a stone in the Watauga River, stripped the heavy, shining clusters of ripe fruit into your tin "bucket," carried them back to camp, and made your pudding; for your true blackberry

PEAKS OF GRANDFATHER MOUNTAIN

pudding must be flavored with warm sunshine glinting between green leaves, the sparkle of running water, and the remembered fragrances of herbs and trees and bushes, with memories of pleasant reveries, and it does it no harm to be spiced with scratches.

There is a certain sensuous pleasure to be derived from the scratches of a berry patch. The hot rip of the thorn through the skin, the crimson line of blood that appears at the surface, but does not overflow, the tingling sensation that courses over your whole body for a moment—for this you willingly endure the smart that comes for hours afterwards whenever your wounded members touch anything. Moreover, you would endure the scratches so soon forgotten for the memory that lasts of the feel of the sun, of the beleaguering fragrances, and for the rich booty you carry home.

And your blackberry pudding, to be perfect, must be eaten in a tent, or sitting on a rock by a brookside, or in a shakedown bower under a big tree. Our dining-room is a bower roofed with evergreen boughs. Out through the open front, through the overhanging ends of the evergreen boughs, we see the top of the Grandfather Mountain and the clouds that come and go over it.

The country people bring us food, apples, butter, eggs, and milk. The butter comes out of a tall earthenware churn whose dasher is moved up and down by a mountain friend whom we see sitting in the doorway of her house busily churning, with a background of the black interior in which are faintly outlined the kitchen utensils. Under the slopes of the Grandfather we go down the valley to picturesque houses shaded by fruit trees.

Sometimes we spend the day on the Grandfather Mountain and such days cannot come too often. Sometimes we walk over the gap under Hanging Rock, or we cross over to Banner Elk, or go down to Linville, and wherever we walk the air stimulates like wine and the wayside is abloom with summer flowers, among them goldenrods and asters for memories of life in the North, and the hillsides are solid masses of white bloom, or they are yellow or pink with flowers—but the slopes along the northern bank of the Watauga River are distinct in your mind from everything else. In the late summer they may be a mere tangle of flowers and plumy grasses, but did you not come along here once and discover them carpeted with strawberries? You could not then walk over them without dyeing your feet in the juice of the ripe fruit. Above the strawberries red-clover was thickly blooming, and above the clover ox-eye daisies. The odor of this field was perceptible before you otherwise noticed it—a chorus of sweet smells seemed shouting to you to come up. As soon as the land is left untilled about here, wild strawberries rush in as pink azaleas do about Traumfest. You can buy them for five cents a gallon, but you will be foolish to do that when you can stain your own fingers with their juices, and fill your tissues with sunshine and fresh air and fragrances out on the slopes when strawberries are ripe.

Shading our camp is the remains of a grove, for most of the trees lie on the ground, bleached skeletons, which, however, prove to be a blessing rather than a misfortune for us. For towards night the air grows cold—and then comes the crowning pleasure of the day: a royal camp-fire suddenly blazes forth.

We have a perfect firemaker in the mountain man who lives in the canvas-covered wagon that brought us here, bag and baggage. Every mountain man is a perfect firemaker, though he is by no means a fire worshiper. He makes his fire for homely uses, not for any spiritual cause such as we imagine kindled those fires of early man in the Far East, fires that yet burn in poetry to warm the heart even at this distant time. The mountain man always starts his fire with a stick whittled into a brush. He scorns paper even when he can get it, seeming to whittle into his brush a sort of magic, for try as you will you cannot whittle a brush that will burn like his. It never fails, and he uses only one match. Our back-log is the trunk of an ash tree seasoned to perfection. Against this is laid various kinds of wood, each kind giving forth its own flames and its own sparks; for trees do not all burn alike. The oak, for instance, expresses itself as distinctly in its flames as in its leaves and fruit, or in its voice in the wind, or its color or the odors it sends forth. Even the different species of oak burn differently. One can sit in reverie before the calm blaze of a white-oak fire, but your Spanish oak explodes and sputters and shoots out sparks in a way to induce anything but reverie. Hickory burns with a steadfast glow, but the unstable chestnut pops and sputters worse, if anything, than Spanish oak. Your firemaker says it is linwood that sends out those fascinating broods of fiery dragons that leap with lashing tails high into the air.

There are some things one would like to know about trees. One would like to know from the flames what tree is burning, how old it is, and what have been its experiences in life, as well as how to tell, by the sound of the wind among the leaves, beneath what tree one is passing, and by the smell of the opening buds as you go along what trees are about you.

As we lie on the fragrant earth watching the flames and the fiery serpents ascend into the black vault above, this seems to us no common fire, but rather the sudden rush into elemental freedom of those patient giants of the forest that have lain here waiting for us to come and free them.

Sometimes a bat flies across the fire, and one night a dark toad was discovered sitting close to your ear. But he had nothing important to say. He sat still for a while, his eyes glistening in the firelight that seemed to fascinate him. Then he attempted to enter the heaven thus suddenly opened to his imagination. In pursuit of his dream he went straight into the fire. What he expected to find, who can say? And what a disillusionment it must have been when he found himself sitting on a red-hot fagot! He made a quick backward movement, to be swept into safety by a merciful human hand. If a toad had the wings of a moth, it would doubtless fly into the fire in the same way. A toad followed a lantern a long distance one night. It is impossible not to like the toad when you once really know it. Besides its friendly manners it has the most beautiful eyes in the world. Those eyes so soft and bright betoken a good heart. What is the old fable of the toad wearing a jewel in its head? The truth of that is, the toad wears two jewels, and they are its lovely golden-brown eyes.

As the fire dies down, talking ceases, the black trees come out more plainly, and the head of the Grandfather wears a crown of stars where great Scorpio lies along the sky.

If you chance to waken in the night, out through the triangular space between the open tent-flaps you see the slopes of the Grandfather bathed in moonlight, or dimly looming in the faint light of the stars, or shrouded in white mists like a ghost. One sleeps soundly in the keen, thin air and at daybreak wakens, not slowly but all at once with a sense of buoyancy in every member. How the cold spring water stings the skin and makes it glow suddenly hot! And as we step out of doors we see the mountain emerging from its robe of white mists, its colors fresh and fine as though it, too, had slept well.

Oftener than anywhere else we go up on the mountain. One can easily, by jumping from stone to stone, cross the Watauga's pretty rippling water, where the trout hide. Some of our little party may stop to fish, and that is good for those of us who come home hungry at night—and how hungry we do come home!—but the Watauga has better uses than fishing, an occupation apt to absorb one's attention too closely, withdrawing it from matters more important than trout. There is a matter of real interest, however, connected with fishing in this region. For it was either here or in the Linville that we saw the sacred piscatorial art pursued with woolen mittens instead of rod and fly. Thus equipped you wade in and grab the fish where they lie in the clear pools.

The path beyond the river is cut through the dense kalmia and *Rhododendron maximum* that make a wide band along the base of the mountain, then it leads up and up and up through the more open forest. There is no sweeter walk in the world than that up Grandfather Mountain, where the path winds among the trees, a canopy of leaves screening the sky, the forest shutting from view the outer world. Once, there were large wild cherry trees on the slopes of the Grandfather, but the wood being valuable—it is what the people call mahogany—there are only saplings left, and a few patriarchs that, though useless for lumber, give an air of dignity to the forest in company with the clear gray shafts of the tulip-trees, the grand old chestnuts, the oaks, the maples, beeches, birches, ashes, and lindens that mingle their foliage with that of the pines and spruces.

You pass beside or under large detached boulders covered with saxifrages, sedums, mosses, and ferns, and in whose crevices mountain-ash trees and twisted hemlocks have taken root as though for purposes of decoration; and in the damp hollows away from the path great jack-vines hang from the treetops. The rock ledges sometimes make caves where bears were wont to live, for the Grandfather was once a famous place for bears. Squirrels still "use on the mountain," as the people say, and a "boomer" will be apt to bark down at you as you go along. You hear the waters of a stream in the ravine below, and here and there you cross a natural garden of "balimony" or some other precious herb that the people gather in the season. About two thirds of the way up you take a path that branches off to the left and leads you over the mossy rocks to an open place on the edge of a gorge where looking off you see the clear-cut profile of the Grandfather sculptured on the edge of a rocky bluff, the bushy hair that rises from the forehead consisting of fir trees that when whitened by the winter snow give a venerable appearance to the stone face. Somewhat above this profile from this point is also visible another, with smaller and rounder features, which of course is the Grandmother.

Returning to the main path and continuing the ascent, the way grows wilder and if possible sweeter. One has a sense of rising spiritually as well as physically. At the base of a high cliff, framed in foliage and crowned with the rosy-flowered *Rhododendron Catawbiense,* gushes out the famous Grandfather Spring that is only ten degrees above freezing throughout the summer. Up to this point there is a bridle path; beyond here it is necessary to walk. The rose-bay still in bloom clings to the rocks, in whose crevices little dwarf trees have taken root along with the mosses, ferns, and saxifrages.

The path gets very steep and rocky. You are now among the balsam firs, those trees to name which is to name a perfume, and you go climbing up over their strong red roots. The pathway becomes a staircase winding about moss-trimmed rocks in whose crevices are tiny contorted balsams like Japanese flower-pot trees. Enormous coal-black lichens hang from the cliffs and the ground is softly carpeted with mossy growths and oxalis, out from whose pretty pale leaves look myriads of pink-and-white blossoms. Long after the *Rhododendron Catawbiense* is done blooming below, one finds it in its prime on the high peaks of the Grandfather.

Up among the balsam firs and about the rocks grow large sour gooseberries and enormous sweet huckleberries, and it was here we found a new and delicious fruit. The bushes crowding the woods in places were loaded with bright red globes the size of a small cherry, each dangling from a slender stem. These

The Grandfather Profile

delightful berries were mere skins of juice, tiny wine-bottles full of refreshment for a summer day. The natives were afraid to eat them, but having decided that they were cousins to the huckleberries, we ventured, and added these jocund fruits to the many attractions that called us again and again to the top of the Grandfather. One wishes it could truthfully be said that these berries grow only on the Grandfather Mountain, but the fact is we discovered them on other mountains, though never much below an altitude of six thousand feet. Finding them thus among the mossy rocks up in the sweet, keen air on the summit of our favorite mountain gave them a charm that was enhanced by the fact that they belonged to us and the birds. Now we shall have to share them with every passer-by, for when we ate and survived, our mountain friends ventured to partake, and doubtless they will spread the news that you can eat with impunity the juicy red berries on top of Grandfather Mountain. One woman even took home a pailful and made from them the most exquisite jelly imaginable, ruby-red, clear, sparkling, and with a delicate wild-flower flavor that made one think of the sweet things growing on the mountain-top. We named them "Our Berries," and with them quenched our thirst instead of carrying water when we went above the spring.

Up through the spruces and the balsams you mount in the resplendent day, lingering at every step. The trees below you are sending up songs as the wind sweeps over them, the balsams about and below you are pouring a vast cloud of fragrance into the blue bowl of the sky, and you yourself someway seem to be a part of the general rapture.

Thus climbing up through the wonderful day, you reach the summit, "Calloway's High Peak," the highest point on the mountain, but from which one cannot command the circle of the horizon. It is necessary to get the view from two points, which is all the better. The rocks at the lookout towards the south being covered with "heather," one can lie on a delightful couch studded all over with little white starry flowers, to rest and receive the view. Lying thus on the earth, warmed by the sun and cooled by the fragrant breeze, one looks over a sea of blue mountains that breaks against a bluer sky. Out of the sea of mountains rises many a well-known form, among them the big beech with its memories of lovely pastures and groves of beech trees, for it is needless to say that a mountain of beeches is a sort of enchanted place. In the distance lies White Top on whose summit three states meet, a heaven for the moonshiner, one should think, if he is able to take advantage of the situation.

Leaving this place and walking on to the point that looks to the south, one shares the feelings and almost the faith of Michaux. The view is very impressive, because of that steep descent of the mountain into the foothills, the long spurs sweeping down in fine lines to a great depth. Above them one looks off over scores of noble forms overlapping and blending in the hazy distance. The Black Mountains stand forth very high and very blue, and beyond them, among the many familiar forms, are distinguished what one supposes to be the faint blue line of the Smokies—or is it the nearer Balsams?

The greater mass of the Grandfather lies on the south side, where those long buttresses sweep down into the valleys of the Piedmont region, glorious ridges with broad bald shoulders where cattle pasture and rhododendrons, laurel, and azaleas stand in regal beauty. Between the long spurs, as well as between the many smaller ridges, glance rivulets that finally become the John's River, whose valley one sees from Blowing Rock winding so prettily between the foothills.

Sooner or later you will find your way to McRae's, which is to the south side of the Grandfather what Calloway's is to the north side, a farmhouse where one can stay awhile. There is a trail over the end of the Grandfather by which you can go directly from Calloway's to McRae's, but to strike this trail you have to walk down the Linville River, which, rising in an open space but a stone's throw from the head of the Watauga, flows in quite the opposite direction, and through so narrow a pass that you have to keep crossing and recrossing it, no small matter in a season of rains. For there are no foot-logs at all. Evidently you are not expected to walk along this road, and if you do you must cross the river, jumping from rock to rock as best you can. But the Linville is one of the streams you are glad to know through all its sparkling length, from the spring behind the Grandfather to where it escapes in wild glee through the gorge below the falls.

There are peacocks at McRae's, and Mr. McRae has not forgotten how to play on the bagpipes those ancient airs that have so stirred the blood of his race. One of the pleasant memories of this side of the Grandfather is Mr. McRae walking up and down before the house playing the pipes. But you will have to coax him to do it.

McRae's stands on the Yonahlossee Road that connects Linville, just below the mountain, with Blowing Rock—Yonahlossee, trail of the bear—but one need fear no bear on the Yonahlossee Road today. From McRae's there is a path up the Grandfather, not to Calloway's High Peak, but to another peak reached by a very sweet climb through the balsams, which, in all this region, are smaller and more companionable than the straight giants of the Black Mountains, these of the Grandfather being twisted and friendly and profoundly fragrant. From this peak one can see in all directions, excepting where one of the Grandfather's black summits obstructs the view.

It is the lichens growing on the rocks that give so sombre an appearance to the top of the Grandfather, those big, black lichens with loose and curled-up edges. Grandfather's black, rocky top is eight miles long, and once Mr. Calloway and our friend the post-master—he who brought us our mail, walking four miles every day for the pleasure of doing a kindness—and the men of the camping party blazed out a rude trail so that we could all take that wonderful knife-edge walk up in the sky over the peaks of the Grandfather; Indian ladders—that is, a tall tree trunk from which the branches have been lopped, leaving protruding ends for steps—helping us up otherwise insurmountable cliffs. It was

THE YONAHLOSSEE ROAD

the great event of the season, a very wonderful walk, and one seldom taken by anybody.

The Yonahlossee Road ought to be followed early in the summer. For then the meadowy tops of the long spurs are like noble parks created for man's pleasure. The *Rhododendron Catawbiense* lies massed about in effective groups and covered with rosy bloom, beyond which one looks out over a wide landscape of mountains and clouds. From these open, flower-decked spaces the road passes into the shadowy forest, to emerge upon a bushy slope where blazing reaches of flame-colored azaleas astound your senses. There are other flowers along the way, but you scarcely see them, intoxicated as you are with the glory of the rhododendrons, and after them the azaleas, for these marvelous growths almost never blossom within sight of each other. You would say they know, like ladies at a ball, how important it is to avoid each other's colors.

Under the trees along the roadside the earth is covered with a superb carpet of large and handsome galax leaves, for the Grandfather is distinguished by the great beauty and abundance of its galax. Laurel, too, claims standing-room on the side of the grand old mountain, and here as elsewhere one notices the apparent capriciousness of the laurel, which forms an impenetrable jungle for long stretches and then stops short, not a laurel bush to be seen for some distance, when with equal suddenness it appears again.

The splendid slopes of the Grandfather are enchanting also when autumn colors them—deep red huckleberry balds, trees wreathed in crimson woodbine, vivid sassafras, tall gold and crimson and scarlet forest trees—it seems more like the brilliant display of a Northern forest. You would say the outpouring of fragrance must pass with the summer. Not so. As you walk among the trees in their thin, bright attire you have a feeling of their friendliness. The forest, as it were, breathes upon you, you are drowned in the sweetness of resinous perfumes that distill from a thousand pines, firs, and hemlocks. When the leaves of the trees are growing scarce and changing to duller hues, into the open spaces witch-hazel weaves its gold-wreathed wands and brightens the woods like sunshine.

Turning to the right from the Yonahlossee Road, a short distance up from McRae's, you walk along under the chestnut trees just beginning to open their burrs, away from the Grandfather out over a beautiful spur that ends in an open, rounded summit. The road to this place has side paths that lead you to high cliffs, whence you look off towards Blowing Rock, and where the sweetest of mountain growths cling to the crevices and drape the edges of all the rocks. For some reason the trees here are small, the chestnuts being not much larger than bushes, but the nuts are proportionately large, the largest nuts one ever saw on our native chestnut trees, and they are peculiarly sweet, again a hint to the fruit-makers who from this could doubtless create a nut as large as the chestnuts of France and as sweet as those of America. The summit of this little mountain of the large chestnuts is one of your favorite places to go for a day of rest and contemplation. It is a lovely, soothing place, as it ought to be, for it is the Grandmother Mountain.

The Holiday of Dreams

Back to Traumfest one comes, after each expedition out over the mountains. And one day the truth dawns upon you—the title so arbitrarily bestowed upon Traumfest belongs to the whole region. Yes, this whole stretch of enchanting and enchanted mountains is the "Holiday of Dreams." And thinking back over those days of happy wandering, how many interesting places appear before the mind's eye that have not been so much as mentioned in this book; how many lovely scenes have been witnessed, how many pleasant adventures encountered that have not been recorded, how many flowers have blossomed without mention, how many birds have sung unchronicled, how many quaint native phrases have been passed over in silence!

And as the years have slipped by, with what pangs of regret one has watched the passing of the primitive life of the mountains, and with what pleasure one reverts to those old days when everybody was uncomfortable and everybody happy. How many today, seeing the train with its line of Pullman sleepers come in on time at Traumfest, remember those days when the track went only as far as Hendersonville, and when, with the old-time courtesy of the Southern man, the conductor politely stopped his two cars on request of any lady passenger who wished to gather a few wild flowers, willing to please so long as he could get in before dark.

Since then, like a cosmic spider, the Southern Railroad has woven its meshes below the Carolina mountains on either side, and thrown its steel threads across them in several places, while now yet another line is being surveyed across the Blue Ridge to the north of Tryon Mountain, up the Broad River Valley, past Chimney Rock, and on as far as Bat Cave where it follows a devious route of escape by way of the Pigeon River Gorge. The Blue Ridge that looks so ethereal in the distance presents almost insuperable obstacles to the civil engineer, as do also the guarding ramparts of the valleys of the plateau, but the great transcontinental line, that is to reach from the Atlantic coast of North Carolina to Seattle on the Pacific, will doubtless find a way.

Occasionally one sees an old-fashioned, boat-shaped wagon covered with a canopy of white cloth, a survivor of those trains that crossed from Tennessee to the Carolinas over the hard-won roads where no longer move trains of wagons, droves of cattle, hogs, and sheep, all these now passing over another form of highway behind the iron horse that pulls the contents of a hundred caravans in one load.

And what means that sudden appearance of two dozen automobiles on Traumfest's modest "Trade Street" the other day? Two or three of these wonders of the age belong to people living here, and those others came on a mission, which was, to further their own interests by making plans for the extension of the road that brought them here. They came up from Spartanburg, a sign of the new era that has dawned to transform the mountains. For already from Spartanburg there comes a wide, new road, a great red serpent whose head is pointed up the Pacolet Valley, and that will never stop until it has coiled and writhed its way over the helpless rampart of the Blue Ridge to its goal—in Asheville? No, not in Asheville, but through it and on and down out into the now teeming Western world beyond. The automobile, which is doing for this country what the military power has so long been doing for Europe, networking it with perfect roads, will soon speed from Jacksonville, Florida, across the plains, the foothills, and the astonished mountains, down to Knoxville, Tennessee, over the broad highway now being constructed for that purpose.

Wherever you go the portable sawmill is ahead of you, the temporary railway of the lumberman disdainfully penetrating the "inaccessible" places. And wherever you go the people of the mountains are waking up out of the care-free, simple life of the past into the wearing, tumultuous life of the present, and that is what causes those pangs of regret. The comforts that are pouring in are not in themselves regrettable; it is only the price one has to pay for them, the exchange of Arcadia for Gotham.

Social transitions are always trying, and perhaps peculiarly so here, where the awakening consciousness suddenly sees the glitter of the prize without understanding the law of exchange. But the people are sound. To native intelligence they add a rude but strong sense of honor and of justice which with the passing of time will undoubtedly mould them happily into the new conditions.

The world is coming; the old-time mountaineer is going, but he will never be wholly metamorphosed so long as human nature remains fundamentally unchanged and the sun continues to exact obedience to its great command, "Thou shalt not hurry." And so long as human nature remains as it is, the newcomer will in time have the sharp edge of his "ambition" dulled by the same resistless force: "Thou shalt not hurry" applies to all alike.

And now, into the increasing turmoil of many interests there comes like an emblem of peace the great Appalachian Park, that, lying in calm expanse over the slopes of the Blue Ridge and the Smoky Mountains, shall save forever for the happiness of the people a part of this glorious wilderness. With the park will come a new world to the mountains. Not only will railroads and highways open up all parts of the country, but an increasing number of those people who need to rest or to play will find their way here, and build themselves homes. Summer homes for the Southerner, winter homes for the Northerner, all-the-year-round homes for many from both sections are already growing up in the laurel thickets and under the trees.

Those who desire an estate in the forest primeval can no longer, it is true, buy a whole mountain covered with virgin forest for a few cents an acre, as was the case not so long ago, when "inaccessible" localities were looked upon as encumbered rather than benefited by their burden of big trees. But whoever wants a mountain-side, with a laurel-bordered stream and a wide view of enchanting heights, can have it, and if all the forest is no longer primeval it is nevertheless charming. The half-grown trees and the saplings, with the few large trees that generally manage to escape destruction, afford a starting-point for the creation of delightful landscape effects. And although the mountains have no great agricultural value, frequent statements to the contrary notwithstanding, they are capable of responding cordially to him who, desiring a garden, a fruit orchard, or a vineyard, goes about it in the right way. New methods will doubtless increase the bearing capacity of the earth, but when all is said neither soil nor climate is as well suited to the production of food crops for man's needs as they are for the production of laurel and azaleas for his pleasure.

Where the mountains stand supreme is in their gracious climate that seems to caress the world-weary; in that and in the subtler beauties of nature that everywhere cover them as with a garment. The chance to build a castle out of fancies and a few firmer materials, to snare the vagrant fragrances that float free, to fix the rose-bay on the cliff, to clear a vista to the heavenly heights, moves the desire of every lover of beauty who comes here sighing for release from the bondage of icy winds or city conventions. Nor is a lordly mansion full of cares the proper housing for this country. Far better for those who seek their freedom is the restfully-proportioned "bungalow," with spreading roof and broad porches, appropriate to the climate and harmonious in the landscape, and which is now growing so greatly in favor.

The world may be coming, but the colors and the fragrances, the wonderful air and the ardent sun remain the same, and ever will. The change that is going on may have its trials, but one has only to project the imagination far enough into the future to see these heights transformed from glorious wildness into glorious order. One looks ahead with undaunted courage to the time when both visitor and native will enjoy without destroying the charming efforts of nature; to the time when man will—to adapt Emerson—name the birds without a gun, love the wild rose and leave it on its stalk; to the time when, undisturbed, the arbutus will again carpet the woods close to the houses, and the flaming azaleas cover the slopes, pressing down as they once did against the wheels of the carriage as you drove along the more frequented roads. For Nature is long-suffering and very kind, so kind, indeed, that in moments of discouragement one has only to remember that even if the worst were to happen, and these beautiful mountains become devastated by ignorant invaders, when the time came, as come it would, that the profaner departed, Nature would begin anew her beneficent task of creating beauty. These mountains, with their tremendous fecundity and their resistless allies of sun and rain, in half a century would erase all but the ineradicable signs of the presence of the destroyer, presenting to some future generation the privilege of joining the beauty of the wilderness to the graces of civilized life. For the whole world is now one population, all knowing each other, and it is incredible that the work of the future will not be in the direction of abolishing war, misery, and ugliness.

When the vitality of man and the energy of money are freed from the barbaric waste of today, physical and municipal, as they will be freed, and can be diverted into making the earth beautiful, then, if not before, this enchanting region will be transformed into the paradise which is so evidently its function in the scheme of nature. For these mountains have been preserved as though on purpose for man's pleasure. Nowhere else does such variety of beautiful trees grow in natural forests, nowhere else do such flowers bloom in gardens of nature's planting. The long line of the Appalachian Mountains, the oldest land in this country, perhaps in the world, having in its southern part escaped the cold death of the glacier, is probably the original home whence many of our hardwood trees have spread over the Northern Hemisphere. Once connected by land with eastern Asia, North America shared the flora of that part of the world, and when the Ice Age spread its destroying mantle over the whole northern part of the earth, the plants of the New World—which is, geologically speaking, a very old world—receding before it, took refuge in these mountains where soil and climate were alike favorable to their sustenance. So that here has been preserved in a great natural botanical garden and arboretum some of the choicest growths of recent millenniums, growths which but for these friendly heights would have been numbered with the long list of forms of beauty that doubtless lived and vanished before man came upon the scene to witness and enjoy.

And here today it is man's privilege to enhance the loveliness of the earth by use of the wonderful trees and flowers that grow spontaneously, as well as by the introduction of the many beautiful forms that recent years have made accessible to us from that sister continent where the people of the Celestial Empire and the Flowery Kingdom have so long made their part of the world enchanting with flowers, foliage, and trees; and where they have created a form of beauty expressing the personality of their race. Seeing the exquisite results obtained by them, one imagines our own civilization expressing itself with equal force and originality, and here in the Southern mountains, with every natural advantage to draw upon, evolving a form of landscape gardening sympathetic to the region, as beautiful as that of any nation, and free from those traditional conventions of ours, which introduced here would convert a possible paradise into a stupid repetition of buildings and gardens that whatever may be their excuse in other climates and other regions, are utterly out of place here.

Already lovely homes, and grounds beautifully planted with the natural growths of the mountains, testify to the possibilities of the country, and form, let us hope, the beginning of a vast domain of beauty, a domain created, not by a few great landholders, but by the many who shall come to take possession.

The Italians have a graceful way of placing in their village parks a notice to the effect that the park is entrusted to the honor of the people for whose pleasure it was made, and in the same spirit one would like to confide nature's great park of the Southern Appalachian Mountains to the loving care of the people. May it be the pleasure of all to assist the charming efforts of nature and to pass on, as a rightful inheritance to future generations, an ever more enchanting Holiday of Dreams.

The End

INDEX

Where applicable, text references are listed first, followed by photographic references in bold.

The Photography of Margaret W. Morley

This edition of *The Carolina Mountains* is supplemented with photographs attributed to Margaret W. Morley and taken during the years she spent in Tryon. The pictures within the text were reproduced by scanning an original 1913 volume of *The Carolina Mountains,* the only book known to be illustrated with Morley's photographs.

Our primary source for additional photographs was the North Carolina Museum of History. A body of work attributed to Margaret Morley has been there since its accession in 1945, though it is believed to have come into their possession at a much earlier date. The photos were presumably captioned by Morley, though some evidence suggests her friend Edith Watson may have cataloged and captioned them. As far as it is possible to determine after nearly a century, the following gallery contains only photos taken by Margaret Morley. Several of the images have been used in books and brochures, often without attribution, perhaps from copies owned by other institutions. We have not included all the available Morley photographs but have chosen a representative grouping of the most reproducible images.

It is unknown what kinds of cameras Margaret Morley used. The staff at the Museum of History believes many of the prints were developed from glass-plate negatives. In 1888, George Eastman produced his first roll-film camera, a less bulky alternative to the equipment in use since the Civil War. At the turn of the century, a variety of inexpensive photographic methods were available to the average American, and photography was becoming a popular hobby. A roll-film camera may have been used for some of Morley's photos.

The photographs in the original book feature landscapes sometimes containing people. In contrast, the following photos focus primarily on Southern Appalachian people going about their everyday tasks. Miss Morley's photographs of children are especially appealing, and it is often noted that she seems to have captured her subjects as she found them rather than costuming and staging them.

The following images provide a visual complement to Morley's written descriptions of the people of the Carolina mountains, whom she clearly admired. Few photographs originally bore useful captions, and individuals were rarely identified by name; available information for specific images follows the picture gallery on page 358.

Notes on Selected Photographs

Page 29: Constance Snow
Page 305: Miss Belle Keeter riding on Daisy
Page 308 (bottom): Circuit rider Norris and his wife, Katherine, from Tryon
Page 309: Caesar's Head profile
Page 314: On Mount Mitchell
Page 315 (bottom): A wayside cabin near Blowing Rock
Page 324: Grinding sorghum to make molasses
Page 326: Big Tom Wilson, the famous wilderness guide
Pages 327–328, 329 (top): Birch bark stills
Page 328: cropped from a larger image
Page 329 (bottom): A moonshine still in the Tennessee mountains
Page 330: A pug mill for processing clay
Page 330 (bottom): Sam Whelchel and his kiln
Page 331: Rich Williams of Greenville County, South Carolina
Page 332: Sam Whelchel
Page 335: Checking on the bee gums
Page 340 (bottom) : Drying apples for winter; note the turkey feather duster!
Page 342: Spinning wool on a great, or walking, wheel
Page 344 (top): Students pose in front of their Carolina mountain school
Page 344 (bottom): Close-up of children, cropped from a larger image
Page 347: Mother and children, cropped from a larger image
Page 355: cropped from a larger image